MW01517819

Bhagat Singh
Revisited
Historiography, Biography and Ideology of the Great Martyr

Chander Pal Singh

Originals
Delhi-110052

ISBN 10: 81-8454-106-6 (HB)
ISBN 13: 978-81-8454-106-9 (HB)
ISBN 10: 81-8454-110-4 (PB)
ISBN 13: 978-81-8454-110-6 (PB)

Published by
Originals
A-6, Nimri Commercial Centre,
Ashok Vihar Phase-IV, Delhi-110052
Phones: 011-27302453, Fax: 011-47061936
e-mail: info@Lppindia.com
url: www.Lppindia.com

Printed at
D K Fine Art Press P Ltd.
Delhi-110052

PRINTED IN INDIA

Contents

Contents

Foreword

It all began in February 2006. While roaming in the World Book Fair held at Delhi, I came across in the Hindi section, a bookstall from Lucknow drenched in the colour of Bhagat Singh. The banners, posters, stickers, songs and even the markings on the shirts of the workers all bore the stamp of Bhagat Singh. I was thrilled. Since my childhood Bhagat Singh as a great patriot and martyr, had been my hero. I went inside, purchased several small pamphlets and a bulky book in Hindi titled, *Bhagat Singh Aur Unke Sathion Ke Sampoorn Uplabdh Dastavej* (Complete Available Documents of Bhagat Singh and His Comrades), edited by Satyam and published by the Rahul Foundation of Lucknow. It had been published just a month back, in January 2006. Reaching home, I impatiently began scanning its pages and was struck by an eighteen pages long *Introduction* penned by the Editor.

I was shocked to discover that the Editor, ignoring Bhagat Singh's ardent patriotism, his quest for the freedom of the motherland and therefore inviting his own martyrdom in a planned manner, had tried to paint him only as a Marxist ideologue. The Editor's disdain for Bhagat Singh's iconic image as 'The Great Martyr' was too obvious. He could barely hide his anguish that, barring a few diehard Left activists, the vast mass of educated Indians recognized Bhagat Singh as a great martyr only. The Editor felt that Bhagat Singh's ideology, more than his martyrdom was relevant to our times, when all the parliamentary parties and pseudo-leftists had been exposed. Writing in the year 2006, he felt convinced that the world had entered a decisive phase of its war against the demonic imperialist- capitalist forces. He was eager to use Bhagat Singh as a beacon light in this decisive war. He gave long quotations attributed to Bhagat Singh to convince readers that the war against imperialist-capitalist forces, begun by Bhagat Singh was continuing. He exhorted his readers to build a new Communist Party in the true Leninist mould as well as to reinvent the class character of Gandhi and his Congress. Writing this in 2006, the poor Editor could hardly have imagined that the eminent Prof. Bipin Chandra, whose authority he had used again and again to support his line of argument, would in the year 2010 announce that in his next work he would be presenting Bhagat Singh, had he chosen to avoid the gallows, as a would-be 'Gandhian Marxist' (a contradiction in itself). The Editor also rued the untimely martyrdom of Bhagat Singh, for in his view, had Bhagat Singh managed to escape the gallows, he would have built a Communist Party, rooted in his own brand of Marxism, which was closer to Mao Tse Tung and Ho Chi Minh. This, the Editor believed, would have given a new turn to the history of not only the Communist movement but of India as a whole.

This interpretation of the great martyr kindled in me a desire to have a look into the recent Marxist writings on Bhagat Singh. I found that Satyam was only articulating the general Marxist position on Bhagat Singh. Each fragment of the Communist movement in India, whether parliamentary parties like CPI, CPM or those who do not believe in the parliamentary democracy like the Maoists, is keen to present Bhagat Singh in its own light, and each is desperate to use Bhagat Singh to reach the youth for whom Bhagat Singh is an icon. They are fully conscious of Bhagat Singh's vast popularity among the Indian masses in general and the youth in particular. Recognizing the iconic image of Bhagat Singh, late Vinod Mishra, ex- General Secretary of CPI(ML) a group actively associated with the naxalite movement, wrote in the year 1998:

> "Even today, Bhagat Singh's portraits are the most widely sold in the country. His portraits are seen adorning the walls of common people's houses, and thousands of martyr's columns

are found in all parts of the country erected at people's own initiative. If there is a single person who can be awarded the status of people's hero in the struggle for independence, it is only Bhagat Singh. Bhagat Singh is not only a great source of inspiration to the revolutionary mindset of the Indian youth, he is its lighthouse too." (*Liberation*, March 2006)

Another Marxist intellectual, J.N.U.'s Prof. Chaman Lal, is more explicit in exploiting Bhagat Singh's popularity to sell the ideology. He writes in his blog, "One needs to have heroes from one's own tradition to have emotional appeal among masses. Bhagat Singh is one such hero, who has mass appeal, and who has the best enlightened leftist ideas during freedom movement." Perhaps with an eye on Bhagat Singh Chair instituted by the Government of India in his birth centenary year, Chaman Lal is trying to project himself as the greatest expert on Bhagat Singh. He claims to have got Bhagat Singh centenary included in Government of India's programs with the help of the left parliamentary parties.

A striking aspect of the Marxist historiography on Bhagat Singh is that Gandhi is held squarely responsible for not doing enough to save Bhagat Singh and thus robbing the left movement of a great leader who could have given it a new direction. Some, like Vinod Mishra, go so far as to charge that "Bhagat Singh's popularity was fast becoming one of the greatest challenges to the Gandhian leadership.... Still more important was Bhagat Singh's transformation from a revolutionary terrorist to a Marxist. It formed the main basis of the tacit agreement between British rulers and the Congress leadership to send Bhagat Singh to the gallows." (*Liberation*, op. cit.) In fact the Communist movement in India since its inception has looked upon Gandhi as its main rival (see S.A. Dange's *Gandhi vs. Lenin* (1921) M.N. Roy's *India in Transition* (1922) and Rajni Palme Dutt's *India Today* (1940). They have tried their best to pit Bhagat Singh's popularity against Gandhi and to beat Gandhi with the stick of Bhagat Singh's martyrdom. Are these Marxist intellectuals really not aware that

Bhagat Singh himself was persistently inching towards his own martyrdom and frustrating all efforts to dissuade him from doing so? In view of the determination with which Bhagat Singh courted martyrdom, it is legitimate to ask how he could have allowed Gandhiji's efforts to save him succeed. And hypothetically, had he chosen to escape the gallows, as a result of Gandhiji's attempts, would he not have lived at the mercy of his rival Gandhiji and would he have emerged the icon he happens to be today? And then, would the various communist factions and fragments have found him useful to market their failed and outdated ideology? Finally, if Bhagat Singh had lived a long life, and retained the same revolutionary and idealist fervour of 1930s, would he have really liked to be labelled a Communist at all? Significantly, Bhagat Singh did not embrace martyrdom for any ideology, rather for the freedom of the motherland. His patriotism was rejected by his contemporary Communists as 'emotional, romantic and anarchism'. Had he not embraced martyrdom and had chosen to lead the life of a Communist worker, he would also have been lost in oblivion like many of his comrades who lived long lives as Communists.

Unmindful of all such questions, all the leftist groups and fragments planned enthusiastically a three year celebration, commencing with the 75th martyrdom anniversary in 2006 through the birth centenary in the year 2007-2008, to propagate the various brands of their Marxist ideology amongst the youth of this country. When the Government of India on 2nd May 2006 included this inspiring event of national importance in its official programmes, many left organizations hurried to form a Bhagat Singh Commemoration Front on 28th September 2006, to hijack Bhagat Singh's legacy. It is difficult to believe that the group of intellectuals and activists, who claim to be rational, scientific and progressive, could think of replaying 1931 in the twenty first century. Are they really not aware that much water has flown in the rivers – Ganga, Volga and Yangtze? Decades long sincere efforts to build a society free of exploitation and inequality on the Marxist model, were made by the 'Dictatorship of the Proletariat' in Russia, China, East European countries and the far off Cuba have completely failed. After the collapse of the Communist regimes, horrifying details of torture, exile and mass massacres have tumbled out of the cupboards of those regimes. Firsthand accounts of insiders like Khrushchev, Solzhenitsyn and Pasternak etc. have completely exposed the false propaganda of the Stalin days, which had mesmerized many idealist revolutionaries like Bhagat Singh, unaware of these ugly realities. By now, all the Communist icons from Marx to Lenin, from Stalin to Mao-tse Tung have been consigned to the dustbin of history by those very people who had once revered them as demi-gods. The philosophical foundations of Marxism have been found wanting in the light of the expanding frontiers of science and the understanding of human aspirations in the light of the civilizational experience of the last century and a half.

There is no denying the fact that in the last two or three years of his short life of 23 years, Bhagat Singh showed some inclination to the idea of Socialism and in some of his statements he used Marxist slogans and clichés also. Bhagat Singh's attraction to Marxism has to be seen its context, a distant untested dream backed by a powerful propaganda campaign. But interestingly, throughout his life, Bhagat Singh's Communist contemporaries like Sohan Singh Josh were not prepared to accept him as a Marxist. They denounced him as an anarchist or a bookish revolutionary. Up to 1950's many of his comrades such as Ajoy Ghosh, Bejoy Kumar Sinha and Yashpal etc. who at some later stage joined the Communist movement, testified that though Bhagat Singh in his last days showed some romantic inclination towards Marx, Lenin and Soviet Union, he had not become a Marxist in real sense and Communists also never owned him.

Infact, the Communist project of appropriating Bhagat Singh was launched in the 1950s when after the Second World War geopolitical equations underwent radical changes. India had attained independence, Communist armed struggle in Telengana had reached a dead end, Soviet Russia was caught in a Cold War with U.S.A. and befriending independent India became its geo-strategic compulsion. The emergence of Communist China under the leadership of Mao Tse Tung in October 1949 led to Mao-Stalin rivalry on one hand and to divided political loyalties in CPI on the other. CPI, because of its betrayal of the freedom struggle and its support to Pakistan movement was completely alienated from the Indian masses. Therefore, on Stalin's order, in 1950 a delegation of the top CPI leaders made a secret visit to Moscow, where Stalin gave them a severe dressing down and ordered them to withdraw the Telengana movement and in order to win the confidence of Indian masses, identify themselves with the freedom struggle from the 1857 revolt up to the Gandhian phase which included the revolutionary stream also. (For details see my book: *Did Moscow Play Fraud on Marx? The Mystery of Marx-Engels' Articles on 1857*, Historians Forum, Delhi, 2007). It was in this background, that an official biography was commissioned by the CPI and was published in 1953 by its own People's Publishing House. Curiously, this small biography was written by G.M. Telang but was published under the pseudonym Gopal Thakur.

The process of giving a Marxist colour to the ideology of Bhagat Singh received a further boost from 1969 onwards, through the efforts of L.V. Mitrokhin, a Soviet scholar researching Lenin's impact on India. In 1979, Professor Bipan Chandra reached the conclusion that Bhagat Singh was a *pre-eminent* early Marxist ideologue of India. After 1986, beginning with Shiv Varma's edited *Selected Writings of Bhagat Singh* and Jagmohan Singh and Chaman Lal's edited *Bhagat Singh Aur Unke Sathion ke Dastawej*, the dissemination of the Marxist image of Bhagat Singh was undertaken by the publication of over two dozen compilations of documents attributed to Bhagat Singh. The number of documents in successive compilations kept on increasing. No effort was made to check the authenticity of these ever increasing documents. While Bhagat Singh's niece, Virendra Sindhu, was able to produce only 34 writings of Bhagat Singh in her collection *Sardar Bhagat Singh: Patra aur Dastavej*, published in 1975, the latest compilation of by Professor Chaman Lal (*Shaheed Bhagat Singh: Dastavejon Ke Aaine Mein*, 2007) attributes an astounding number of 107 documents to Bhagat Singh. Most of the compilers of Bhagat Singh's documents have left ample scope for the addition of future discoveries of Bhagat Singh's writings. They are convinced that there would still be a number of Bhagat Singh's writings waiting to be discovered. They are hopeful that manuscripts of the four major works supposedly written by Bhagat Singh: (1) *Autobiography* (2) *Ideals of Socialism* (3) *Revolutionary Movement in India* and (4) *At the Door of the Death*; which are considered lost, will surface some day in some personal collection or archive. After all, Bhagat Singh's Jail Notebook had been discovered after almost half a century.

In this background, I felt strongly that Bhagat Singh's life and ideological journey should be re-examined in its context. It is gratifying that my young colleague Dr Chander Pal Singh readily agreed to undertake this onerous task. For four years he painstakingly went through almost all the available primary and secondary sources on Bhagat Singh. It will not be an exaggeration to claim that as far as possible, nothing published in Hindi and English on Bhagat Singh has escaped his eyes. The book owes its present shape to the numerous discussions, which the author had with me regularly for the last four years. It has evolved through many drafts, with practically every chapter rewritten several times over to accommodate the constant inflow of publications on Bhagat Singh on the eve of his birth centenary. The purpose behind this work is to present Bhagat Singh in true light, re-examine the historical questions surrounding him, explain the correct context in which Bhagat Singh was inclined towards socialism in the last few years of his short but glorious life and also expose the Left's dubious claims on the legacy of Bhagat Singh.

The present work has dealt with several unique dimensions of the history related with Bhagat Singh. It, for the first time, re-examines the authenticity and authorship of every document attributed to Bhagat Singh and selectively quoted by the Marxist publicists to push their political agenda. This book examines threadbare the estranged relationship between Bhagat Singh's Naujawan Bharat Sabha and Sohan Singh Josh's Kirti group of the CPI. The book examines minutely all the available evidence on Gandhiji's efforts to save Bhagat Singh's life till the last moment and why he did not succeed. The book also documents the making of the legend of Bhagat Singh and also his persistent quest towards martyrdom.

I am confident that the readers will find many new facts, insights and interpretations in this work. Their comments and observations will help in its improvement and will be eagerly awaited. At the end, I am beholden to Prof. Bimal Prasad, who in spite of his many intellectual preoccupations, on my request, went through an earlier draft and made very valuable and concrete suggestions which helped in making the book more crisp and focused. I am also thankful to my friend Pradip Mittal of the reputed Low Price Publications to have published it.

Devendra Swarup

Preface

Armed revolutionaries were a minor but conspicuous stream in the struggle for Indian independence. They were organized into small bands of heroic and inspired young men who were convinced that British rule over India was established through sword and it could be removed through sword only. To achieve this purpose, an armed uprising was considered inevitable for which people could be motivated only through self-sacrifice and by terrorizing the British officials. It goes to the credit of the revolutionaries that unlike other streams, the British failed to entice them into the trap of the constitutional development process which was designed to prolong the foreign rule in India by continuously creating new divisions in the Indian society. Though their fight against the British might was very unequal, yet the revolutionaries left indelible mark on the hearts of their fellow countrymen with their bravery and sacrifice.

Among the hundreds of the revolutionary martyrs whom a grateful nation cannot afford to forget, the names of a few are itched stronger in the public memory. They include, among others, Chapekar brothers – Damodar and Balkrishna, Khudiram Bose, Madan Lal Dhingra, Prafulla Chaki, Kartar Singh Sarabha, Ramprasad Bismil, Ashfaq Ullah Khan, Jatin Das, Chandra Shekhar Azad, Bhagat Singh, Sukhdev, Rajguru and Surya Sen. Even in this elite gathering, one name that stands out and has become synonymous with the highest ideals of patriotism and martyrdom is Bhagat Singh. Seventy nine years after his martyrdom, Bhagat Singh still remains a symbol of courage, valour and supreme sacrifice for the nation. He is one of the most popular figures of the struggle for Indian independence, an object of pride for countless millions, and above all, a national icon.

Though Bhagat Singh is known for participating in the killing of the police officer Saunders and bomb explosions in the Central Assembly, his most rewarding exploits were related not to his life as an underground revolutionary, but to his two years stay in jail. While other martyrs earned fame for their heroic acts outside the jail, Bhagat Singh's iconic stature and legend is the product of his jail life. He courted arrest in the Central Assembly with a definite purpose and plan. Every act of his, during his trial and after the conviction, was aimed towards popularizing the ideals and objectives of the revolutionary party, and to electrify the nation with his sufferings and sacrifice. Under his leadership, the revolutionary party used the court proceedings to popularize their cause and struggle to such an extent that Government became nervous and was forced to take legally questionable steps to hasten the trial, including the trial in absence. Thus Bhagat Singh exposed the reality of the oft-repeated British boast of their 'rule of law'. In the course of his struggle in jail, including an epic 113 days long hunger strike, Bhagat Singh received sympathy and love from all the classes, some of whom in the past had been skeptical of identifying with the revolutionary cause and methods. He thus singlehandedly changed the image of revolutionaries from misguided patriots to popular heroes and gave the revolutionary movement a human face. He invited and planned his martyrdom and embraced it at the height of his popularity to cause the maximum impact. His martyrdom unleashed powerful waves of patriotic sentiment in all corners of India. No Indian revolutionary or martyr, before or after Bhagat Singh, was able to achieve all this.

No wonder, Bhagat Singh is also the most written about revolutionary in India. Last few years, in the wake of the 75th anniversary of his martyrdom (2006-2007) and his birth centenary (2007-2008), have witnessed a spate of writings on Bhagat Singh. A cursory look at the recent literature is sufficient to bring home the impression that most of it has been penned to project Bhagat Singh as a Marxist ideologue rather than highlight his role in the freedom movement. In these works there is overemphasis on

Bhagat Singh's attraction towards Socialism in the last few years of his life. For this purpose they are recklessly attributing writings to Bhagat Singh without carefully settling the authorship. In short they are using the iconic status of Bhagat Singh to revive the Communist movement's fortunes in India so much so that there is competition among various Communist groups about their claims on Bhagat Singh.

In the process of depicting Bhagat Singh in a Marxist mould, the role of early influences, traditions and events in shaping Bhagat Singh is being ignored. Apart from the ideological bias, there are several other lacunas in the available literature on Bhagat Singh. It may shock an informed reader that even the chronology of events of Bhagat Singh's life is not yet fixed. There is no consensus on the dates of several important events of the great martyr's life, such as his date of birth and events of his early revolutionary career. Also not fixed is the number of writings attributed to Bhagat Singh, nor is there any consensus on some of the writings attributed to Bhagat Singh. Many compilers of Bhagat Singh's writings, rather than working on the authorship and authenticity of writings are unfortunately competing among themselves to attribute maximum number of documents to him.

Among the multitude of books available on Bhagat Singh, the present work claims its relevance in the light of the issues raised above. Besides revisiting Bhagat Singh and his times, this book also examines critically the historical presentation of Bhagat Singh. It emphasizes that patriotism, not socialism, constituted the core of Bhagat Singh's ideology. Burning patriotism and a strong urge to sacrifice his life for the freedom of the motherland were the consistent features of his short life until the last moment. Socialism enters in the last few years but remains at periphery. The readers will find in this work many new contemporary sources as well as several new aspects of the debate on Bhagat Singh, which, it is hoped, will stimulate further research on the subject.

The book is divided into three sections- Historiography, Biography, and Ideology. The first section presents a survey of the sources available on Bhagat Singh. A reconstruction of the chronology of his life, based on a chronological analysis of the events, and marked by the use of some new sources is also a part of this section. This section also includes, for the first time, a detailed investigation of the writings attributed to Bhagat Singh in terms of their authorship, date of writing, publication history and controversies associated with them.

The second section deals with the biographic aspect of Bhagat Singh. First two chapters in this section are about his family background and his formative phase and his activities as the member of the revolutionary party before going to the prison. Third chapter in this section deals with the political platform of revolutionary groups in Punjab, the Naujawan Bharat Sabha, of which Bhagat Singh was one of the founders. Sabha's relationship with the Communist Kirti group has been explored here for the first time. Fourth chapter of this section is about the fascinating tale of Bhagat Singh's struggle in jail leading to his transformation from an unknown revolutionary to the most popular figure of his time, rivaling even Mahatma Gandhi's popularity. The last chapter presents the persona of Bhagat Singh as a man in the words of his friends, colleagues and contemporaries.

The third section deals with the ideological debates associated with Bhagat Singh. The first chapter in this section brings out the fact that whatever ideological tags may have been attached to Bhagat Singh, intense patriotism only remained the fundamental ingredient of his creed, independence of the motherland his cherished goal and martyrdom his lifelong passion. Next chapter in this section successfully challenges the commonly held notion that Mahatma Gandhi did little to save Bhagat Singh whom he supposedly regarded as an ideological rival. Some critics of Gandhi have gone as far as to accuse of Gandhi of having reached a tacit understanding with the British on the fate of Bhagat Singh. The fact which emerges after a thorough perusal of all the evidence available is that Gandhi did his best to save the lives of Bhagat

Singh, Sukhdev and Rajguru till the last moment. Third chapter of this section puts a question mark on the claims of Bhagat Singh being a Marxist ideologue as such. This chapter places Bhagat Singh's attraction towards Socialism in the context of the contemporary Bolshevik propaganda of creating a dream society in Russia, their promise of help against imperialistic powers and help to the Indian revolutionaries in exile etc. The chapter concludes with the contemporary Communist position regarding Bhagat Singh and his fellow revolutionaries up till 1951 as '*terrorists*', their concept of revolution as the '*psychology of revenge and not revolution*', and their methods simply '*not permissible in Marxism*'. The last chapter traces the Indian Communists' stand on Bhagat Singh since 1950's to the present day, from condemnation to appropriation, including the shifts and contradictions in the Marxist historiography of Bhagat Singh, and the competition among the different factions of the Communist movement to present Bhagat Singh of their own mould.

In the preparation of this book I received help, guidance and material from many sources. My first and foremost gratitude is reserved for Sh. Devendra Swarup who conceived this project and guided me from the start to the last draft. I have benefitted greatly from his vast knowledge, penetrative analysis, and huge collection of books. Numerous hours which I spent in his exalted company are among my most precious treasures. I am also indebted to Mrs. Virendra Sindhu and Sh. Kiranjeet Singh, niece and nephew of Bhagat Singh, for their ever willingness in sharing valuable information on the great martyr. Sh. Rudravir Kapur, son of Late Comrade Ramchandra, made available out of print works by Comrade Ramchandra. Mrs. Manorama Dewan, daughter of Principal Chhabildas, also provided me a biography of her parents besides encouragement. I am grateful to Historians' Forum for a research stipend which sustained me for two years. Brig. Raj Bahadur Sharma twice went through an earlier draft of the manuscript minutely and saved me from much embarrassment by rectifying copious flaws of language. Dr. Meenakshi Jain and Dr.

Ramchandra Pradhan also read an earlier draft and gave valuable suggestions along with continuous motivation. Professor Bimal Prasad also spared his valuable time and energy to read an earlier draft and gave extremely useful comments. Sh. Ranjan Agarwal, out of his interest in this work, arranged for the typing of the first draft and he himself typed several chapters. Sh. Shiv Kumar Goyal readily parted with some rare books in his collection. Dr. Isha Sharma lent her Ph. D. dissertation and other books. Sh. T.C. Ghai and Deepak Kumar Sharma contributed in the translation of Hindi quotes. I am indebted to all of them. However, for all errors of facts, interpretation or language, I alone am responsible.

I am also grateful to the librarians and staff of the libraries which I consulted for this work- National Archives of India, Nehru Memorial Museum and Library, Central Secretariat Library, Delhi Public Library, Ajoy Bhawan Library, Sapru House Library, Lajpat Bhawan Library, all in Delhi; Martyrs' Memorial and Freedom Struggle Research Centre, Lucknow; M.M.H. College Library, Ghaziabad; and C.C.S. University Library, Meerut. Among them, Sh. Rajmani and Dr. Pradeep Kumar, both of National Archives of India, deserve special mention for their friendly back-up and cups of tea. I also acknowledge my indebtedness to my family, friends, and well-wishers for their support and encouragement. In the end, I am much obliged to Sh. Pradeep Mittal for taking a keen interest in the publication of this work.

Chander Pal Singh

Historiography

Historiography

1

A Survey of the Sources

More than 79 years have passed since Bhagat Singh attained martyrdom on 23rd March 1931. Being one of the most popular icons of India's freedom struggle, much has been written about him. Large volume of literature is available on Bhagat Singh, both in the form of full length biographies as well as articles in newspapers and journals. In keeping with the historical tradition, Bhagat Singh's birth centenary (2007-2008) provided an opportunity to look back and review his historiography. Historiography, as generally understood, is the history of historical writing. In other words, it is writing *about* history rather than *of* history. In the present context, historiography of Bhagat Singh focuses on the examination of the writings on Bhagat Singh upon issues such as sources, use of evidence, interpretation, method of presentation etc.

Aim of the present chapter is to present a synoptic view of the sources available for a study of Bhagat Singh. These sources can be divided into five broad catagories: his own writings, government record, reminiscences of contemporaries, press reports, and secondary sources including biographies and articles etc.

Bhagat Singh's name suddenly burst upon the national scenario with a bang when along with Batukeshwar Dutt he made headlines for throwing bombs in the Central Assembly in Delhi on 8th April 1929. His subsequent emergence as a legend in less than two years of his remaining life has been analysed in detail in a separate chapter. Contemporary press, which took a deep interest in Bhagat

Singh, is a very valuable source of his historical reconstruction. Particularly indispensible are the files of *The Tribune* (Lahore), *The People* (Lahore), *Abhyudaya* (Allahabad), and *Bhavisya* (Allahabad). Life sketches and patriotic poetry centered on Bhagat Singh had begun to appear in print in different parts of the country during his jail life. His execution was followed by a spurt in the published material which included special numbers of several newspapers. Nearly all such publications before independence were proscribed by the British Government; some of them are available in archival files and library of National Archives of India (NAI), in Hindi, English, Tamil, Telugu, Punjabi (Gurumukhi), Urdu and Gujarati. A handy account of such sources is provided by two booklets published by NAI entitled *Patriotic Writings Banned by the Raj* (New Delhi, 1982) and *Patriotic Poetry Banned by the Raj* (New Delhi, 1982) and also N.G. Barrier's *Banned Controversial Literature and Political Control in British India (1907-47)* (New Delhi, 1977). A recent work, Gurudev S. Sidhu's *Hanging of Bhagat Singh: The Banned Literature* (Chandigarh, 2007) provides information about 153 pieces of literature, in both prose and poetry, which appeared after the hanging of Bhagat Singh.

Home Political records at NAI are not of much help to know the early career of Bhagat Singh. They provide precious details only for the period after April 1929 when Bhagat Singh was arrested in the Assembly Bomb Case. Papers of the Assembly Bomb Case (1929) and the Lahore Conspiracy Case (1929-1931) available at NAI and Nehru Memorial Library and Museum (NMML) in New Delhi are essential for any study on Bhagat Singh. They provide detailed account of the activities of the revolutionary group known by the name of Hindustan Socialist Republican Association of which Bhagat Singh was one of the founder leaders. Of particular interest are the notes on the margins of Lahore Case proceedings, in the handwriting of Sukhdev, which throw new light on the case. Important selections from the Lahore Conspiracy Case papers are also available in Malwinder Jit Singh

Waraich, and Gurudev Singh Sidhu, (eds.), *The Hanging of Bhagat Singh, The Complete Judgement and Other Documents* (Chandigarh, 2005).

Secondary sources on Bhagat Singh are scattered among biographies, articles in newspapers and journals, and reminiscences of his contemporaries. More than fifty biographies of Bhagat Singh are at present available in English and Hindi only, the latest being M.M. Juneja's *Biography of Bhagat Singh* (Hisar, 2008). Among them, two by Bhagat Singh's revolutionary colleagues- Jatindra Nath Sanyal and Ajoy Ghosh, both co-prisoners in the Lahore Conspiracy Case, stand apart. J.N. Sanyal's *Sardar Bhagat Singh* (Allahabad, May 1931) was one of the earliest biographies of Bhagat Singh, published within two months of his execution. Written in the face of the danger of being banned by the Government (which eventually it was), Sanyal had to hold back many facts. This handicap was done away by the author in the post-independence edition of the book (Mirzapur, 1970). In between the two editions, a Hindi translation of the book by Snehlata Sehgal (Allahabad, 1947) appeared in 1947. Snehlata was the daughter of Ram Rakha Sahgal of Hindi monthly '*Chand*' fame, who had also published Jatindra Nath Sanyal's original work in 1931. Snehlata's volume comes with some very useful information for a Bhagat Singh reader in the form of contemporary press clippings and detailed accounts of the proceedings of the two Lahore Conspiracy Cases. Snehlata's Hindi version of J.N. Sanyal's book was almost lost to public memory when National Book Trust brought out a reprint in 1999. A reprint was also published by Rahul Foundation of Lucknow in 2004, but for reasons best known to them, they chose to drop Purhsottam Das Tandon's forward to Snehlata's Hindi version. Ajoy Ghosh's *Bhagat Singh and His Comrades* (Delhi, 1945) contains only 15 pages on Bhagat Singh, but it is often cited for its brevity and authenticity, coming from someone who was Bhagat Singh's comrade in the revolutionary party and was also involved in the Lahore Conspiracy Case. Other biography by a contemporary worth mentioning is *Bhagat Singh and His Times*

(New Delhi, 1977) by Manmathnath Gupta. Gupta, who as a seventeen year old, had participated in the famous Kakori train decoity (1925) and thus was a colleague of Bhagat Singh in the revolutionary movement.

Among the other notable biographies of Bhagat Singh, one by his niece Virender Sindhu (daughter of his younger brother Kultar Singh), *Yugdrista Bhagat Singh Aur Unke Mritunjaya Purkhe* (Delhi, 1968) stands out for its extensive use of family memories, documents, and contemporaries' memoirs and also for its literary style. Gur Dev Singh Deol's *Shaheed Bhagat Singh: A Biography* (Patiala, 1968) was the first to use archival records. Malwinder Jit Singh Waraich's *Bhagat Singh: The Eternal Rebel* (Delhi, 2007) is also significant as it brings to light some archival documents on Bhagat Singh, hitherto unknown. Among the non-biographical works mention must be made of *Bhagat Singh and His Legend* (Patiala, 2008), edited by J.S. Grewal and A.G. Noorani's *The Trial of Bhagat Singh* (Delhi, 1996). Former is a collection of essays by eminent scholars on the subject and latter has analyzed in detail the bias and unfairness of British judicial system evident during the trial of Bhagat Singh.

The Communist perspective on Bhagat Singh is represented by three biographies: Gopal Thakur's *Bhagat Singh: The Man and His Ideas*, (New Delhi, 1953); A.B. Bardhan's *Bhagat Singh: Pages from the Life of the Martyr* (New Delhi, 1984); and P.M.S. Grewal's *Bhagat Singh: Liberation's Blazing Star* (New Delhi, 2007). A well documented work, *To Make the Deaf Hear: Ideology and Programme of Bhagat Singh and His Comrades* (Delhi, 2007) by S. Irfan Habib, not exactly a biography, is the most eloquent presentation of Marxist position on Bhagat Singh. But the largest and also the latest compendium of Left scholarship on Bhagat Singh is *Rethinking Radicalism in Indian Society: Bhagat Singh and Beyond* (Jaipur, 2009), edited by Jose George, Manoj Kumar and Avinash Khandare. This compendium of 28 papers has 18 papers devoted to Bhagat Singh.

Reminiscences of Bhagat Singh's contemporaries are a significant source for historical reconstruction of Bhagat Singh, both as a man and as a freedom fighter. Based on close personal contact, they provide intimate yet multi-dimensional glimpses into his personality. But as these reminiscences were penned dawn long after the events, they have their limitations as layers of the intervening time make the memories hazy, hence their proper use requires cross checking and verification. The present work has used the reminiscences of contemporaries such as Jogesh Chattarjee, Sohan Singh Josh, Yashpal, Prakashvati Pal, Comrade Ramchandra, Sachindra Nath Sanyal, Satyabhakta, Chatur Sen Shastri, Raja Ram Shastri, Guru Dutt, Principal Chhabildas, Shiv Varma, Bejoy Kumar Sinha, Bhagwan Das Mahaur, Vishwanath Vaishampayan, Nand Kishore Nigam, Jayachandra Vidyalankar, Dinanath Sidhantalankar, Durga Devi Vohra, Lajjavati, Mathura Das Thapar, Prithvi Singh Azad, Manmathnath Gupta, Jitendra Nath Sanyal, and Sadashiv Malkapurkar. Transcriptions of the interviews of some of the contemporaries preserved in the oral history section of NMML have also been very useful in this regard.

For a study of Bhagat Singh, histories of freedom struggle and revolutionary movement are indispensible for the context and the background they provide. General histories of revolutionary movement form a significant portion of bibliography, earliest of which are- Manmathnath Gupta's *Bharat Mein Sashastra Kranti Ki Chesta Ka Romanchkari Itihas* and Chandra Shekhar Shastri's *Bharatiya Atankavad Ka Itihas*, both published in 1939. In tracing the history of the revolutionary movement, great help is also provided by the compilations of intelligence reports prepared by senior officers of British Intelligence. Two such compilations covering the period of Bhagat Singh are: J. M. Ewart's *Terrorism in India, 1917-36*; and H. Hale's *Political Trouble in India, 1917-37*.

In order to understand the Communist perspective on Bhagat Singh, histories of the Communist movement in India in general and the 'Left' writings on Bhagat Singh in particular are essential readings. They include works by Communist leaders who were also contemporaries of Bhagat Singh like Shaukat Usmani, S.A. Dange, Muzzaffar Ahmad, and Sohan Singh Josh. Some of Bhagat Singh's colleagues in the revolutionary party like Ajoy Ghosh and Shiv Varma became Communists later in their life. Their reminiscences of Bhagat Singh deserve special attention. During the last few years, Indian Communist movement has also published a number of pamphlets on Bhagat Singh. These pamphlets and recent writings on Bhagat Singh are importants source to understand the leftist interest in Bhagat Singh. Compilations of British intelligence reports on Communist activities in India, covering a period from 1919 to 1934, by three Directors of Intelligence Bureau viz. Cecil Kaye, David Petrie and Horace Williamson, have also been consulted although they, out of 'Russo-phobia', reveal signs of British over-reaction to the 'Bolshevik threat' to the Empire. Among the works on history of Communism which appeared after the disintegration of Soviet Union and end of the communist regime in Russia, a special mention must be made of Sobhanlal Datta Gupta's *Comintern and the Destiny of Communist Movement in India, 1919-1943*. Importance of Datta's work lies in the fact that it is based on new material, collected from once forbidden Comintern archives in Moscow and archives of the Communist Party of Great Britain, which became accessible for the first time in 1990's and provides a refreshing new insight into the working of Communist organizations quite different from the official Communist version.

2

Bhagat Singh's Chronology Reconstructed

It indeed is a travesty of Indian history that even after 79 years of the martyrdom of one of the most popular symbols of our national movement, the chronological fixation of Shaheed Bhagat Singh's lifespan of merely 23 years, is still far from satisfactory. About 50 biographies and numerous articles which have appeared so far, have failed to resolve the conflicting opinion on the dates of certain important events in the life of the great martyr such as: date of his birth; movement to Kanpur and back; organization of the reception to Jaiton *jattha*; and birth of Naujawan Bharat Sabha. Following is a humble attempt to reconstruct the chronology of Bhagat Singh.

Chronologically, Bhagat Singh's life span of twenty three years can be divided into three parts: (i) 1907 to 1923: Bhagat Singh's life at home and as a student; (ii) 1923 to 8th April 1929: the phase when Bhagat Singh was involved in revolutionary activities; and (iii) 8th April 1929 to 23 March 1931: the last phase of his life spent in British jails as an under trial prisoner and as a convict awaiting execution. Except the last phase of his life for which detailed official record is available, chronology of the rest of twenty one years of Bhagat Singh's life has to be reconstructed with the help of related events.

Bhagat Singh was born in 1907 in village Banga of district Lyallpur in Punjab. There are at least eight different versions of his date of birth according to different authors: 7th September 1907[1] – *Encyclopedia Britannica, Indian History Modern*; 25th September 1907[2] – Hansraj Rahbar ; 27th September 1907[3] –

G.S. Deol, K.K. Khullar; 28th September 1907[4] – Virender Sindhu; 5th October 1907[5] – Mathura Das Thapar, Shiv Verma; 19th October 1907[6] - K.C. Yadav; 27th October 1907[7] – J.N. Sanyal; and 28th December 1907[8] – Ram Chandra, Manmath Nath Gupta. Apart from these dates there is a date of birth based on Hindu calendar – '*Ashwin Triyodashi Shukla Vikrami Samvat* 1964, Saturday'. This date of birth appeared in the short biographies of Bhagat Singh which appeared in '*Bhavisya*' of 16 April 1931 and '*Abhuyudaya*' of 8th May 1931 (Bhagat Singh number) and some authors have also mentioned it.[9] Lack of concensus on Bhagat Singh's date of birth justifies the opinion of Prithvi Singh Azad,a noted revolutionary himself, in his write up on Bhagat Singh in *Dictionary of National Biography* that exact date of birth of Bhagat Singh is not known.[10]

Bhagat Singh completed his primary school education in his village Banga.[11] Later, he was admitted to D.A.V. school, Lahore.[12] Bhagat Singh left D.A.V. School in 1921 during the Non-Cooperation movement.[13] He also worked as a Congress volunteer and actively participated in the boycott of foreign goods during the Non-Cooperation movement. To enroll the non-cooperating students, Congress had planned to establish national schools and colleges throughout the country. Consequently the Punjab Provincial Congress formed a Board of National Education in early 1921.[14] As a result, a national university under the name of 'Punjab Qaumi Vidyapeeth' was established with Lala Lajpat Rai as its Chancellor and Bhai Parmanand as its Vice Chancellor. Lala Lajpat Rai had earlier established the 'Tilak School of Politics' in December 1920 with the objective of evolving a band of life members to be trained in different departments of national work.[15] With the starting of Non-Cooperation movement, Tilak School of Politics was practically suspended in favour of National College, Lahore (under the auspices of Punjab Qaumi Vidyappeeth).[16] National College, Lahore was formally started on 16 May 1921.[17]

Bhagat Singh was in ninth class when he left D.A.V. School to join National College where the students could take admission only after passing the matriculation. Bhai Parmanand gave Bhagat Singh some time to prepare and after a thorough test found him fit to admit in first year of the College in year 1921.[18] There he met some of his future associates in revolutionary activities like Sukhdev, Bhagwati Charan Vohra and Yashpal.

Yashpal writes that after the suspension of Non – Cooperation movement in 1922, Bhagat Singh had started participating in *Gurdwara* movement. He had started keeping long hair, and wearing black turban and sword.[19]

While studying in National College, in 1923, Bhagat Singh came in contact with the famous revolutionary Sachindra Nath Sanyal through Jaichandra Vidyalankar.[20] In the same year, he ran away from home to escape marriage and reached Kanpur with a letter from S. N. Sanyal for Jogesh Chandra Chatterji.[21] Bhagat Singh went to Kanpur in the later part of 1923.[22] At that time he had passed F.A. and had taken admission in B.A. At Kanpur Bhagat Singh came in contact with Batukeshwar Dutt, Ajoy Ghosh, Jogesh Chandra Chatterjee, Suresh Chandra Bhattacharya, Bejoy Kumar Sinha, Ganesh Shankar Vidyarthi, Manilal Awasthi, and Vir Bhadra Tiwari, all members of the revolutionary party.

Meanwhile, Jaidev came to know about Bhagat Singh's Kanpur address through his letter. As a result of the efforts of friends and father, Bhagat Singh returned home in early 1924, after about 6 months of absence. Punjab in those days was witnessing *Gurdwara* movement against corrupt *Mahants*, who were under active protection of the British Government. In April 1924, Bhagat Singh successfully organized a welcome to the *Akali* Jatha participating in '*Jaiton*' Satyagraha, in his village against the Government orders.[23] He had to go in hiding as arrest warrants were issued in his name. After staying for one month in Kanpur, Bhagat Singh is said to have worked for three months in a National School as headmaster, at village Shadipur of Kher tehsil of Aligarh district established by Thakur Todar Singh.[24]

By the end of the year 1924, Bhagat Singh was working in Delhi, in the office of '*Arjun*', a Hindi newspaper edited by Indra Vidyavachaspati.[25] There he stayed with Satyaketu Vidyalankar. According to Satyaketu Vidyalankar, Bhagat Singh distributed a revolutionary pamphlet in Delhi on 31st December 1924.[26] In the beginning of 1925 he was back at Lahore. At that time he, along with Comrade Ram Chandra, Bhagwati Charan Vohra, Master Guru Dutt, Sukhdev, Jai Dev and Principal Chabildas amid others, established the Naujawan Bharat Sabha (NBS).[27] Comrade Ramchandra, in his book *Naujawan Bharat Sabha and HSRA* has stressed that the Sabha was founded 'towards the end of 1924'[28] and by early 1925 its constitution had been finalised.[29] At another place Ramchandra wrote that NBS was founded in 1924-25.[30] But taking into account the evidence cited above about Bhagat Singh's presence in Delhi up to the last days of year 1924, beginning of 1925 as the year of establishment of NBS appears to be more plausible. Initially Guru Dutt, Bhagat Singh and Bhagwati Charan Vohra had been elected as President, General Secretary and Treasurer respectively.[31] Bhagat Singh continued to work in the capacity of General Secretary of the Sabha till October 1928.[32]

Meanwhile Hindustan Republican Army had conducted Kakori Train Decoity on 9th August 1925. By October 1925 all the participants of Kakori action except Chandra Shekhar Azad were arrested. During the trial of Kakori conspiracy case (which started on 4th January 1926 in the court of Special Magistrate and continued upto 21 May 1926), Bhagat Singh went to Lucknow to attend trial in the lower court.[33] According to J.N. Sanyal he established secret communication with the under trials of the case confined in the District Jail.[34] Bhagat Singh also attempted to free Ram Prasad Bismil from Jail in 1926 and again in the beginning of 1927. For this purpose he lived with Shiv Verma in Kanpur at the end of 1926 and again in the beginning of 1927.[35] During September – October 1926, Bhagat Singh was in Lahore.[36]

It was the time of electoral campaigning for Provincial Councils and the Central Assembly due to be held in November 1926.[37] Naujawan Bharat Sabha decided to support Swaraj Party against independent Congress Party of Lala Lajpat Rai and Madan Mohan Malviya.[38]

It was in 1926 that Raja Ram Shastri came to Lahore and worked as Librarian of Dwarka Prasad Library till 1931. In his memoirs he has described in detail his interaction with Bhagat Singh from 1926 to 1928.[39] During this period Bhagat Singh used to visit Dwarka Das Library frequently. Yashpal has written that during the later part of 1926 Bhagat Singh was quite agitated due to his inability to speed up revolutionary work and pressure from his father to quit such activities.[40] On 29th May 1927, Bhagat Singh was arrested in Lahore.[41] Police had some clues to suspect Bhagat Singh's links with the Kakori group and so they arrested him on the false pretext of his suspected involvement in a bomb blast in Lahore on the occasion of Dussehra on 16th October 1926.[42] Bhagat Singh was released on bail on 4th July 1927.[43]

The year 1928 witnessed the full bloom of Bhagat Singh's versatility. Most of his writings in periodicals were published in this year. Naujawan Bharat Sabha also became more vigorous and *Kirti* Group joined it. Revolutionary party was also revamped.

Though the journal '*Kirti*' in Punjabi had started in February 1926[44], Bhagat Singh's first writing in '*Kirti*', under the pen name- 'Vidrohi', was published in May 1927.[45] Bhagat Singh came into contact of chief editor Sohan Singh Josh for the first time in the first week of April 1928 in connection of the first Naujawan Bharat Sabha Conference in Jallianwala Bagh, Amritsar on April 13 and 14.[46] According to Sohan Singh Josh, Bhagat Singh also worked in the editorial board of Urdu *Kirti* (the first issue of Urdu *Kirti* was published in April 1928)[47] for about three months[48]. The largest numbers of articles of Kirti, attributed to Bhagat Singh, were published between May 1928 and August 1928 and so this period may be taken as the one in which he worked on the editorial board of *Kirti*.

At about the same time Bhagat Singh had cut all links with his family and became fully engrossed in the revolutionary work.[49] In July 1928, a meeting was held at Kanpur to reorganize the revolutionary party and form a central Committee.[50] Bhagat Singh and Bejoy Kumar Sinha also started touring different places to revive the old contacts and make new contacts. Finally, a meeting of revolutionaries was held at Feroj Shah Kotla grounds in Delhi on 8th and 9th September 1928 in which the name of the party was changed from Hindustan Republican Association to Hindustan Socialist Republican Association (HSRA) and its organization and policies were revamped.[51] It was at this time in Delhi that Bhagat Singh met Phanendra Nath Ghosh and Manmohan Bannerji for the first time.[52]

Here onwards, the movements of Bhagat Singh are difficult to trace because as a revolutionary all his movement must have been incognito. The responsibilities entrusted to him required constant travelling to different places. In the middle of September, Bhagat Singh was in Ferozpur (Punjab) where he cut his hair.[53] Towards the end of September, Bhagat Singh went to Bettiah (Bihar) with Chandra Shekhar Azad for a decoity which could not take place.[54] In October, Bhagat Singh resigned from the post of Secretary of Naujawan Bharat Sabha because his revolutionary activities left little time for the work of the Sabha.[55]

Simon Commission's arrival in Lahore on 30th October was protested against by demonstrators shouting 'Simon Go Back'. Police lathi charge on the demonstration injured Lala Lajpat Rai who later died as a result of his injuries on 17th November 1928. HSRA decided to take revenge and most of the members of the party were called to the Punjab. HSRA also decided to loot the Punjab National Bank in Lahore on 4th December to solve the financial problems of the party.[56] However the plan had to be abandoned at the last moment due to unavailability of a car.

On 10th December, the Central Committee of HSRA in Lahore drew a plan to kill Mr. Scott, Superintendent of Police as he was responsible for attack on Lala Lajpat Rai.[57] At first, the date of murder of Scott was fixed for 15th December but later it was postponed to 17th December. Scott proved to be lucky, in his place, due to mistaken identity, Assistant Superintendent of Police Mr. Saunders was killed by Raj Guru and Bhagat Singh, on the designated date. Next morning, HSRA pamphlets owned responsibility for the murder and also explained the reasons behind the attack.[58]

Bhagat Singh left Lahore on 20th December[59] to escape the police net and reached Calcutta on 22nd December. In Calcutta, Bhagat Singh met Phanindra Nath Ghosh, Jayachandra Vidyalankar, Jatin Das, Sohan Singh Josh, Bhagwati Charan Vohra, Sushila Didi, Trailokya Nath Chakraborty and Manmohan Bannerjee. It is not clear when Bhagat Singh returned from Calcutta.[60]

In the beginning of February 1929, Jatin Das taught Bhagat Singh, Phanindra Nath Ghosh and Kamal Nath Tiwari the art of making bomb at Arya Samaj Mandir at Cornwallis Street in Calcutta.[61] Soon after a bomb factory was established at Agra which had been the party headquarter since November 1928 (shifted from Jhansi). Those who were present at Agra to learn bomb making from Jatin Das were: Bhagat Singh, Chandra Shekhar Azad, Phanindra Nath Gosh, Sukh Dev, Bejoy Kumar Sinha, Shiv Varma, Sadashiv and Lalit Kumar Mukherjee.[62] The immediate plan of the party was to rescue Jogesh Chandra Chatterjee on 16th February during his transfer from Agra to Lucknow Jail.[63] But the rescue operation could not take place due to lack of accurate information. On 19th February members of Central Committee decided to attack Simon Commission with bomb.[64] Bhagat Singh and Azad left Agra to raise funds for this purpose.

In the last week of February 1929, the Central Committee decided to cancel the plan of attacking Simon Commission due to tactical problems. In its place they decided to bomb the Central Assembly.[65] During those days Bhagat Singh travelled continuously, shuttling between Lahore, Delhi and Agra. By the end of March Agra headquarters was abandoned by HSRA and in its place

Saharanpur was chosen as the new headquarters.[66] Bhagat Singh and Batukeshwar Dutt were chosen as the volunteers to carry out the bomb attack in the Central Assembly. Both of them reached Delhi where first they lived at Bazar Sita Ram and then shifted to Nai Sarak.[67] On 8th April they threw bombs in Central Assembly along with some copies of a pamphlet and surrendered to the police.

The chronology of Bhagat Singh after 8th April 1929 upto 23rd March 1931 is well recorded in minute details in the official records and contemporary press.

Chronological Sketch of Bhagat Singh (1907-1931)

1907		Bhagat Singh born in village Banga of district Lyallpur in Punjab
1909		Ajit Singh leaves India
1910		Swarn Singh passes away
1913-15		Ghadar movement in Punjab
1915- 16		Elder brother Jagat Singh passes away
1915	November 16	Kartar Singh Sarabha hanged in Lahore jail
1918	July 22	First available letter of Bhagat Singh; written while studying in 6th class to his grandfather Sardar Arjun Singh
1919	February 6	Government introduces Rowlett Bills in Central Assembly
1919	April 13	Jallianwala Bagh massacre in Amritsar
1919	April 21	Martial law imposed in Punjab
1920- 1922		Non-Cooperation Movement
1920	December	Tilak School of Politics founded in Lahore by Lala Lajpat Rai

1921	May 16	National College Lahore formally started
1921		Bhagat Singh (studying in 9th class) left D.A.V. School, Lahore on Mahatma Gandhi's call to boycott government backed schools. He was able to get admission in National College, Lahore as a student of 11th class
1922		Bhagat Singh started keping long hair, and wearing black turban, and a sword as a mark of sympathy with the ongoing Gurudwara Reform movement
1923		*Babbar Akali* movement in Punjab. Bhagat Singh passed Intermediate, took admission in B.A. but soon ran away from home to Kanpur under guidance from Sachindra Nath Sanyal. Joined Hindustan Republican Association (HRA)
1924	Beginning of year	Returns home after six months
1924	April	Organises Jaiton *jattha* reception in his village
	May-June	Goes to Kanpur and remains there for a month
	July-Sep.	Works as headmaster in a national school in Aligarh district
	Octob. onwards	Worked in *Arjun* in Delhi
1925	January 28	Distributed pamphlet *Revolutionary* in Delhi
Early part of 1925		Formation of Naujawan Bharat Sabha in Lahore
	March 9	Participated in a decoity
	August 9	Kakori train decoity

1926		Rajaram joins Dwarkadas library at Lahore
	October 16	Bomb explosion in Lahore during Dussehra
	End of the year	Bhagat Singh made efforts to rescue Kakori prisoners
1927	May 29	Bhagat Singh's first arrest in Lahore
	July 4	Released on bail
		Kishan Singh sets up dairy at village Khasaria near Lahore
	December 17	Rajendranath Lahiri hanged
	December 19	Ramprasad Bismil, Ashfaqullah Khan, and Master Roshan Lal hanged
1928	February	Quashing of the bail of Bhagat Singh
	March	Naujawan Bharat Sabha reactivated
	April 11-13	Naujawan Bharat Sabha conference at Amritsar. *Kirti* group associated with Naujawan Bharat Sabha
	April- May	Family loses contact with Bhagat Singh
	July	HRA meeting at Kanpur
	September 8-9	Meeting at Feroz Shah Kotla in Delhi. HRA rechristened HSRA
	Sep. (middle)	Bhagat Singh got his hair and beard removed at Ferozpur
	October	Resigned from the post of General Secretary of Naujawan Bharat Sabha
	October 30	Protest demonstration against Simon Commission at Lahore

	November	HSRA headquarters shifted to Agra from Jhansi
	November 17	Death of Lala Lajpat Rai due to injuries caused by police lathi charge
	December 4	HSRA's bank decoity plan at Lahore failed
	December 9-10	HSRA meeting at Lahore to plan assassination of Scott
	December 17	Saunders murdered
	December 20	Bhagat Singh leaves Lahore for Calcutta incognito with Durga Bhabhi
	Dec. 25-31	Congress session in Calcutta
1929	January	Bhagat Singh in Calcutta
	Feb.(beginning)	Jatin Das at Agra to teach bomb making to HSRA members
	February 16	Rescue operation for Jogesh Chatterji fails
	February 19	Central Committee of HSRA deided to attack Simon Commission
	Feb.(last-week)	Decision to bomb Central Assembly
	March	Bhagat Singh shuttles between Agra and Delhi
	March 4	Gandhi arrested at Calcutta
	March 20	Arrest of labour leaders
	March (end)	Agra headquarters of HSRA abandoned, Saharanpur chosen as the new headquarters

Last week of March-

First week of April	Bhagat Singh and Batukeshwar Dutt live in Delhi, first at Bazar Sita Ram and then at Nai Sarak
April 8	Bhagat Singh throws bombs in the Central Assembly and courts arrest along with Batukeshwar Dutt
April 15	Lahore bomb factory raided; Sukhdev, Jaigopal and Kishori Lal arrested
May 7	Trial begins in Assembly Case in District jail, Delhi
May 13	Saharanpur bomb factory raided. Shiv Varma and Jaidev Kapur arrested
June 4	Trial in Assembly Case in Sessions Court in Delhi
June 6	Joint statement of Bhagat Singh and Batukeshwar Dutt in Sessions Court
June 10	Trial ends in Sessions Court
June 12	Sessions Court awards life imprisonment to both Bhagat Singh and Batukeshwar Dutt. Bhagat Singh sent to Miawali Jail and Dutt sent to Lahore Central Jail
June 15	Bhagat Singh and Dutt begin their hunger strike
July 10	Trial starts in Lahore Conspiracy Case
July 13	Some other under-trials of Lahore Conspiracy Case also join hunger strike
July 24	Jatin Das joins hunger strike
September 2	Punjab Jail Enquiry Committee appointed. All except Jatin Das abandoned the strike

	September 4	Bhagat Singh and Dutt resumed their hunger strike
	September 13	Jatin Das becomes a martyr
	September 30	Rajguru arrested at Poona
	October 5	Bhagat Singh and others end their hunger strike
	Nov. (first week)	Yashpal and Bhagawati Charan Vohra meet Chandra Shekhar Azad for the first time
	December 23	Bomb attack on Viceroy's train near Delhi by HSRA
	Dec. 25-31	Annual Session of Congress at Lahore
1930	January 2	Mahatma Gandhi criticizes revolutionaries' violent acts in an article "The Cult of the Bomb" in his paper *Young India*
	January	Bhagat Singh and Dutt's statement in the High Court
	January 13	High Court uphelds the judgment of the Sessions Court
	January 26	HSRA distributes the pamphlet "*Philosophy of the Bomb*" as a reply to "*The Cult of the Bomb*"
	February 4	Hunger strike resumed
	February 19	Government issues a press communiqué on the classification of convicted prisoners and undertrials.
	May 1	Special Tribunal to try Lahore Conspiracy Case set up
	May 28	Bhagwati Charan Vohra attains martyrdom while testing a bomb near

		Lahore during the preparations to rescue Bhagat Singh and Dutt from jail.
	June 1	Date of the proposed rescue of Bhagat Singh and Dutt. Rescue operation could not take place
	June 6	HSRA conducts Gadodia Stores decoity in Chandni Chowk Delhi
	July 19	Explosions at six places in Punjab by HSRA
	October 7	Judgment of Lahore Conspiracy case announced. Date of death sentence fixed for 27th October 1930
	October 16	Petition in Privy Council filed
	October 28	Kailash Pati arrested in Delhi
	November 1	Dhanvantri arrested in Delhi
	December 4	N.K. Nigam arrested
	December 23	Hari Krishan fires at Governor of Punjab
1931	February 6	Moti Lal Nehru passes away in Luknow
	February 11	Privy Council rejects appeal of the Defence Council
		Vaishampayan arrested in Kanpur
	February 14	Madan Mohan Malviya appeals to the Viceroy to commute the death sentences
	February 16	A special petition by Jiwan Lal, Baljit Singh, and Shyam Lal in High Court
	Feb.17-Mar. 5	Gandhi –Irwin talks at Delhi. On 18th February Gandhi raised the issue of Bhagat Singh's commutation

February 27	Chandra Shekhar Azad attains martyrdom in an encounter with the police in Allahabad
March 3	Bhagat Singh's last meeting with family
March 5	Gandhi- Irwin Pact signed
March 18	Punjab Government decided to carry out death sentences on the evening of 23rd March
March 19	Gandhiji met Irwin, requested to commute the death sentences
March 20	Bhagat Singh, Sukhdev and Rajguru, in a memorandum to the Governor, ask to be shot dead in place of hanging. Gandhiji meets Home Secretary
March 20 &21	Gandhiji meets the Viceroy
March 23	Gandhiji writes the final letter to Viceroy to save Bhagat Singh in the morning. At 7 PM Bhagat Singh, Rajguru and Sukhdev were executed.
March 24	Government makes the news of hangings public. Whole India goes into mourning. In Calcutta, police fires into protesting crowds resulting in the death of 141 persons.
March 25	Riots break out in Kanpur on the question of closure of shops as a mark of respect to the martyrs. Ganesh Shankar Vidyarthi done to death while attempting to stop the riots.
March 26-30	Karachi session of Indian National Congress

Notes & References

[1] *Encyclopedia Britannica, Indian History Modern, p. 34 CB.*

[2] Hansraj Rahbar, *Bhagat Singh: Ek Jwalant Itihas*, 2004, p. 34.

[3] G.S. Deol, *Shaheed Bhagat Singh: A Biography*, 1985, p.10; K. K. Khullar, *Shaheed Bhagat Singh: Kuchh Adhkhule Prasth,* 1981.

[4] Virender Sindhu, *Yugdrista Bhagat Singh Aur Unke Mritunjaya Purkhe,* 2004, p. 129.

[5] Mathura Das Thapar, *Mere Bhai Shaheed Sukhdev*, 1992, p. 22.;Shiv Verma, *Samsmritiyan,* 1974, p. 11.

[6] K.C. Yadav and Babar Singh, *Bhagat Singh: Making of a Revolutionary, Contemporary Portrayals*, 2006, pp. 28-29.

[7] J.N. Sanyal, *S. Bhagat Singh,* 1983, p. 10. In 1931 edition of his book, J.N. Sanyal did not give exact date of birth of Bhagat Singh but only mentioned that he was born on a Saturday in the month of October in 1907. (J.N. Sanyal, *Sardar Bhagat Singh,* May 1931, p. 5).

[8] Ram Chandra, *Naujawan Bharat Sabha and Hindustan Socialist Republican Association* 1986, p. 87; Manmathnath Gupta, *Bhagat Singh and His Times,* 1977, p. 69.

[9] Both of these papers were popular Hindi weeklies with nationalist flavour, published from Allahabad. Chandra Shekhar Shastri, Virender Sindhu, G.S. Deol, and K.K. Khullar have also mentioned this Indian calendar date.

[10] S.N. Sen, ed., *Dictionary of National Biography,* p. 154.

[11] According to Jaidev, his school mate, Bhagat Singh was in class IX in 1921. (Virender Sindhu, op. cit., p. 135). It is quite logical to say that he would have been in class I in 1913. K.K. Khullar, op. cit. (p.118) gives the date of admission in primary school as September 1911 but does not give any source.

[12] Khullar also writes that Bhagat Singh was shifted to D.A.V. School, Lahore in May 1912. Where as Bhagat Singh has admitted in his essay *'Why I am an Aethiest'* that he moved to Lahore after completing his primary education (Shiv Varma, *Selected Writings of Shaheed Bhagat Singh,* p. 122).

[13] Though D.A.V. Schools did not receive any government aid, they could not dissociate themselves from the Universities set up by Government. Jaidev (transcript of interview, NMML) and Yashpal (*Simhavalokan,* 2005, p. 21) have mentioned Bhagat Singh's boycott of D.A.V. School.

[14]   *The Tribune,* 19 February, 1921.

[15]   *The People,* Lala Lajpat Rai Number, 13 May, 1929, p. 46.

[16]   Ibid.

[17]   N.A.I., Home Political file, 88, Congress, 1942 cited in Ramchandra, *Naujawan Bharat Sabha and Hindustan Socialist Republican Association,* 1986, p. 11.

[18]   *Abhyudaya,* Bhagat Singh number, 8 May, 1931 and Jaidev Gupta (Transcript of interview, NMML).

[19]   According to Yashpal, Bhagat Singh and his brothers did not keep long hairs as required by Sikh religion as Sardar Kishan Singh did not follow the '*Panch Kakars*' (*Simhavalokan,* op. cit., p. 23).

[20]   Sachindra Nath Sanyal started the re-organisation of revolutionaries in north India after Gaya Session of Congress (26-31 December, 1922). Sometime later he reached Lahore (*Bandi Jeewan,* 1963, pp. 260-271).

[21]   J.C.Chatterji, *In Search of Freedom,* p. 220.

[22]   Ajoy Ghosh, recalled meeting Bhagat Singh for the first time in Kanpur in 1923. He was introduced to Bhagat Singh by B.K. Dutt. (Ajoy Ghosh, *Bhagat Singh and His Comrades,* 1929, p. 17). G.S. Deol and Hansraj Rahbar have given the year of Bhagat Singh's arrival in Kanpur as 1924.

[23]   According to Sohan Singh Josh (*Akali Morchon Ka Itihas,* 1974, pp. 417-418) fifth *shaheedi jattha* started from Lyallpur city on 12 April 1924. A Punjab Government report (Home Political Punjab, 67, 1924, pp. 211-212) cited by M. S. Waraich (*Bhagat Singh: The Eternal Rebel,* 2007, p. 27) stated that "...in 1924, he (Bhagat Singh) went to Chak No.105, GB, where his father's land was situated. While being there, he took care of Lyallpur Saheedi (martyrs) *Jatha.* Consequently he was booked under Criminal Law Amendment Act, section 17 (1) whereupon he absconded". G..S. Deol (op. cit., p. 24), Hansraj Rahbar (op. cit., pp. 77-78), K.K. Khullar (op. cit., p. 118) give a wrong year of incident of *Jaiton* jatha incident as 1925.

[24]   J.C.Chatterji, op. cit., p. 230. Bhagat Singh's stint at National School is also corroborated by Punjab Government report cited by M. S. Waraich (op.cit.)

[25]   *Arya Samaj Ka Itihas,* Vol. VI, 1987, pp. 55-57.

[26]   Ibid.

[27]   Comrade Ram Chandra, *Naujawan Bharat Sabha and HSRA,* 1986, p. 14.

[28] Ibid., p. 18.

[29] Ibid., p. 20. On page 19 of the same book, Comrade Ram Chandra refers to his speech on 17th May 1931 in Rawalpindi that Naujawan Bharat Sabha was formed seven years back. G.S. Deol, S.R. Bakshi, K.K. Khullar, Hansraj Rahbar, K.C. Yadav, Vishnu Prabhakar and Kamlesh Mohan among others give 1926 (March) as the year of formation of Naujawan Bharat Sabha. Their information is based on a report by the Punjab CID on Naujawan Bharat Sabha dated 2nd August 1929. The report is based on an erroneous report on early history of NBS by Punjab CID (N.A.I., Home Political, 130 & K.W. 1930).Contemporaries of Bhagat Singh never mentioned 1926 as year of birth of NBS. Ajoy Ghosh, Gopal Thakur, Prithvi Singh Azad and Yashpal have also mentioned 1925 as the year of formation of NBS.

[30] Comrade Ramchandra, *Ideology and Battle Cries of Indian Revolutionaries* , 1989, p. i, 228.

[31] Chief Secretary, Punjab to Home Deptt., 21 [st] May 1929, (Home Political, 130 &KW, 1930) ; Ram Chandra op.cit, p. 20, Also see Guru Dutt, *Bhav aur Bhavna*, 2000, p. 8; V. Sindhu, op. cit, p. 15; Rahbar, op. cit, p. 90; G.S. Deol, op. cit, p. 25; Manmathnath Gupta, op. cit., p. 103 among others have named Ramkishan as the first president of the Sabha which is wrong, Ramkishan became the president of the Naujawan Bharat Sabha on 30th March 1929 (Home Political, 130 &KW, 1930).

[32] Comrade Ram Chandra, *Naujawan Bharat Sabha and HSRA*, 1986, p. 89.

[33] Jogesh Chandra Chatterji, op.cit, p. 324.

[34] J.N. Sanyal, op. cit., p. 18.

[35] According to Shiv Verma (*Sansmritiyan*, 1974, pp. 15-21), Bhagat Singh met Shiv Varma and Jaidev for the first time during the end of 1926 in Kanpur.

[36] Comrade Ramchandra mentions Bhagat Singh's presence on 19th September 1926 during election campaign of Independent Congress Party at Lahore. (*Naujawan Bharat Sabha &HSRA*, p. 28).

[37] Bipin Chandra, *India's Struggle for Independence*, 1987, p. 244.

[38] It was on this issue that Guru Dutt and Bhai Parmanand got alienated from NBS.

[39] Raja Ram Shastri, *Amar Shaheedon ke Sansmaran,* 1981.

[40] Yashpal, op. cit., p. 85.

[41]   Recently discovered letters published in *Jansatta*, 25 Mar 2007; *The Tribune*, 8 April 2007. Virendra Sindhu, op. cit (p. 154); Ram Chandra (*NBS & HSRA*, p. 37) and K.C. Yadav and Babar Singh have given the date 29 July, 1927 for the first arrest of Bhagat Singh. But in his essay – '*Why I am an Atheist*' Bhagat Singh himself gives date of his arrest as May 1927. Manmathnath Gupta (op. cit., p. 124) gives 1928 as year of arrest. K.K. Khullar (op. cit., p. 118) gives the date of arrest as 23 October 1927. G.S. Deol (op. cit., p. 27) also writes that Bhagat Singh was arrested in October 1927.

[42]   N.A.I., Home Political, p. 254, 1926.

[43]   Recently discovered letters published in *Jansatta*, 25 March 2007; *The Tribune*, 8 April 2007.

[44]   Sohan Singh Josh, *My Meetings with Bhagat Singh and on Other Early Revolutionaries*, 1976, p. 11.

[45]   See the chapter: Literary Heritage of Bhagat Singh: A Re-examination.

[46]   Sohan Singh Josh, *My Meetings with Bhagat Singh Singh and on Other Early Revolutionaries*, 1976, p. 18. To these months largest number of writings are attributed to Bhagat Singh.

[47]   Sohan Singh Josh, *My Tryst with Secularism*, 1991, p. 142.

[48]   Ibid., p. 143.

[49]   Virender Sindhu, op. cit., p. 159.

[50]   J.N. Sanyal, 1983, op. cit., p. 23.

[51]   Judgment of Lahore Conspiracy Case, Chronological account of facts, cited in M.S.Waraich and G.S.Sidhu. (eds.), *The Hanging of Bhagat Singh, The Complete Judgement and Other Documents*, 2005, pp. 100-101. (Here onwards MSW&GSS).

[52]   Ibid.

[53]   Judgment of Lahore Conspiracy Case, cited in MSW & GSS, p. 151.

[54]   Ibid.

[55]   Ram Chandra, *NBS and HSRA*, 2003, pp. 56-57.

[56]   Judgment of Lahore Conspiracy Case, cited in MSW & GSS, op. cit., p. 105.

[57]   Ibid., p. 106.

[58]   Ibid.

[59]   Ibid., p. 109.

60   An intelligence report claims that Bhagat Singh was noticed at Dacca with Pratul Gangualy on 1 February (N.A.I., Home political, 129, 1929).

61   Judgement of Lahore Conspiracy Case, chronological account of facts, cited in *MSW & GSS*, p.111.

62   Ibid., p. 112.

63   Ibid., p. 113.

64   Ibid., pp. 113-114.

65   Ibid., p. 114. According to Shiv Varma, the decision to throw bomb in Assembly was taken in February. (*Selected Writings of Bhagat Singh*, 1996, p. 36).

66   Ibid., p. 115.

67   N.A.I., Home Political File, 129, 1929.

3

Literary Heritage of Bhagat Singh:
A Re-examination

One of the major concerns of historiography is the reliability or the authenticity of the sources. In this context, Bhagat Singh's own writings assume special significance because most of his writings came to light after his execution. Over the years, the corpus of writings attributed to Bhagat Singh has grown in size as new writings are being added to it. A close look reveals the various issues associated with the writings attributed to Bhagat Singh, such as authorship, dating of the writings, different versions, and controversies associated with them. In the following pages an attempt has been made to analyse and investigate the issues concerned with the writings attributed to Bhagat Singh.

Compilations of the Bhagat Singh's Writings (Appendix A)

Soon after his arrest on 8th April 1929, Bhagat Singh was able to capture the imagination of people at large. Press media, which played a leading role in popularizing Bhagat Singh, published all his court statements, messages and available letters etc.[1] These writings formed the content of the first compilations to appear in the special number of some newspapers after his martyrdom. Till date there are 21 major collections of his writings apart from several minor collections as well as appendices of the books, attributing in all about 107 documents to Bhagat Singh, comprising articles, letters, statements and messages from jail. First and second editions of Shiv Varma's memoirs '*Sansmritiyan*', published in 1969 and

1974 respectively, had eight documents related to Bhagat Singh in the appendix. In 1972, some left intellectuals of Delhi took the initiative to publish a collection of Bhagat Singh's documents in '*Mukti*', a Hindi monthly.[2] The first collected works of Bhagat Singh in Punjabi was published in 1974.[3] The collection of Bhagat Singh's documents in Hindi- '*Sardar Bhagat Singh: Patra Aur Dastavej*' edited by Bhagat Singh's niece (daughter of Kultar Singh) Virender Sindhu, was published for the first time in 1975. It contains 34 documents out of which there are 23 letters, 2 court statements, 2 pamphlets and 7 articles. Virender Sindhu brought out another compilation under the name-'*Mere Krantikari Sathi-Sardar Bhagat Singh*' in 1977. It is a collection of biographical accounts of 47 revolutionary martyrs, ascribed to Bhagat Singh. These accounts were first published by the Hindi monthly '*Chand*' of Allahabad, in its famous *"Phansi"* (execution) number of November 1928, which was banned immediately after its publication. Shiv Varma, a close associate of Bhagat Singh in Hindustan Socialist Republican Association (HSRA), who became a prominent communist leader after he was released from Andaman in 1946, brought out '*Selected Writings of Bhagat Singh*' in 1986. Shiv Varma's compilation consisted of 28 selected writings including '*Why I am an Atheist*'. Many of them appeared in English for the first time. The *Selected Writings* began with a lengthy forward by veteran communist leader B.T. Ranadive.[4] Shiv Varma's introduction entitled '*Ideological Development of the Revolutionary Movement (from Chapekars to Bhagat Singh)*' was successively used in later collections of Bhagat Singh's writings by other compilers too.

The *Selected Writings of Bhagat Singh* was soon followed by '*Bhagat Singh Aur Unke Saathiyon Ke Dastavej*', compiled jointly by Jagmohan Singh (a nephew of Bhagat Singh) and Chaman Lal, in 1986. This collection comprising 109 documents, largest so far, had also included the documents of Bhagat Singh's colleagues- Sukhdev, Mahabir Singh, Balukeshwar Dutt, Bhagwati Charan Vohra, Jatin Das and some anonymous write-ups. Its compilers have claimed that the collection included for the first time the Hindi translation of Bhagat Singh's articles in the '*Kirti*' (Urdu and Punjabi monthly, a mouthpiece of Kirti Kisan Party in Punjab in late 1920s). The 1991 edition of this collection omitted Balukeshwar Dutt's writing '*Krantikari Jeewan Darshan*' with the reasoning that 'this document does not reflect the ideological development of Indian revolutionary movement of 1925-31'.[5] Subsequent collections also chose to ignore this article. The deliberate omission of this document reflects a predetermined ideological bias behind the compilation.

Bhagat Singh's jail note book containing notes and extracts from books read by him in jail is also presented as a part of his documents. Excerpts from this note book were first serialised in *Indian Book Chronicle* from 1991. The notebook itself was first published in 1994 under the title '*A Martyr's Notebook*'.[6] Its Hindi translation was published by Rahul Foundation in 1999. Another Hindi translation, by Ved Swaroop Narang and Gyan Kaur Kapur was published in 2002. This translation also contains a biographical sketch of Bhagat Singh over five chapters.

The year 2006 saw four compilations of Bhagat Singh's documents edited by Chaman Lal, Satyam, Raj Shekhar Vyas and the duo of K.C. Yadav and Babar Singh.[7]

Chaman Lal in '*Bhagat Singh Ke Sampoorna Dastavej*' has attributed in all 73 documents to Bhagat Singh. Two extra documents in this collection, which were not present in the 1991 edition of Jagmohan and Chaman Lal, are '*Jail Notebook*' and '*Letter to the Editor of 'Maharathi*' (27 February 1928).

Satyam's (ed.) '*Bhagat Singh Aur Unke Sathiyon Ke Sampoorna Uplabdha Dastavej*' contains all the documents available in Chaman Lal (2006) and Jagmohan and Chaman Lal (1991) besides including some other writings attributed by the editor to comrades of Bhagat Singh, or, according to the editor, representing the ideology of the great martyr. In addition, it also has two write-ups on Bhagat Singh's jail notebook by Alok Ranjan and L.V. Mitrokhin.

'*Mein Bhagat Singh Bol Raha Hoon*', edited by Raj Shekhar Vyas (2006) is spread over three volumes.[8] This work includes editor's articles on Bhagat Singh, Bhagat Singh's letters, writings attributed to Bhagat Singh including short biographies of martyrs from Chand's *'Phansi'* number, and articles and excerpts from the writings of Hansraj Rahbar, Shiv Varma, Gopal Thakur, and Madhulekha Vidyarthi. But the jail note book of Bhagat Singh is conspicuous by its absence in the compilation.

'*Fragrance of Freedom: The Writings of Bhagat Singh*' is a part of the 15 volume series which its editors- K.C. Yadav and Babar Singh planned on Bhagat Singh. It is a collection of 64 'selected' writings of Bhagat Singh[9] and excludes his jail notes which have been published in a separate book. '*Fragrance of Freedom*' for the first time presents the English version of some of the Bhagat Singh's documents.[10] A short collection of Bhagat Singh's documents in English has also been published under the title '*Bhagat Singh: Select Speeches and Writings*' by D.N. Gupta (2007).[11] The latest and largest collection of Bhagat Singh's writings has been edited by Chaman Lal under the title, *Shaheed Bhagat Singh, Dastavejon Ke Aieene Mein* (2007)[12]. It contains 107 documents in total, an increase of 34 documents over the compiler's previous collection published in 2006. While in 2006 Chaman Lal attributed 4 articles of *Chand* to Bhagat Singh, a year later he increased this number to 33 without ascribing any reason for this sudden inflation.

Apart from these there are some smaller collections of Bhagat Singh's documents such as *Amar Shaheed Bhagat Singh: Vyaktitwa aur Vichar* (Allahabad, 1987)[13]; *Shaheed-i-Azam: Bhagat Singh. Vichar Aur Sangharsh* (Patna, 2003)[14] and "*Yad Kar Lena Kabhi: Shahedon Ke Khat* (Delhi, 1997)[15]. *Vyaktitwa Aur Vichar* contains 14 documents including 5 letters as appendix. *Vichar Aur Sangharsh* contains 20 documents including 6 writings. *Shaheedon Ke Khat* has 24 letters written exclusively by Bhagat Singh and another 10 letters written by him in association with his comrades in jail. During the centenary year many small booklets containing a few selected documents have also been published by different ideological groups.

Classification of Bhagat Singh's writings

For the sake of convenience Bhagat Singh's writings may be classified into five categories:

1. Letters:

a. Letters to relatives and friends

b. Letters to government authorities from jail

(An annotated list of Bhagat Singh's letters is available in Appendices B &C)

2. Statements in courts. (Appendix D)

3. Pamphlets/posters ascribed to Bhagat Singh. (Appendix F)

4. Writings or articles said to have been written by him for various periodicals before he was arrested in the Central Assembly on 8th April, 1929. (Appendix G) Though these writings in Hindi, Punjabi and Urdu are said to have been published during his life time, none of them carried his real name. Instead, all of them were written under some pen names. One could understand it, for, being part of the revolutionary movement he did not want to expose himself by using his own name. All these articles were attributed to Bhagat Singh only after his execution. A writing which does not meet the above stated criteria but is placed in this category is Bhagat Singh's essay 'Punjab Ki Bhasa Aur Lipi Ki Samasya'.

5. Writings ascribed to Bhagat Singh when he was in jail. These appeared after his execution.

Bhagat Singh's Letters

Among Bhagat Singh's documents, the most authentic are his letters because they were written under his name and the original copies of many of them exit. Still, few letters with doubtful credentials have been attributed to Bhagat Singh by some scholars.[16] G.S. Deol in his work '*Shaheed Bhagat Singh: A Biography*' has given two letters of Bhagat Singh to his father when he left home to escape marriage.[17] Curiously, Deol does not give the universally accepted letter which Bhagat Singh wrote to his father, reminding the pledge his grandfather had taken, at his grandsons' sacred thread ceremony. All the three letters compared together convey a similar message, creating ample ground for doubting the authenticity of the letters given by Deol. Interestingly, K.C. Yadav and Babar Singh (2006) included all the three versions of this letter in their collection.[18] Obviously, Bhagat Singh could not have written three letters with almost the same content to his father on the same date. Two of the three must have been later concoctions. Another doubtful letter ascribed to Bhagat Singh is addressed to Batukeshwar Dutt, informing him of his death sentence and asking those revolutionaries who escaped death to endure hardships. Here too, we find two letters written to the same person with similar contents. Both of these letters are included in a publication of Publication Division of Government of India *Yaad Kar Lena Kabhi—Shaheeedon Ke Khat* (1997).[19] The genuine letter was originally published in *New Era* (Calcutta) in November 1930.[20]

Writings ascribed to Bhagat Singh published before 8th April, 1929 (Appendix G)

This category consists of Bhagat Singh's writings published in *Matwala* (Calcutta), '*Pratap*' (Kanpur), *Maharathi* (Delhi), *Kirti* (Amritsar) and *Chand's Phansi* number (Allahabad). Pen names known to have been adopted by Bhagat Singh while writing for different papers are as: *Matwala* - 'Balwant'; *Pratap* - 'Ek Punjabi Yuvak'; '*Kirti*'- 'Vidrohi'; and *Maharathi* - 'B.S. Sindhu'.

The earliest available writings ascribed to Bhagat Singh were published in *Matwala*. '*Vishwa-prem*' was published in *Matwala* in two instalments on 15th and 22nd November 1924 under the name 'Balwant'. '*Yuvak*' was published under the same name in

'*Matwala*' on 16th May 1925. All the compilations of Bhagat Singh's documents give the name of the author as Balwant Singh whereas the original articles carried the name – 'Balwant'.

Though Bhagat Singh is said to have worked with '*Pratap*' (Allahabad) during 1923-24, his earliest available writing in that paper entitled '*Holi Ke Din Rakt Ke Chheetain*' is dated 15th March 1926. Author's name is given as 'Ek Punjabi Yuvak'. Compilers have also attributed two documents published in *Maharathi* to Bhagat Singh –'*Kooka Vidroh*' (published in February 1928) and '*Chitra Parichaya*' (March 1928). Author of the first is named as B.S. Sindhu while the second writing does not carry any name.

'*Punjab Ki Bhasa Aur Lipi Ki Samasya*' (The problem of language and script in Punjabi language)

'*Punjab Ki Bhasa Aur Lipi Ki Samasya*' was written by Bhagat Singh for an essay competition held by 'Punjab Hindi Sahitya Sammelan'. Bhim Sen Vidyalankar, president of the Sammelan, preserved the essay and published it in '*Hindi Sandesh*' of 28th February 1933. The problem with documentation of this writing is its date. Virender Sindhu in *Patra aur Dastaraj* (1975) and Rajshekhar Vyas (2006) give the date of its writing as 1922-23, Shiv Varma (1986) and K.C. Yadav (2006) as 1923 and Jagmohan and Chaman Lal identify the year of this writing as 1924.

But the testimonials of Yashpal and Bhim Sen Vidyalankar's biography prove beyond doubt that this writing cannot be dated prior to 1925. Yashpal was the co-winner of the above mentioned essay competition, along with Bhagat Singh. He has written about the subject in *Simhavalokan*:

"I recall an event in 1925. Hindi Sahitya Sammelan had been newly established in Punjab ... The Sammelan had announced a prize of Rs. 50 for the best essay on a topic. I also wrote an essay for this competition. After waiting for the result for several months, we came to know that the prize could not be given to any individual, because the judges had found three essays of the same highest standard. It also became known that my essay was among the three best essays. The other two were found to be by Bhagat Singh and Jaychandraji's niece."[21]

According to the biography of Bhimsen Vidyalankar, written by his daughter Shanta Malhotra, Bhimsen Vidyalankar recorded in his diary that he reached Punjab in 1925 only.[22] Before that Vidyalankar had worked in the editorial department of *Arjun* in Delhi from 15 August 1923 to 13 January 1925.[23] It is also well established that he was the president of Punjab Hindi Sahitya Sammelen when Bhagat Singh wrote this eseay. All these facts are sufficient to prove that the essay '*Punjab Ki Bhasa Aur Lipi Ki Samasya*' was written in 1925 or later.

'*Kirti*' Writings

'*Kirti*', initially a Punjabi monthly, was started by Santokh Singh of the '*Kirti*' group in February 1926 in Amritsar. In all, 16 writings published in '*Kirti*' have been attributed to Bhagat Singh, out of which 11 happen to be unsigned. Jagmohan Singh and Chaman Lal (1986, 1991) attribute 14 writings from *Kirti* but do not include '*Yugaantkaari Maa*' (September 1928) and '*Lala Lajpat Rai Aur Naujawan*' (August 1928). These two writings were included in Bhagat Singh's documents by K.C. Yadav and Babar Singh (2006) and Chaman Lal (2007)[24] respectively.

Writings published in *Kirti* attributed to Bhagat Singh

S. No.	Name of the Writing	Date of Pub.	Author's Name
1.	*Kakori Ke Veeron Se Parichay*	May 1927	Vidrohi
2.	*Kakori Ke Shaheedon Ki Phansi Ke Halaat*	Jan. 1928	Vidrohi
3.	*Madan Lal Dhingra*	March 1928	Vidrohi
4.	*Arajaktavaad I (Anarchism)*	May 1928	Unsigned

5.	*Dharam Aur Hamara Swadheenta Sangharsh*	May 1928	Unsigned
6.	*Arajaktavaad II*	May 1928	Unsigned
7.	*Sampradayik Dange Aur Unka Ilaaj*	June 1928	Unsigned
8.	*Satyagriha Aur Hartalain*	June 1928	Unsigned
9.	*Achhoot Samasya*	June 1928	Vidrohi
10.	*Arajaktavaad III*	July 1928	Unsigned
11.	*Vidyarthi Aur Rajniti*	July 1928	Unsigned
12.	*Naye Netaon Ke Alag Alag Vichar*	July 1928	Unsigned
13.	*Roos Ke Yugaantkari Naashwadi*	August 1928	Unsigned
14.	*Lala Lajpat Rai Aur Naujawan*	August 1928	Unsigned
15.	*Yugaantkaari Maa*	Sep. 1928	Unsigned
16.	*Kuka (II) Vidroh**	Oct. 1928	Vidrohi

* *Kuka Vidroh (I)* was published in Maharathi in February 1928. Numbering in bracket has been given for the sake of convenience.

The first '*Kirti*' writing ascribed to Bhagat Singh- '*Kakori Ke Veeron Se Parichay*' was published in May 1927 and the last writing is dated October 1928. According to Sohan Singh Josh, the chief editor of '*Kirti*' since 21st January 1927, Bhagat Singh was approached to join Urdu '*Kirti*', first issue of which came out in April 1928 (while Punjabi '*Kirti*' was working since February 1926). Sohan Singh Josh recalled, "Bhagat Singh joined the '*Kirti*', worked for about three months and then vanished."[25] From the above table it can be observed that 10 out of 16 writings belong to the months- May, June and July of the year 1928. So May-July 1928 may be the period when Bhagat Singh worked on the editorial board of '*Kirti*'.

Coming back to Josh's statement, it seems logical that Bhagat Singh 'vanished' in July/August 1928, i.e. he was not available to '*Kirti*'. This was also the time when Bhagat Singh must have been busy preparing for September 8-10 meeting of HRA in Delhi. But then writings of August, September and October 1928 have also to be accounted for. '*Kirti*' writings also raise the question of unsigned articles. 11 out of 16 articles are unsigned.[26] It may be argued that Bhagat Singh, when he was on the editorial board of '*Kirti*', wrote his articles unsigned as the editors usually do, but there is an article from the months when Bhagat Singh was supposed to be working as an editor- *Achhoot Samasaya* (June 1928) signed as 'Vidrohi'. Thus, authorship of at least the unsigned articles is doubtful.[27] Significantly, some of these articles are being used by the Communist propagandists against their political and ideological opponents. '*Kirti*' being a pro-Communist paper most of its published articles reflect their ideology. Attributing such unsigned articles to Bhagat Singh would obviously serve their ideological purpose.

Hindi translation of *My Fight for Irish Freedom*

Dan Breen (1894-1969) was an Irish revolutionary, involved in armed struggle against British occupation of Ireland. He became well known in India through his autobiography *My Fight for Irish Freedom*[28], published in 1924, an inspiring account of the Irish struggle for freedom during the period 1915-1921. Soon after its publication, this book became a kind of text book for Indian revolutionaries in the 1920s. It was also one of the favourite books of Bhagat Singh. A Home Department file[29] at National Archives of India regarding proscription of the Hindi translation of Dan Breen's book on 27 May 1929, under the name '*Ireland Ki Swatantrata Ka Yudh*', provides the information that it was published from *Pratap* Office, Cawnpore and printed by Babu Ganesh Shankar Vidyarthi. The translator's name was given as 'Balwant'. It is well known that Bhagat Singh used to write under this name in '*Pratap*'. Date of the file establishes the fact that

Bhagat Singh had translated Dan Breen's book before his arrest in the Assembly bomb Case on 8th April 1929. Government report also stated that Gurumukhi translation had already been proscribed.

It was also staed in the file, Raj Shekhar Vyas has claimed that Bhagat Singh's translation was secretly published through the efforts of late Pt. Surya Narayan Vyas (Rajshekhar Vyas' father) in 1931 under the title- '*Meri Kahani*'.[30] This statement needs to be verified. Raj Shekhar is convinced that '*Meri Kahani*' is also one of the so called 'lost manuscripts' of Bhagat Singh. '*Meri Kahani*' was later reprinted by Raj Sekhar in 1989 and again in 2006 in his compendium on Bhagat Singh.

In the context of Bhagat Singh's translation of the Dan Breen's classic, both Raj Shekhar Vyas and Shiv Varma (writing in his preface to '*Meri Kahani*' in Raj Shekhar's book) have made wrong statements that Bhagat Singh translated the work while lodged in his condemned cell.[31] The translation had already been banned by the British authorities before Bhagat Singh went to jail. This translation does not find mention in Shiv Varma's '*Sansmritiyan*' (1969) and '*Selected Writings of Bhagat Singh*' (1986).

Authorship of biographical sketches in Chand's *'Phansi'* number (November 1928) (Appendix H)

'*Chand*', a Hindi monthly published from Allahabad brought out a special number entitled '*Phansi*' (execution) in November 1928 which became very popular and was immediately banned by the British Government. It contained a separate section of eighty pages namely '*Viplav Yagna Ki Ahutiyan*' consisting of short biographical articles on 48 revolutionary martyrs. 46 of these articles were attributed to Bhagat Singh by Virender Sindhu in her compilation-'*Mere Krantikari Sathi*' (1977).[32] If the test of Bhagat Singh's known pen names is applied to *Chand* articles, then Bhagat Singh's tally comes to three articles – *Awadhbehari* (Vidrohi), *Basanto Kumar Viswas* (Vidrohi), and *Kartar Singh Sarabha*

(Balwant). In the preface of her book, Virender Sindhu cited Kulbir Singh (younger brother of Bhagat Singh) and Acharya Chatursen (editor of Chand's *'Phansi'* number) to conclude that Bhagat Singh had indeed authored all these biographical sketches. She further elaborated that some of these sketches were originally written by Bhagat Singh in Hindi while others he had got translated from Gurumukhi. Raj Shekhar Vyas (2006) went further to attribute all the 48 biographical articles compiled in the *Phansi* issue to Bhagat Singh, including *Gendalal Dikshit,* which is the only article in the compilation where the real name of the author is given - Ram Prasad Bismil. Chaman Lal (2006) attributed 4 articles of *'Chand'* to Bhagat Singh; *'Sufi Amba Prasad'* (author: Agyat), *'Balwant Singh'* (Mukund), *'Mathura Singh'* (Brijesh) and *'Kartar Singh Sarabha'* (Balwant). K.C. Yadav and Babar Singh (2006) have attributed four more (along with the above four included by Chaman Lal)- *'Basant Kumar Biswas'* (Vidrohi), *'Dalip Singh'* (Kapil) and *'Heroes of Battle of Munder'* (*'Phansi'* number gives this title as *'Shri Banta Singh Dhamiyan'* and author's name is given as 'Senapati'). In his latest compilation, Chaman Lal (2007) has increased the number of biographical sketches supposed to be authored by Bhagat Singh to 33 without any explanation.[33]

Investigation into the authorship of *'Chand'* articles should start with the origins of the *'Phansi'* issue. Writing 35 years after the event, Acharya Chatursen Shastri, editor of this special issue, gave a brief account of the origins of *'Phansi'* number in his autobiography *'Meri Atmakahani'*:

> "*Chand's* financial condition was not well those days. Perhaps only a thousand copies were printed ... One day the idea of improving *'Chand'* cropped up all of a sudden. I proposed a scheme to publish six special issues. Among them, the first was to be the *'Phansi'* (Execution) number. I took up the task in the right earnest. My approach was that the special issue, on one hand, must express our disapproval of the death sentence,

and on the other hand to make the issue more interesting, we should include an account of death sentences given to the martyrs. Moreover, on this pretext, a record of political executions in the twentieth century would also be made ... But the problem was I could not obtain any authentic accounts of political executions. Luckily, at that time, Sardar Bhagat Singh came to me for some financial assistance and I handed over this difficult task to him ... He worked hard travelling from house to house and was able to give me over 70 authentic biographical accounts. In return 'Chand' paid him Rs. 700/- only. In the beginning Bhagat Singh introduced himself as Balwant Singh."[34]

A comparison of Chatursen's account with the accounts of other key persons who were involved with Chand's 'Phansi' number such as Acharya Chandra Shekhar Shastri and Shiv Varma (both omitted by Chatur Sen), points out the unreliability of Chatur Sen's attribution of above mentioned articles to Bhagat Singh. Chatursen's account is full of factual errors too. For example, he writes that "by that time he had killed Saunders."[35] Whereas 'Phansi' number (November, 1928) was published before Saunder's murder (17 December 1928). Chatur Sen has also described in detail how Bhagat Singh himself took Chatur Sen and his wife in a taxi to witness Assembly bombing on 8th April 1929. This account does not tally with revolutionaries' accounts of that fateful day.

Chandra Shekhar Shastri, another editor associated with 'Phansi' number, gives a different version of the story in third person:

"In the middle of 1928, 'Chand', the famous Hindi monthly, announced a special 'Phansi' (execution) number, to start a movement to abolish the death sentence all over the world. Chatursen Shastri, a story writer from Delhi, was appointed as the editor of this special issue. Now it was thought that the issue will remain incomplete if it did not include the biographical sketches of those executed for revolutionary activities. Hence, the editor of this number assigned Chandra Shekhar Shastri, another writer from Delhi, to write and edit these sketches. Chandra Shekhar Shastri, in this work, took the help of Shiv Varma (Harnarayan Kapur) and some others. Chandra Shekhar Shastri had written a full historical account of the 'Kakori' episode. But the management of '*Chand*' did not publish the entire history, restricting only to the biographical sketches. Many imaginary names were also added and Chandra Shekhar Shastri was denied his due reward."[36]

Chandra Shekhar Shastri makes no mention of Bhagat Singh. His account makes it amply clear that several persons were involved in writing the biographic sketches in the '*Phansi*' number. The judgement of the Lahore Conspiracy Case has also established that Shiv Varma authored certain articles for the Phansi number. It has cited the evidence of Jaigopal (a member of HSRA who turned approver) and Chandra Shekhar Shastri:

"Jaigopal has deposed that Sheo Verma came to Gaya Parshad's home at Ferozepur about the end of September, 1928, being then known as Ram Narain or "Elder Brother"…(He) was writing biographies of men who had been executed in various conspiracy cases which were to be contributed as articles to the 'Phansi' (execution) issue of the *'Chand'* magazine, a copy of which is Ex. P570 and the articles at pages 244 to 323 of which are attributed by Jai Gopal to Sheo Verme… There is also corroboration of the fact that Sheo Vema wrote certain articles for the Chand Magazine which were published and paid for in October, November and December, 1928, in the evidence of Chatar Sen Shastri (P.W.350), Chander Shekhar Shastri (P.W.438) and K Seigal (P.W.432) of whom only Chander Shekhar Shastri (P.W.438) has identified Sheo Verma whom he knew fairly well. The signatures of Sheo Verma on the receipts which he gave for the payments due on his articles and which he made in the name of

Har Narain Kapur, are proved by Mr Scott (P.W.423) to tally with the proved handwriting of Sheo Verma…"[37]

In 1986, Shiv Varma himself made a definitive statement about Bhagat Singh's author ship of these articles. In his preface to the 'Selected Writings of Bhagat Singh' (1986), Shiv Varma categorically stated, "in Hindi, to my knowledge, he (Bhagat Singh) wrote biographies of four martyrs: Baba Ram Singh of 'Kooka' movement, Sufi Amba Prasad, Dr. Mathura Singh and Kartar Singh Sarabha. The first two were published in 'Maharathi', a Hindi monthly from Delhi (defunct now). Subsequently, with little variations, they were again published in the 'Phansi' number, of 'Chand', a Hindi monthly from Allahabad. The last two were written by him in 'Chand' office where he stayed with me for three or four days."[38]

It was a known fact among the revolutionary circle that Virender Sindhu had wrongly attributed all sketches to Bhagat Singh. Several persons including Manmathnath Gupt had repeatedly urged Shiv Varma to openly come out on the issue. As a result, Shiv Varma wrote a full article in 1992 clarifying the Bhagat Singh's authorship of the biographic sketches published in the special issue of *Chand* of November 1928.[39] According to Shiv Varma, the task of writing these sketches was taken up in October 1928. In the beginning both Bhagat Singh and Shiv Varma were supposed to take up the work of writing. But the task of writing fell upon Varma as Bhagat Singh became busy preparing for an 'action' in Punjab. Apart from mentioning above mentioned four sketches, Varma added new information that he also translated (with the help of Jaygopal) the articles on Ghadar heroes which had been originally written by Bhagat Singh in *Kirti*. Varma further wrote that Bhagat Singh had also authored biographic sketches of Babbar Akali martyrs but they were quite shallow. Consequently, Shiv Varma had to rewrite them in the light of the newly available court proceedings and judgements (which were not available to Bhagat Singh). Shiv Varma concluded that Bhagat Singh's contribution was limited to the articles related to Baba Ram Singh of 'Kooka' movement, Sufi

Amba Prasad, Dr. Mathura Singh, Kartar Singh Sarabha and other Ghadar martyrs. Shiv Varma attributed to himself the articles on martyrs of Bengal, Kakori case, Babbar Akalis and Chapekar brothers. Interestingly, Shiv Varma makes no mention of Chandra Shekhar Shastri's contribution.

Jail Writings of Bhagat Singh

The Philosophy of the Bomb

On 23rd December 1929, HSRA revolutionaries made an attempt to blow up the train in which Lord Irwin, the Viceroy of India, was travelling. Irwin escaped unhurt but this act of violence drew sharp condemnation from Gandhiji who responded through an article '*Cult of the Bomb*' in '*Young India*' of 2nd January 1930 denouncing the use of violence by revolutionaries in their struggle against British Government. '*Philosophy of the Bomb*' was the response of the HSRA (which had several intellectuals in its ranks apart from Bhagat Singh, Sukhdev, Bejoy Kumar Sinha, and Shiv Varma) in the form of an exposition of revolutionary ideology justifying the use of violence and a sharp criticism of the Congress. The pamphlet was widely distributed in public on 26th January 1930.

There is some confusion about Bhagat Singh's role in writing of '*The Philosophy of the Bomb*'. According to Virender Sindhu, this was Bhagat Singh's own work. Citing the testimony of Bhagat Singh's colleague J.N. Sanyal, she claims that Bhagat Singh wrote this pamphlet while in jail.[40] Jagmohan and Chaman Lal in their collections published in 1986, 1991, 2006 and 2007 have taken the position that the original document was prepared by Bhagwati Charan Vohra but its final shape was given by Bhagat Singh in jail. Whereas according to Nand Kishor Nigam, a member of HSRA, with whom Azad lived for some time around December 1930 in Hindu College hostel in Delhi, '*The Philosophy of the Bomb*' was exclusively written by Bhagwati Charan Vohra on directions from Chandra Shekhar Azad.[41]

Durga Devi Vohra alias *Bhabhi*, wife of Bhagwati Charan Vohra, and a revolutionary herself in an interview stated, "it was prepared by Shri Bhagwati Charan Vohra and Yashpal in Lucknow".[42] Yashpal himself has placed on record that his own contribution in the preparation of the above mentioned document was about one fourth while three fourth of the effort was of that of Bhagwati Charan Vohra. A copy of the document was shown to Bhagat Singh (in jail) and he liked it very much.[43] Yashpal also provides the information that this document was written in Aminabad in Lucknow and its printing was arranged by Chandra Shekhar Azad in a secret press in Kanpur.[44]

'Why I am an Atheist'

'Why I am an Atheist' is one of the most quoted writings of Bhagat Singh. He apparently wrote it in jail, a few days before the pronouncement of the judgement of the Lahore Conspiracy Case (7th October 1930).[45] Sometime before his execution, he sent his writings and papers to Lajjavati, Secretary of the Bhagat Singh Defence Committee. Lajjavati recalled giving these papers to Feroz Chand (the other secretary of the Defence Committee and editor of 'The People', a weekly paper published from Lahore), to see the papers and publish anything which he found worthwhile. One of the writings selected by Feroj Chand was 'Why I am an Atheist'.[46] Feroj Chand published it in 'The People' in its issue of 27th September 1931 under a heading –'Literary Remains of Bhagat Singh'.[47] The newspaper published it with the following introduction:

> "By special arrangement The People is permitted to print some of Bhagat Singh's writings in jail. The things placed at our disposal are mostly non – political. Copy- right rests with S. Kishan Singh".-(Editor)

The writing was also translated in Tamil and published in 1934 under the title-'Nan Nasththeegan Ain? Sardar Bhagat Singh'.[48] 'Rediscovery' of this article is attributed by the Left publicists to Bipan Chandra, who published it with an introduction in the year 1979.[49] While Raj Shekhar Vyas claims to have published this essay in 1971 in his booklet entitled *Aag Laga Do Aise Dharm Ko* (Set such a Religion on Fire).[50]

Bhagat Singh wrote this essay in reaction to the charge of vanity by some friends (whom he did not name). In Bhagat Singh's words, "conversation with some friends has given me a hint that certain of my friends….are inclined to conclude from the brief contact they have had with me, that it was too much on my part to deny the existence of God and that there was a certain amount of vanity that actuated my disbelief."[51] Shiv Varma has opined that Bhagat Singh wrote this article in reply to the sarcasm of Baba Randhir Singh, a former Ghadarite and a fellow prisoner. In the introduction to *'Why I am an Atheist'*, Varma wrote the following:

> "Baba Randhir Singh, a freedom fighter, was in Lahore Central Jail in 1930-31. He was a God-fearing religious man. It pained him to learn that Bhagat Singh was a non-believer. He somehow managed to see Bhagat Singh in the condemned cell and tried to convince him about the existence of God, but failed. Baba lost his temper and said tauntingly: "You are giddy with fame and have developed an ego which is standing like a black curtain between you and the God."[52]

The writing is autobiographical in nature and provides an authentic account of journey of life of Bhagat Singh.

'Introduction to The Dreamland'

This is an introduction written by Bhagat Singh to a composition in English verse authored by Lala Ram Saran Das, a fellow revolutionary. Ram Saran Das was one of the earliest revolutionaries from the Punjab and had worked with S. Ajit Singh and Sufi Amba Prasad. In 1908 he joined the Bengal revolutionaries and in 1910 he became associated with Ras Behari Bose. He also participated actively in the Ghadar movement. He was arrested on 23rd February 1915 and sentenced to death along with Bhai Parmanand and others. The death sentence was later commuted to life imprisonment. He was released on 25th September 1927. Later, he was tried again as a co-accused in the Lahore Conspiracy Case. He turned an approver initially but later retracted from his statement. He was awarded two years of jail which was reduced on appeal to six months.

Full name of the book is '*The Dreamland or Ram Rajya: The Kingdom of God on the Earth*'. The author himself has admitted that the book was composed in 1926 in Penetentiary Jail, Madras. Author claims that it is a divine revelation of an ideal society, in 665 verses, based on the teachings of *Tulsi Ramayan* and *Bhagwad Gita*. On the request of the author, Bhagat Singh wrote an introduction to his book while in Lahore Central Jail on 15th January 1931. The introductory piece turned out to be more of a critique of the utopia dreamt by the author. But Bhagat Singh's and the manuscript of *Dreamland* were discovered many years later. The hand written manuscript of the book along with Bhagat Singh's introduction is at present a part of the Gopichand Bhargava Papers preserved in Nehru Memorial Museum and Library, Delhi. The preface of *The Dreamland or Ram Rajya* is dated August 17, 1961, implying thereby that the introduction itself must have come to light after that date. Introduction is also written in Ram Saran Das's handwriting, below which is mentioned 'Sd. Bhagat Singh' and dated 15 January 1931. It was published for the first time in 1969 as appendix to the *Sansmritiyan* of Shiv Varma,[53] who acknowledged receiving it from Bhagat Singh's nephew Prof. Jagmohan Singh.[54] Jagmohan Singh has acknowledged that he received the writing from Ram Saran Das himself.[55]

The above narrative leaves some questions unanswered- why this writing of Bhagat Singh remained unknown for three decedes? Bhagat Singh had become too big a name in his lifetime. Then why did Ram Saran Das waited so long to keep this writing out of public knowledge? How this manuscript reached Gopi Chand Bharagava papers? The author, in his preface, gives no clue to answer these questions.

To the Young Political Workers

The history of this document is mired in mystery and controversy. An abridged version of this document was published in '*The*

People' (Lahore) on 29th March 1931 under the heading *"Bhagat Singh on Compromise.*[56] *'Bhavisya'*, a popular Hindi weekly from Allahabad, in its issue dated, 16th April 1931, published a longer version of this document, with the title *'Kaum Ke Naam Swargiya Sardar Bhagat Singh Ka Akhiri Sandesh'.* The under mentioned note followed:

> "We have reproduced the following letter from our associate *'Punjab Kesari'*. According to the associate this letter was sent by the late Sardar to one of his friends, when the negotiations on the pact between the Viceroy and Congress had started. The original letter was in English and was longer. *All its important points have been incorporated here.*"[57] (Emphasis added)

The text of the letter published in *'Bhavisya'* was later reproduced by Shiv Varma in *'Sansmritiyan'* (1969) along with the above mentioned note. According to Manmathnath Gupta, "a letter was published in *'Punjab Kesari'* under his (Bhagat Singh's) name. This letter could only be published on 2nd February 1931[58]. By that time movement (Civil Disobedience) was over. Letter was written when talks were going on. Original letter is said to have been written in English but we have not seen it."[59] *Abhyudaya* (Allahabad) of 8th May 1931 also published the *Bhavisya* version with the following note: "Even though we disagree with the author on many counts, this letter is being published here so as to show the depth to which he could analyze political issues and also to know the evolution of his thought through his experience."[60]

The contents published in *The People*, *Bhavisya* and *Abhyudaya* are almost similar and focused on Gandhi-Irwin negotiations only. It can also be surmised that it was first published in *Punjab Kesari*. But how could it be published on 2nd February 1931 because the negotiations between the Viceroy and Mahatma Gandhi had started on 17th February 1931 only. The credibility of this document was in doubt since the very beginning. Even Manmath Nath Gupta was constrained to write, "How far this letter is authentic, it is not known."[61] But Shiv Varma added a new twist to the controversy after 51 years of its first publication, when in 1986 he claimed to have discovered a fuller version of the document in a Government report entitled *"Note on the Development of the United Front Movement in Bengal (1936)"*.[62] C.E.S. Fairweather, writer of the report, in a note dated 1st November 1933, wrote that this revolutionary programme was drafted by Bhagat Singh (hanged) and was found in the house search of (detenu) Mrs. Bimala Pratibha Devi in Calcutta on 3rd October 1931.[63] A question naturally arises is why this fuller version was not known to the above mentioned papers who published it much before 3rd October 1931? How could it have travelled to far away Bengal and was discovered in the house of Bimala Pratibha Devi, a comparatively unknown name while Bhagat Singh's close colleagues (of HSRA) in north India were completely unaware of it. The known life history of Bhagat Singh does not reveal any contact with Bimala Pratibha Devi. Even after her release (in 1937), Bimala Pratibha Devi or any other revolutionary in Bengal never mentioned any thing about the existence of such a document. Doubts about the authenticity of the document become stronger if one sees the Government report in the context of British phobia of the Bolshevik threat to India during 1920s and 1930s.

Armed with this report, Shiv Varma (in 1986) went on to claim that the earlier versions of the document were actually "…a mutilated form. All references to Soviet Union, Marx. Lenin and the Communist Party were carefully deleted."[64] Strangely, Shiv Varma had no such apprehensions when he published the earlier version of the document in '*Sansmritiyam*' in 1969. Shiv Varma (in 1986) had signalled the end of the document where (in the Fairweather's report) 'Long Live Revolution' was cited in bold letters along with the date 2nd February 1931. Soon after, Jagmohan and Chaman Lal (1986), without offering any explanation, further doubled the size of this document by adding what was written beyond that end from the Government report. The subsequent collections, Jagmohan and Chaman Lal (1991), Satyam (2006),

K.C. Yadav (2006), Raj Shekhar Vyas (2006) followed the Jagmohan and Chaman Lal (1986) tradition, giving no explanation for accepting the extended version. The later part of the document, adopted by Jagmohan & Chaman Lal (1986) and others is nothing less than the political programme of the Communist Party and presents Bhagat Singh as a confirmed Communist activist. If it was so, then why a top Communist leader and a colleague of Bhagat Singh like the late Ajoy Ghosh should put on record in 1945 that "it would be an exaggeration to say that he became a Marxist".[65]

Of late, compilers of Bhagat Singh's documents (except Satyam who in the latest edition (2008) has retained the extended size) have reverted to the length of this document given by Shiv Varma in 1986.[66] In this *volte face,* most pathetic is the case of Chaman Lal who in 1986, 1991, and 2006 had presented the extended version (beyond Shiv Varma) but suddenly, in his latest compilation (2007), found it prudent to adopt the version given by Shiv Varma in 1986, without giving an iota of explanation.

The Jail Note Book of Bhagat Singh

The year 1991, sixty years after the martyrdom of Bhagat Singh, saw for the first time the serialized publication of a new and important document, commonly known as his jail note book, annotated by Bhupendra Hooja, in issues of *Indian Book Chronicle*. Bhupendra Hooja also broght out the notebook in book shape in 1994 under the title *A Martyr's Notebook*. In his introduction, Hooja narrated the story behind the 'discovery' of martyr's note book. According to Bhupendra Hooja, G.B. Kumar Hooja, his elder brother and Vice Chanceller of Gurukul Kangri University (Haridwar), acquired a copy of Jail notebook from Swami Shaktivesh of Indraptrastha Gurukul (Delhi) in 1980s.[67] Swami Shaktivesh had claimed to have discovered this notebook in an underground cellar in the Indraprastha Gurukul. Unfortunately, Shaktivesh was murdered soon after passing the notebook to G.B. Kumar Hooja, and the notebook thus remained with Hooja. At about the same time an Indian scholar Dr. Prakash Chaturvedi found a typed copy of the notebook in a Moscow archives, which was probably taken to Moscow by Mitrokhin. Both these copies matched. Subsequently the Hindustani Manch of Jaipur (with which G.B. Kumar Hooja was associated) decided to publish the contents of the note book, first as a series in Indian Book Chronicle in 1991 and finally in book shape in 1994.

Bhagat Singh was for the first time issued a blank note book for his use in jail on 12th September 1929. Its every page was numbered. The notebook carried the signatures of jail authorities as well as of Bhagat Singh at the beginning. Bhagat Singh used this note book for taking down notes from the books which he read while in jail, i.e. for a period lasting about 18 months. A photo copy of this jail note book is now available in the manuscript section of Nehru Memorial Museum and Library, New Delhi. Of the original 404 page note book, only 304 pages are available; out of which 145 pages carry notes in Bhagat Singh's own hand writing, 159 pages are blank. Nothing is known about the missing 100 pages.

As to how and when this note book reached Bhagat Singh's family is also not known.[68] As mentioned earlier, Bhagat Singh transferred all his papers before his execution to Lajjavati.[69] Lajjavati is on record (interviewed in November 1981) that she received all the papers of Bhagat Singh. But, she was unable to recall anything specifically about the notebook. She recalled that Kishan Singh made desperate attempts to acquire the papers but she did not oblige him. Later, she transferred those papers to Bejoy Kumar Sinha.[70] Bejoy is said to have given those papers to an acquaintance for safe keeping who panicked fearing Government reprisal during Quit India Movement and destroyed them.[71]

That a jail note book of Bhagat Singh actually existed became known for the first time in 1968, some 37 years after his martyrdom, through an article written by G.S. Deol in *People's Path*.[72] At another place, Deol wrote that the notebook is at present (in 1968) with Kultar Singh who had settled at Saharanpur.[73] This fact was corroborated by Virender Sindhu, daughter of Kultar Singh, in an interview with the author in April 2006 in New Delhi. Virender Sindhu had also used a fascimile of a page of this notebook in her book '*Yugdrista Bhagat Singh Aur Unke Mrityunjay Purkhe*' (1968).[74] In her interview, she also recalled returning the notebook to her father in 1969 when, after her marriage, she went to England, to settle there. It appears that by 1977, the jail notebook was in the possession of Bhagat Singh's younger brother Kulbir Singh at Faridabad.[75] L.V. Mitrokhin, a Soviet historian searching material on Lenin's influence on India, came across Bhagat Singh's note book in 1977 at Kulbir Singh's home in Faridabad. How and when this valuable document changed hands is not known.[76]

In 1979, the Nehru Memorial Museum and Library (NMML), New Delhi started correspondence with Bhagat Singh's family to acquire a copy of the above mentioned notebook. In a letter dated 17th January 1979, Kultar Singh directed the NMML to contact Kulbir Singh in connection with the jail note book.[77] NMML's correspondence with Kulbir Singh and his son Abhay Singh continued till 1981 ending with the acquisition of its copy by NMML. The above facts indicate that the jail notebook reached Kulbir Singh some time between 1969 and 1977. In his book, *Lenin in India* (1981), Mitrokhin quoted extensively from the note book and attempted to establish Bhagat Singh as a follower of Marxism - Leninism.

A comparison of the photocopies available at NMML and the copy published by Indian Book Chronicle reveals that latter is a copy of the former. The title pages of the two copies are exactly the same except that the latter has an extra line at the bottom-'*Copy by Abhay Kumar Singh. Nephew of Shaheed Bhagat Singh*', meaning thereby that Abhay Kumar Singh had a role in transferring a copy of jail notebook to Swami Shaktivesh.

The above narrative raises several questions about the discovery of the jail notebook of Bhagat Singh: Through whom and when was it sent out of jail by Bhagat Singh? Why were Lajjavati and Feroz Chand (both were secretaries of Bhagat Singh Defence Committee) and especially Lajjavati whom Bhagat Singh had entrusted with his papers, not aware of its existence? The story of its existence can be traced upto 1968 and not beyond that. How did it first reach Kultar Singh and then from Kultar Singh to Kulbir Singh? What happened to the missing 100 pages? If Swami Shaktivesh really found it in a cellar of the Gurukul, who took it there and when? If the existence of the diary was known in 1968 to Kultar Singh's daughter Virender Sindhu as well as G.S. Deol, why did it not find any place or mention in any of the compilations of Bhagat Singh's documents published before 1991, when it was first serialised in the Indian Book Chronicle?

The jail notes of Bhagat Singh are a living evidence of the voracious reader that Bhagat Singh was. Under the shadow of death, Bhagat Singh was studying and enriching himself. Notes and extracts jotted dawn from diverse sources are a testimony to his varied interests.[78]

The mystery of the 'missing manuscripts' of Bhagat Singh

Any account of Bhagat Singh's documents will be incomplete without mentioning the controversy related to the missing manuscripts of the four books which Bhagat Singh is said to have written in jail. The story begins with a statement made by Virender Sindhu, in 1968, in her book, *Yugdrista Bhagat Singh Aur Unke Mrityunjay Purkhe* wherein she wrote that Bhagat Singh, while in the condemned cell, authored several books, important among them being: *Ideal of Socialism; The Door to Death; Autobiography* and *The Revolutionary Movement of India with Short Biographic Sketches of the Revolutionaries*.[79] At another place in the same book she gave the name of the last mentioned book as *Swadheenta Ki Ladai Mein Punjab Ka Pahla Ubhaar*.[80] According to her, Bhagat Singh wanted to publish all those books as soon as possible but he was most concerned about the *Ideal of Socialism* as it had great 'political value'.[81] However,

Virender Sindhu does not mention the source of her information about the said manuscripts.

As mentioned earlier, Bhagat Singh had deputed Lajjavati to keep his papers with specific instructions not to give them to any body, not even to his relatives. Lajjavati had refused to part with these papers even to Bhagat Singh's father Sardar Kishan Singh even after repeated efforts by the latter to acquire these papers because she suspected Bhagat Singh's family of making commercial bargain out of the martyr's papers.[82] Virender Sindhu cited Kulbir Singh, who recalled writing in 1933-34 about these papers to Ajit Singh, his uncle in exile. Ajit Singh instructed Kulbir Singh to send him a copy of those papers so that he could get them published in the Europe. According to Kulbir Singh, when he went to Lajjavati, he was told by her that she had given the papers to Jawahar Lal Nehru because they were a national heritage. Nehru, when approached by Kulbir Singh, expressed his ignorance about the matter. Kulbir Singh again questioned Lajjavati who this time replied that she had given the manuscripts to Bejoy Kumar Sinha. Bejoy was released in 1938 only then these papers could have been transferred to him. He admitted having them in his possession and kept on assuring Kulbir Singh till 1946 that he would get them published. Later, he revealed that he had given Bhagat Singh's jail papers to a friend for safe keeping, from where they were lost.[83]

In her interview in November 1981, Lajjavati recalled that she had asked Feroz Chand to publish whatever worthwhile material he could find in Bhagat Singh's jail papers. She could recall nothing about the manuscripts. Feroz Chand chose one or two writings one of which was '*Why I am an Atheist*' (published in *The People* of Lahore on 27th September 1931). At this point two questions arise: First, how Kulbir Singh came to know that jail papers of Bhagat Singh contained manuscripts of four books? Second, why Feroz Chand was not able to find any thing else worth publishing when the above mentioned manuscripts (according to Kulbir Singh) formed an important part of the papers lying with Lajjavati?

Lajjavati is on record that she first hid the papers (some time after 27th September 1931) with Rai Bahadur Badri Das. Later she met Bejoy Sinha in Delhi (after Bejoy's release from jail in 1938) and gave him the papers as she recognised Bejoy as Bhagat Singh's successor in the revolutionary party.[84] Shiv Varma in *Selected Writings of Bhagat Singh* in 1986 provided the additional information that when the Second World War broke out in 1939, Bejoy apprehended "his arrest and a search of his house. In order to save Bhagat Singh's manuscripts from falling into the hands of the police, he passed them on to a friend for safe custody. In 1942, during the Quit India movement, when the government machinery of repression was in full swing, that friend, however, became funky and destroyed the manuscripts."[85] Meanwhile, Bejoy was arrested in 1941 while participating in the *Satyagriha* and was released in 1945. Strangely, his biography written by his wife Srirajyam Sinha, using his personal papers and her own memories (they were married in 1946), nowhere mentions the episode of Bhagat Singh's manuscripts. [86]

With the exception of Chaman Lal (2006), writings on Bhagat Singh appearing after 1968 accepted the episode of Bhagat Singh's missing manuscripts without raising any questions. In his preface to his collection of Bhagat Singh's writings, *Bhagat Singh Ke Sampoorna Dastavej* (2006), Chaman Lal expressed doubts whether Bhagat Singh really wrote four separate books while in jail: "I feel that Bhagat Singh's four manuscripts were in reality copies of his jail notebook only…. It is also possible that the manuscripts namely '*Autobiography*' and '*Door to Death*', may be versions of Dan Breen's autobiography. '*Ideal of Socialism*' has been mentioned at several places in the jail note book. It is near impossible to write '*History of Revolutionary Movement in India*' during stay in jail…Logically, it is impossible to write four books in two years of jail stay."[87] Also it is worth raising the question- how was Bhagat Singh able to get writing material in jail for four full length books?

Notes & References

[1] For example see *The Tribune* of 10th April 1929-full text of pamphlet thrown in Assembly; 8th June 1929-Bhagat Singh's statement in Sessions Court; 4th October 1930- Bhagat Singh's letter to father; 22nd October. 1930 - Bhagat Singh and B.K. Dutt's message to second All Punjab Students Conference; 24th December 1930- Bhagat Singh and B.K.Dutt's letter to editor of '*Modern Review*'.

[2] Suresh Salil, *Rastriya Sahara*, 27th May, 2007. Bibliography of S. Irfan Habib, *To Make the Deaf Hear,* (2007) also gives a reference to '*Mukti*' of July 1972.

[3] Amarjeet Chandan, ed, *Collected Works of Bhagat Singh and his Comradas*, 1974.

[4] 1996 edition of '*Selected Writings of Bhagat Singh*' also contains a second preface by Harkishan Singh Surjeet.

[5] Jagmohan Singh and Chaman Lal, *Bhagat Singh Aur Unke Saathion Ke Dastarej*, second edition, 1991, pp. 5-6.

[6] Edited by Bhupendra Hooja, Indian Book Chronicle, Jaipur, 1994. It carries two annexures, *Bhagat Singh: The Man and His ideology* by Kamlesh Mohan and Shiv Varma's *Ideological Development of Revolutionary Movement.*

[7] Chaman Lal, *Bhagat Singh Ke Sampoorna Dastavej*; Raj Shekhar, 2006; Satyam, 2006, op.cit.; Rajshekhar Vyas, *Mein Bhagat Singh Bol Raha Hoon*, 3 vols., 2006; and K.C.Yadav & Baber Singh, *The Fragrance of Freedom, The Writings of Bhagat Singh*, 2006.

[8] This compendium suffers from repetitions and poor proof corrections.

[9] *The Fragrance of Freedom*, 2006, p. 7.

[10] Bhagat Singh wrote in Urdu, Gurumukhi, Hindi and English.

[11] D.N. Gupta, ed., *Bhagat Singh: Select Speeches and Writings*, 2007.

[12] Chaman Lal, (ed.), *Dastavejon Ke Aaeene Mein*, 2007.

[13] Naresh Suri and Ragini Mitra, *Amar Shaheed Bhagat Singh: Vyaktitwa Aur Vichar,* 1987.

[14] *Shaheed-i-Azam: Bhagat Singh.* Patna, 2003.

[15] *Yad Kar Lena Kabhi: Shaheedon Ke Khat,* 1997.

[16] One of the colleagues of Bhagat Singh, Kishori Lal has himself raised doubts about the authenticity of some letters attributed to the revolutionaries. (Cited in Mathura Das Thapar, *Mere Bhai Shaheed Sukhdev,* 1998, p. 13.).

[17] G.S. Deol, *'Shaheed Bhagat Singh: A Biography'*, 1985, pp. 18-19.

[18] K.C. Yadav and Babar Singh, *Fragrance of Freedom*, 2006, pp. 297-298.

[19] *Yaad Kar Lena Kabhi: Shaheeedon Ke Khat*, 1997.

[20] Shiv Varma, *The Selected Writings of Bhagat Singh*, 1996, p. 102.

[21] Yashpal, *Simhavalokan*, 2005, p. 61.

[22] Shanta Malhotra, *Sreya Marg Ke Pathik*, 2000, p. 59.

[23] Ibid., p. 49.

[24] Chaman Lal in his earlier compilation (2006) did not attribute this article to Bhagat Singh. He has not explained the basis behind the inclusion of this article in his latest compilation.

[25] Sohan Singh Josh, *My Meetings with Bhagat Singh and on Other Revolutionaries*, 1976, p. 18.

[26] See Appendix M.

[27] Unfortunately even the prestigious journals such as '*Mainstream*' have not bothered to check the authenticity of anything passing under the name of Bhagat Singh. For instance, the article- '*Sampradayik Dange Aur Unka Ilaaj*' (unsigned, June 1928) has been published twice under the title '*Bhagat Singh for Today*' on 27 March 1993 and August 11-17, 2006 by Nazirul Hasan Ansari. On both occasions, its year of publication in 'Kirti' was wrongly given as 1927.

[28] Dan Breen, *My Fight for Irish Freedom*, Talbot Press Limited, Dublin, 1924. This reference is courtesy Arpita Sen, "The Proscription of an Irish Text and the Chittagong Rising of 1930," *The Indian Historical Review*, December 2007, New Delhi, p. 96.

[29] N.A.I. Home Political, 28 (II), 1929.

[30] Raj Shekhar Vyas (2006), Vol.III, p. 51.

[31] Ibid., Vol. I, p. 84.

[32] Bhagat Singh, *Mere Krantikari Sathi*, compiled by Virender Sindhu, 1977.

[33] Chaman Lal, *Shaheed Bhagat Singh: Dastavejon Ke Aaine Mein*, 2007.

[34] Acharya Chatursen Shasti, *Meri Atmakahani*, 1963, pp. 152-53.

[35] Ibid. p. 153.

[36] *Chandra* Shekhar Shastri, *Bhartiya Atankwaad ka Itihas*, 1 January 1939, p. 354.

[37] Judgement of the Special Tribunal in Lahore Conspiracy Case, cited in Malwinderjit Singh Waraich and Gurudev Singh Sidhu, eds., *The Hanging of Bhagat Singh: The Complete Judgement and Other Documents*, 2005, pp. 141-142.

[38] Shiv Verma, *Selected Writings of Bhagat Singh*, 1996, p. 16.

[39] *Sangrathan,* September, 1992, republished in Chaman Lal. *Bhagat Singh*, 2009, pp. 240-244.

[40] Virender Sindhu, *Patra Aur Dastavej*, 1975, p. 44.

[41] Nand Kishore Nigam, *Balidaan*, n.d., p. 88.

[42] Durga Devi's interview to Dr. Kaushalya Devi Dublish on 27 February 1976 in Luknow, cited in Kaushalya Devi Dublish, *Revolutionaries and Their Activities in North India*, 1982, p. 210.

[43] Yashpal, *Simhavalokan,* 2005, p. 273.

[44] Ibid., p. 255.

[45] In the course of this essay Bhagat Singh writes: "Judgement is already too well known. Within a week it is to be pronounced." (*Why I am an Atheist*, cited from Shiv Varma, *Selected Writings of Shaheed Bhagat Singh*, 1996, p. 125.).

[46] Transcript of Lajjavati's interview at NMML, p. 130.

[47] Raj Shekhar Vyas has twice given a wrong date of its publication in *The People*- 17 September, 1934 (Raj Shekhar Vyas, 2006, Vol. I, p. 155, p. 221).

[48] Jeevanthan, P., (tr.), *'Nan Nasththeegan Ain? Sardar Bhagat Singh'*, Erode: Bhagvthariya Noor Pathippur Khazhalagam,Erode, 1934, (NAI Lib).

[49] Bipan Chandra, *Why I am an Atheist,* 1979.

[50] Raj Shekhar Vyas, 2006, Vol. I, p. 19.

[51] *Why I am an Atheist*, cited from Shiv Varma, *Selected Writings of Shaheed Bhagat Singh*, 1996, p. 121.

[52] Shiv Varma, *Selected Writings of Shaheed Bhagat Singh*, 1996, p. 121.

[53] But Virendra Sindhu in '*Patra Aur Dastavej*, 1975, p. 69 has claimed its first publication.

[54] Shiv Varma, *Sansmritiyan*, 1974, p. 156.

[55] Jagmohan Singh and Chaman Lal, *Bhagat Singh Aur Unke Saathion Ke Dastavej*, 1991, p. 381.

[56] Jagmohan & Chaman Lal (1986 & 1991), Chaman Lal (2006) and K.C.Yadav and Babar Singh (2006) all have wrongly given the date of publication in *The People* (Lahore) as 29th July 1931.

[57] *Bhavisya*, Allahabad, 16 April 1931, p. 32.

[58] Letter's publication in '*Punjab Kesari*' could not be verified.

[59] Manmathnath Gupta, *Krantidoot Bhagat Singh Aur Unka Yug*, 1972, pp. 214-218.

[60] Published under the title '*Sardar Ka Antim Sandesh Krantikarion Ke Naam*'.

[61] Manmath Nath Gupta, *Krantidoot Bhagat Singh Aur Unka Yug*, 1972, p. 214.

[62] A photocopy of the report is available in the Library of the Martyrs' Memorial and Freedom Struggle Research Centre at Lucknow. Unfortunately the file number or other references are not mentioned. The new version was published for the first time in Shiv Varma, (ed.), *Selected Writings of Shaheed Bhagat Singh* (1986).

[63] Bimala Pratiba Devi was arrested on 20th June 1933 while leading a procession on Deshbandhu Diwas in Calcutta. Later she was taken under Ordinance. She was released in 1937. (Manmathnath Gupta, *Bhartiya Krantikari Andolan Ka Itihas*, 2004, p. 293).

[64] Shiv Varma, *Selected Writings of Bhagat Singh*, 1986, p. 128.

[65] Ajoy Ghish, *Bhagat Singh and His Comrades*, 1979, p. 28.

[66] Chaman Lal, *Bhagat Singh: The Jail Note Book And Other Writings*, 2007; *Shaheed Bhagat Singh: Dastavejon Ke Aaine Mein*, 2007; S.Irfan Habib , *To Make the Deaf Hear*, 2007 and Kuldip Nayar, *Without Fear*, 2007.

[67] Hooja, Bhoopendra (ed.), *A Martyr's Notebook*, 2002, p. xxii.

[68] Though according to K.C.Yadav and Babar Singh, (*Bhagat Singh: Ideas on Freedom, Liberty and Religion; Jail Notes of a Revolutionary*, 2007, p. 17) the notebook was handed over, along with other belongings of Bhagat Singh to his father, Sardar Kishan Singh after Bhagat Singh's execution. This information is not corroborated by any known source.

[69] Virender Sindhu (2004), p. 257; Transcript of Lajjavati's interview at NMML.

[70] Transcript of Lajjavati's interview at NMML, p. 130.

71 Shiv Varma, *Selected Writings of Bhagat Singh*, 1996, p. 16.

72 L.V. Mitrokhin, *Lenin in India*, 1981, p. 116. Chaman Lal is incorrect in stating that an article by A.V. Raikov, '*Bhagat Singh and his Ideological Legacy*'(1971) and Mitrokhin's article of the same year, '*The Books Read by Bhagat Singh*', were some of the earliest studies of the Jail Note Book. Mitrokhin himself came to know about the jail note book of Bhagat Singh for the first time in 1977 (L.V. Mitrokhin, *Lenin in India*, 1981, p. 116).

73 G.S. Deol (1985), p. 108, foot-note 19.

74 Virender Sindhu, 1968.

75 L.V. Mitrokhin, *Lenin in India*, 1981, p. 116.

76 According to K.C.Yadav and Babar Singh, *Bhagat Singh: Ideas on Freedom, Liberty and Religion; Jail Notes of a Revolutionary*, 2007, p. 17, " After Sardar Kishan Singh's death, the notebook (along with other papers of Bhagat Singh) was passed on to his (S. Kishan Singh's) son, Shri Kulbir Singh." This information is not correct as the notebook was with Kultar Singh for about twenty years before it passed on to Kulbir Singh. S. Kishan Singh had died on 30 May 1951.

77 Interview with Mr. Hakip, Incharge of Manuscript Section, NMML, New Delhi.

78 Unfotunately, beginning from Mitrokhin in 1981, some vested interests are busy giving a particular colour to Shaheed Bhagat Singh's ideology by citing extracts from his jail notebook. It must be noted that notes and extracts under question had been randomly taken for the purpose of self study. They can not be termed as 'writings' as writing is a well thought out expression of one's mind. Neither it can be termed as 'jail diary' in the conventional sense as it does not contain a date-wise account of daily events in the jail.

79 Virender Sindhu, *Yugdrista Bhagat Singh Aur Unke Mrityunjay Purkhe*, 2004, p. 287.

80 Ibid., p. 228.

81 Ibid., p. 287.

82 Oral Transcript of Lajjavati's interview at NMML, New Delhi, p. 130.

83 Virender Sindhu, 2004, op. cit., pp. 287-288.

84 Ibid.

85 Shiv Varma, *Selected Writings of Bhagat Singh*, 1996, p. 16.

86 Srirajyam Sinha, *A Revolutionary's Quest for Sacrifice,* 1993.
87 Chaman Lal, *Bhagat Singh Ke Sampoorna Dastavej,* 2006, pp. 28-29.

Biography

4

Background and the Formative Phase

Martyrdom being the highest manifestation of patriotism, the origins of Bhagat Singh's quest are rooted in his ardent patriotism as nurtured and nourished by a host of factors like his illustrious family background, Arya Samaji milieu of Punjab of the early 20th century, inspiration from the heroes of *Ghadar* movement, and deep anguish from the tragedy of Jallianwalla Bagh.

The tradition of resistance to the British in Bhagat Singh's family goes back to Bhagat Singh's ancestor Sardar Fateh Singh, a native of village Khatkar Kalan in Jalandhar district. According to Jagmohan Singh, Bhagat Singh's nephew, Fateh Singh had participated in the Anglo-Punjab wars in the 1840s. But despite the heroics of the Sikh army Punjab was annexed by the British on 22nd March 1849. Fateh Singh was one of those whose land was confiscated by the British as a punishment for defending the motherland. During the 1857 upsurge, the British Governor Lord John Lawrence wanted to enlist the support of the landed class and thus declared to give the confiscated property back in lieu of their support. Sardar Fateh Singh responded by saying, 'Guru Gobind Singh has taught me to stand up for the people fighting for their rights and freedom. The help of the oppressor is tantamount to the betrayal of His teachings.'[1] Khem Singh, Bhagat Singh's great grandfather, according to Kulbir Singh (Bhagat Singh's younger brother), had so much contempt for the foreign rulers that he strictly forbade the study of English at his home. He had also vowed not to visit any government office as it would require being polite to the English officers.[2]

The common folk of Punjab with their tradition of resistance to foreign invasions were shocked but helpless at the establishment of British rule on their land. The situation remained much the same even during the year 1857, the darkest hour of the British in India. The first resurgence from the prevailing despondency in Punjab emerged in the form of *Namdhari* movement under the leadership of Baba Ram Singh. *Namdharis* were also called *Kukas* (shouters) because they used to shout with joy (*'Kuk'*) while worshipping. The Baba preached the ideals of a purified Sikhism based on *Khalsa* of Guru Gobind Singh, emphasising on austerity and equality.[3] The consumption of beef was strictly prohibited. The *Namdhari* vision of a restructured Sikhism, called for a total reshaping of the Sikh community into a militant, religious-political dominion which contained elements of a parallel government, went against British political interests. By 1863, British officers had become quite alarmed over the growth of *Namdhari* sect and even interned Baba Ram Singh for a while. The direct clash with the British occurred over the issue of cow protection in 1871 when *Namdhari* bands began to attack Muslim slaughter houses. The British crushed the movement with a heavy hand. In a single incident on 17-18 July 1872, 66 *Kukas* was summarily executed. Baba Ram Singh was arrested and sent to exile in Burma where he died in 1885. *Kukas* were hunted down and many restrictions were placed on them. Ram Singh and *Namdhari* movement became a symbol of revolution. Bhagat Singh had called the *Namdhari* movement as the first attempt to liberate Punjab.[4] Arjun Singh, Bhagat Singh's grandfather, had also been a *Namdhari* for some time during his young age.[5]

Namdhari movement unnerved the British as Punjab was strategically important for the British Empire in India. After the revolt of 1857 Punjab had become the largest recruiting ground for the British Indian army. Several new steps were taken to strengthen the British hold over Punjab by sowing the seeds of separatism in the Punjabi community: Sikhs were declared as a 'martial race' (read loyal); *Namdhari* missionaries were prohibited from preaching to the Sikh troops of the British Indian army[6]; and second Punjab Census in 1868 officially recognized Sikhs as a separate category (from the Hindus) whereas the first Punjab Census of 1855 had included the Sikhs under the definition of Hindus.[7] Against the multiple Sikh identities in the post-1857 Punjab with indistinct boundaries, the British treated one Sikh identity, the 'Singh' as the only true Sikhism.[8] This way a wedge was created between the *Keshdhari* (keeping long hair) Sikhs and *non-Keshdhari* Sikhs. Here the underlying motive was to delink the Sikh identity from its Hindu milieu and submerge it in *Khalsa* identity by emphasizing external *Khalsa* symbols. As a result of these developments, by the 1890s, the question of Sikh identity had started raising a lot of dust in Punjab.

In this scenario, Swami Dayananda visited Punjab and received an overwhelming response. The first Arya Samaj in Punjab was established at Lahore in 1877. Arya Samaj imparted a new vision to its followers- the greatness of ancient Indian civilization, which gave self confidence and self reliance leading to a feeling of ardent nationalism. Revolutionary message of Arya Samaj also included ideals of social equality, self-dependence, rationality in social and religious fields and national education. An estimate of the contribution of Arya Samaj in generating political consciousness in Punjab can be gauged from the fact that almost the entire nationalist leadership in Punjab during the early 20th century emerged from the Arya Samaj ranks.

Many a patriotic Sikh joined the Arya Samaj. Its first secretary in Punjab was Jawahar Singh, a Sikh. Arjun Singh was also among the first Sikhs to join Arya Samaj in Punjab. Arjun Singh was a remarkable man; he produced in his family some of the best known patriots of Punjab- Ajit Singh, Kishan Singh, Swarna Singh, and Bhagat Singh. Arjun Singh was not content by merely becoming a lay follower of Arya Samaj. He made a deep study of Arya Samaj literature and went on to become a spokesman of Arya Samaj in his region and participated in many debates (*shastrarthas*). He also wrote many pamphlets for Arya Samaj including the one titled '*Hamare Guruban Vedon Ke Pairo The*' (Our *Gurus* were followers of the *Vedas*). When Arya Samajists of Patiala were implicated in a conspiracy and tried on charges of insulting the *Guru Granth Sahib*, Arjun Singh worked on the defence committee. Along with other scholars he was able to present about 700 couplets of *Granth Sahib* and *Vedas* which were similar and on the basis of their similarities, the defence committee was able to prove that *Vedas* and *Granth Sahib* were similar and hence worthy of equal adoration.[9] Arjun Singh also attacked the practice of untouchability and superstition in his village.

Most conspicuous quality of Arjun Singh was his versatility; apart from being a leading Arya Samaji he was also a cultivator, a Unani *hakim* and a *munshi*. When Government offered 25 acres of land to every family settling in northwest Punjab, Arjun Singh did not let go the opportunity and settled in village Banga of District Lyallpur (now in Pakistan). There he worked hard on the virgin land to become a prosperous farmer. Most remarkable trait of Arjun Singh was his progressive and nationalist attitude. He could have become a very rich cultivator or a famous '*hakim*' but he accorded priority to the work of Arya Samaj and Congress. It is said that even Dadabhai Naoroji was attracted towards him.[10] He was one of the first Jat Sikhs to send his sons to Saidas Anglo Sanskrit High School Jalandhar. He participated in all the political movements of his time. What more can be said about the patriotism of a person whose one son (Swarna Singh) died of tortures in jail, second (Ajit Singh) was in exile in foreign lands, third was in jail (Kishan Singh) and he still had the heart to bequeath publicly his grandsons (Jagat Singh and Bhagat Singh) to the cause of the nation.[11]

Impact of Arjun Singh was not limited to his sons, it transcended to his third generation. Bhagat Singh spent his childhood (till he completed his primary school) under the care and guidance of his grandfather, Arjun Singh. Bhagat Singh has mentioned about the influence of his grand father during his formative years.[12] It was Arjun Singh who inculcated the Arya Samaji virtues in Bhagat Singh's life. Bhagat Singh's letters also reveal his affection for his grandfather.

Kishan Singh, Bhagat Singh's father, was the eldest son of Arjun Singh. In the words of Virendra Sindhu, his grand daughter, "he was a born rebel, a revolutionary since birth and remained a revolutionary till his last day."[13] Bhagat Singh later summed up his father's influence on himself in the following words- "It was through his teachings that I aspired to devote my life to the cause of freedom."[14]

While studying at Saidas Anglo Sanskrit School, Kishan Singh along with his younger brother Ajit Singh, was greatly influenced by the patriotic teachings imparted by Sundar Das, the headmaster of the school. Sundar Das was the son of Arya Samaji leader Saidas.[15] Kishan Singh started his public life under the guidance of Lala Hansraj, the noted Arya Samaji leader and head of DAV College, Lahore.[16] Kishan Singh rendered exemplary public service in different parts of India affected by natural calamities viz. the famines in Berar and Gujarat in 1898 and 1900 respectively, the Kangra earthquake in 1904, and flood in Jhelum in Srinagar in 1905. The apathy of the Government towards disaster-struck areas further strengthened his revulsion against the colonial and foreign nature of the British government. In 1905-06, he jumped into extremist politics during Swadeshi Movement along with his younger brother Ajit Singh. In Punjab this movement acquired the nature of a popular upsurge centred around peasant issues like Colonisation Act, Bari Doab Act and revenue hike. To coordinate the movement, 'Bharat Mata Society' was formed by the joint efforts of the leading stalwarts of that time like Sufi Amba Prasad, Ajit Singh, Kishan Singh, Lala Hardayal, Swarna Singh, Kartar Singh Kesargarhiya, Lal Chand Falak, Mahashaya Ghasita Ram, Mehta Anand Kishore, Jia Ul Haq, Kedar Nath Sehgal and Lala Pindi Das. The society also brought out a newspaper "*Bharat*

Mata" in Urdu. It has been aptly said that Kishan Singh was the *arm* of this movement, while Ajit Singh was the *heart*; Sufi Amba Prasad was the *soul*, and Hardayal the *brain*.[17] Kishan Singh also edited the revolutionary organ *Sahayak* for sometime. Kishan Singh possessed the qualities which remain the hallmark of a seasoned revolutionary. As an organizer he was a genius, he could work secretly and effectively even when under heavy surveillance and most importantly, he was able to keep his cool and maintain his mental balance in difficult conditions.

It is on record that during the First World War, Kishan Singh supported the *Ghadar* party movement financially and otherwise. He had links with the leading revolutionaries of his time including Sachindra Nath Sanyal. He also helped Ras Bihari Bose after the Harding Bomb Case. The British Government was aware of the activities of Kishan Singh and considered him a danger to the empire.[18] As a result, he had to face many trials and went to jail several times. While in jail, several times he opposed torture. Interestingly, Kishan Singh was one of the pioneers to hungerstrike for reform in jail rules. His son Bhagat Singh was himself to lead an epic hunger strike some years later for the same cause.

Kishan Singh's younger brother Ajit Singh also grew up in an Arya Samaji environment at home and developed a strong sense of self respect and equally strong hatred for the foreign rulers. He studied up to intermediate in D.A.V. College, Lahore and had great interest in Sanskrit. Later, he took up social and political studies independently. He wrote numerous pamphlets and tracts for Arya Samaj out of which '*Vidhwa Ki Pukar*' (*Widow's Cry*) became very famous.[19]

In politics, Ajit Singh along with his brother Kishan Singh was a follower of Bal Gangadhar Tilak. Tilak was equally impressed with Ajit Singh and saw in him a statesman leading the nation in future. But the limitations of the contemporary Congress politics made it too small a canvas to absorb the dynamic revolutionary zeal of Ajit Singh. As far back as 1903, during the Royal *Darbar* organized by Lord Curzon, Ajit Singh, then a young man of twenty two, had secretly tried to incite the native princes to recreate the 1857 type revolt. [20] The most spectacular work of Ajit Singh was the organisation of the peasant unrest of 1907 (also known as Pagri Sambhaal Jatta movement) under the banner of Bharat Mata Society. The primary functions of Bharat Mata Society were to publish seditious material and awaken the popular spirit through speeches. If Sufi Amba Prasad was in charge of publication work, the star speaker of the Society was Ajit Singh. Oratory of Ajit Singh was legendry. His moving speeches attracted people from far and wide. Even soldiers from the cantonments came to hear Ajit Singh speak, thus creating hopes of an army insurrection. The British government was greatly alarmed by the movement which threatened to create a general revolt among peasants and soldiers. A government report regarded Ajit Singh as "the most violent public speaker at political meetings; he had frequently advocated active resistance to Government, and his utterances are largely directed to exciting discontent among the agricultural classes and the soldiery". [21]

The Government was left with no choice but to arrest Ajit Singh. He was arrested on 2nd June 1907 and kept in Mandalay fort along with Lala Lajpat Rai. While in jail, Ajit Singh wrote a compilation of biographic accounts of famous revolutionaries of world namely '*Muhibbane Watan*'. The book became very popular and the Government had to proscribe it. After his release in November 1907, Ajit Singh again tried to infuse vigour into the work of Bharat Mata Society but soon found that Government was preparing a conspiracy case against him and on the advice of his colleagues decided to secretly leave India. Ajit Singh left India in 1909 and wandered in many countries including Iran, Turkey, Central Asia, Germany, France, Switzerland, Brazil, and Italy. During this long exile he continued his efforts to liberate India. He was able to return to India in 1947 and breathed his last on the morning of 16 August 1947, only hours after India became independent.

Bhagat Singh was about two years of age when Ajit Singh left India but as he grew up he acquired a great deal of knowledge about his uncle's activities.[22]

Like his elder brothers, Swarn Singh, the third son of Arjun Singh was also head and heart into the peasant movement. He was arrested and tried in 1907 and sentenced to one and a half years of rigorous imprisonment. He died at the age of 23 in 1910 due to tuberculosis. At a very young age, he had begun to assist in the public work of his brothers. He worked as in-charge of an orphanage which consisted of children whose parents had been lost in famines, earthquakes or floods. He also functioned as in-charge of propaganda of Bharat Mata Society and wrote sensational articles on the British Government's activities. In jail, he contacted tuberculosis due to excessive hard work, bad food and unhygienic environment. The callous attitude of jail authorities towards his disease made it incurable. When his condition deteriorated he was released prematurely but the tuberculosis had reached a stage where he could not be saved despite the best efforts of his family members.

With this glorious pedigree, Bhagat Singh was born in 1907 to Kishan Singh and Vidyavati in the village Banga of district Lyallpur (now in Pakistan). Thus he inherited the tradition of fighting and suffering for the country. It also removed from his mind the fear of police, jail and even death. Since his early childhood, family environment inculcated in him a dream of throwing out the British rulers and avenging the hardships endured at their hands. There is a legend that once Mehta Anand Kishore asked the four year old Bhagat Singh what he reaps in his fields. Bhagat Singh stunned him by answering-'guns'.[23] Members of his family used to recall how he was greatly affected by woes of his aunts Harnam Kaur (wife of Ajit Singh) and Hukum Kaur (widow of Swarna Singh). He used to console his aunts that he will take revenge and bring back his uncle Ajit Singh.[24]

While still a child, he had gone through the abundant patriotic literature available in his home which included newspapers files, court judgments and propaganda material. Such studies, even though the limits of a child's understanding must be kept in mind, were enough to incite and inspire him. His studies made him aware of the early extremist movement and role of various leaders including his family members. At the same time, repressive and exploitative image of the British rule filled him with contempt.

The deepest impact on the impressionable mind of the young Bhagat Singh was made by Kartar Singh Sarabha, the Ghadar martyr. Ghadar movement (1913-1915) was planned on the lines of 1857 Revolt mainly by Punjabi immigrants settled on west coast of United States of America. But Ghadar leaders failed to keep their plans secret and British Government was able to arrest most of them when they returned to India to execute their plans. In the ensuing trial in 1915, as many as 275 persons were tried, out of which 46 were sentenced to death, youngest of them being Kartar Singh Sarabha.[25] Bhagat Singh was just nine years old when Kartar Singh, a lad of nineteen years was hanged on 13th September 1915. Bhagat Singh has written that during his trial, Kartar Singh acted very defiantly and preferred death to life-imprisonment. When awarded death sentence, he smilingly thanked the judge[26]. According to Vidyavati, his mother, Bhagat Singh was so fond of Kartar Singh that he always carried a photograph of Kartar Singh with him and used to call him his 'hero, friend and companion'. She also recalled that Bhagat Singh used to often sing the favourite couplet of Kartar Singh:

"Seva desh di jindarye bari aukhi

Gallan karian dher sukhalian ne

Jinhan desh seva wich pair paya

Unhan lakh musibtan jhallian ne" [27].

(Hard is the path of patriotism, easy enough uttering of speeches; those who follow the path of service to motherland, have to bear countless torments).

Ghadar movement and its trials had captivated the minds of Indian patriots and Punjab was the most affected province as most of the Ghadarites belonged to Punjab. In popularizing these heroes and their ideals, crucial role was played by '*Ghadar*', the mouth piece of the Ghadar party. It was published in several languages besides Urdu and Punjabi. More lasting impact on the public mind was made by '*Ghadar Ki Goonj*', selection of inspiring poems and couplets from the '*Ghadar*', first edition (1914) of which had sold ten thousand copies.[28] Poems of '*Ghadar Ki Goonj*' became very popular throughout Punjab. Bhagat Singh himself used to recite some of them. Audacity, heroism and sacrifice of Ghadar heroes and particularly of Kartar Singh Sarabha continued to inspire Bhagat Singh throughout his life. He aspired to become another Sarabha.

Wounds left by the trial of Ghadar movement had not healed when on 13 April 1919, Jallianwala Bagh tragedy left the whole nation shell shocked. Most inhuman and brutal face of the British rule laid exposed as hundreds of unarmed and unwarned people, with no means to escape, fell to the bullets of an army contingent led by General Dyer. Jallianwala Bagh tragedy left a deep impact on the psyche of Bhagat Singh, then hardly a child of twelve. He felt so disturbed that he went alone to Amritsar from Lahore and brought back blood laced soil from the site of killings in a small bottle. According to his sister Amar Kaur, Bhagat Singh and she herself worshiped that bottle for many days. Bhagat Singh's childhood friend, Jaidev Gupta recalled later that after 1919 massacre, atmosphere in Sardar Kishan Singh's home became very tense. Prominent nationalists of Lahore including Kedar Nath Sehgal, Bhai Parmanand, Mehta Anand Kishore, Lala Pindi Das and Lal Chand Falak used to come there and talk about martial law and killings etc.[29] Such discussions increased his understanding about the prevailing situation and also steeled his resolve to devote his life for the cause of the nation.

In 1921, when Non-Cooperation Movement was launched under the leadership of Mahatma Gandhi, students were exhorted to leave Government backed schools. For such students, National College was established in Lahore. At that time, at the age of thirteen, patriotic spirit in Bhagat Singh had become so intense that he left D.A.V. School against the advice of his father. In those days he was keenly following the events around him. In a letter dated 14th November 1921, he informed his grand father in a cryptic manner about the impending railway strike. He enthusiastically participated in the boycott of foreign goods. Bhagat Singh's family had already been wearing *Khadi* for long.

In those days he also sympathized with the Babbar Akali movement in Punjab. His article in *Pratap* 'Holi ke Din Rakta ke Cheetain' (15th March, 1926) is a testimony to his admiration for Babbar Akali heroes. When *Gurudwara* movement was started for taking the control of Sikh shrines from the hands of the government backed corrupt *Mahants*, Bhagat Singh started keeping long hair, black turban and *kirpan* as symbol of his support for the movement.

Bhagat Singh's association with *Arya Samaj* was part of his family heritage. Early part of his life was spent in the company of his grandfather who, as mentioned before, was a staunch *Arya Samaji*. Under his influence Bhagat Singh was brought up as a cultured and disciplined boy. In keeping with the *Arya Samaji* tradition, *Yagnopavit Sanskara* (sacred thread ceremony) of Bhagat Singh was duly held. After the ceremony Arjun Singh declared that he was offering both his grandsons, Bhagat Singh and Jagat Singh (elder brother of Bhagat Singh, died in 1915-16), in the service of the nation. Bhagat Singh always remained fully conscious of the significance of that sacred ritual. When he left home in 1923 to escape marriage he reminded his father:

"My life has already been bequeathed to a noble cause - the cause of the freedom of India. For that reason comforts and worldly desires have no attraction in my life. You might remember that at the time of my sacred thread ceremony, when I was quite young, Bapuji (grandfather) had declared that I was being pledged for the service of the country. I am therefore honouring the pledge of that time."[30]

When Bhagat Singh completed his primary studies, his father got him admitted to D.A.V. School of Lahore where morning and evening *Vedic* prayers and *Yagnas* were part of the daily routine. Bhagat Singh wrote: "After finishing my primary studies, I joined D.A.V. School of Lahore and stayed in its Boarding House for full one year. There, apart from morning and evening prayers, I used to recite '*Gayatri Mantra*' for hours and hours. I was a perfect devotee in those days".[31] Bhagat Singh's letters of those days to his grand father begin with '*OM*' (a fact that has been deliberately missed in several collections of Bhagat Singh's documents), he was quite proficient in Sanskrit (Bhagat Singh attained 110 marks in Sanskrit in comparison to 68 in English out 150).[32] Bhagat Singh continued to study Sanskrit even in National College. Yashpal has also ascribed this to the Arya Samaj background of Bhagat Singh.[33] In the National College, Bhagat Singh was a favourite student of Bhai Parmanand. Bhai Parmanand was the chief administrator as well a teacher of history in National College. He was a living legend for students because of his participation in First Lahore Conspiracy Case and Ghadar movement. He was subsequently awarded death punishment which was later commuted to life sentence and had a stint at Andaman's Cellular Jail. In the words of Comrade Ramchandra who was also a product of National College, "of all teachers Bhai Parmanand inspired us [the] most. He taught modern European history with full revolutionary fervour. Recounting in detail one European revolution after the other he inspired the students to resolutely adopt revolutionary methods to free the country."[34] Lala Feroz Chand, editor of *Bandematram* and *The People*, who also taught in the National College for a brief period, recalled later in an interview:

"Real strength of National College was Bhai Parmanand. The biggest contribution of National College was not to produce great scholars but great patriots......In my view Bhai Parmanand was responsible for it. Those teachers or students who came in his contact imbibed it (patriotism)."[35]

For Bhagat Singh, Bhai Parmanand was an object of double reverence as he was the one who had guided and inspired Kartar Singh Sarabha, the hero of Bhagat Singh since childhood.[36] Bhai Parmanand used to encourage the students to participate in plays such as *'Rana Pratap'*, *'Bharat Durdasha'*, and *'Samrat Chandragupta'*. Bhagat Singh participated very enthusiastically in these plays. Once Bhai Parmanand appreciated Bhagat Singh's performance in *Samrat Chandragupta* so much so that he hugged Bhagat Singh on the stage and declared, "Bhagat Singh will prove to be the Chandragupta of the future".[37] Bhai Parmanand taught Bhagat Singh the virtues to be followed by a true revolutionary and Bhagat Singh followed them throughout his life.

Another teacher of National College who influenced Bhagat Singh greatly was Jayachandra Vidyalankar. A graduate of India's first national university, Gurukul Kangri, he was also a great historian as well as a great teacher. His historical insights had convinced Bhagat Singh that an armed revolt was inevitable to free India from foreign bondage. Patriotic impulse of Bhagat Singh was given a revolutionary direction by Jaychandra Vidyalankar who had links with Bengali revolutionaries and also Sachindra Nath Sanyal. About Jayachandra's role in revolutionary movement, Sachindra Nath Sanyal wrote in *Bandi Jiwan*:

"Full credit of the foundation of revolutionary movement in Punjab goes to Sri Jayachandraji. Without him, I could not have succeeded in Punjab in so little time. It was only through his efforts that I became acquainted with the students of Tilak School of Politics. With his help I acquired men, whom I could send to the most difficult and dangerous places."

When Bhagat Singh reached Kanpur at the suggestion of Sanyal, he worked under the leadership of Jogesh Chandra Chatterjee who himself was impressed by Arya Samaj and its principles. Jogesh Chandra Chatterjee writes in his memoirs:

"I read *'Satyartha Prakash'* very thoroughly and was very impressed. Though the basis of the book is the Vedas, the feeling of overwhelming patriotism is its outstanding feature. I realised the intense national feeling that Swami Dayanand Saraswati had. .... Swami Dayanand too was a great soul who gave a nationalist and patriotic lead to the Hindu society... I was further thrilled to know that Shyamji Krishna Verma, who was a great supporter of the Indian revolutionaries in London, and who afterwards shifted to Paris, was a devotee of Swamiji and a staunch believer in Arya Samaj"[38]

Arya Samaj's role in Bhagat Singh's life was not limited to the formative period alone. He continued to have deep faith in the patriotism and steadfastness of individuals connected with Arya Samaj. Due to the secret nature of revolutionary work there was always a great scope for betrayals and conspiracies. In this context Bhagat Singh always found in Arya Samaj, a safe sanctuary for his activities. Memoirs of Satyaketu Vidyalankar, Bhimsen Vidyalankar, Dinanath Siddhantalankar (all of them worked with Bhagat Singh in *'Arjun'* in Delhi during 1924) and Kamal Nath Tiwari, revolutionary colleague of Bhagat Singh who was sentenced to life in the Lahore Conspiracy Case, provide details of their association with Bhagat Singh which continued till he was arrested in the Assembly Bomb Case in April 1929.[39]

Notes & References

[1] *Frontline*, October 20 - November 2, 2007.

[2] Transcript of interview of Kulbir Singh at Nehru Memorial Museum and Library (NMML), New Delhi, pp. 3-4.

[3] Kanneth W. Jones, *Socio Religious Reform Movements in British India*, 2003, pp. 90-91.

4   Chaman Lal, *Bhagat Singh Ke Sampoorna Dastavej,* 2006, p. 97. Bhagat Singh wrote two articles on *Kuka* movement; in *Maharathi* (February 1928) under the name B.S. Sindhu and second in October 1928 in *Kirti* under the name 'Vidrohi'.

5   Virender Sindhu, *Yugdrista Bhagat Singh Aur Unke Mritunjay Purkhe,* 2004, p. 4.

6   Kanneth W. Jones, op.cit, pp. 92.

7   Kanneth W. Jones, "Religious Identity and the Indian Census," in N.G. Barrier, (ed.), *The Census in British India: New Perspectives,* 1981, p. 79.

8   Fox, Richard G., *Lions of the Punjab: Culture in the Making,* 1985, p. 7.

9   Virender Sindhu, op. cit., p. 19.

10 Ibid., p. 16.

11 Bhagat Singh's letter to his father, cited in Virender Sindhu, *Patra Aur Dastavej,* 1996, p. 18.

12 *Why I am an Atheist,* in Shiv Varma, ed., *Selected Writings of Bhagat Singh,* 1996, p. 122.

13 Virender Sindhu, *Yugdrista Bhagat Singh Aur Unke Mritunjay Purkhe,* 2004, p. 26.

14 *Why I am an Atheist,* op. cit., p. 122.

15 Satyaketu Vidyalankar, *Arya Samaj Ka Itihas,* Vol.VI, p. 52.

16 Virender Sindhu, *Yugdrista Bhagat Singh Aur Unke Mritunjay Purkhe,* op.cit., p. 27.

17 Ibid., p. 28.

18 Judgement of Lahore Conspiracy Case I, 1915, cited in G.S. Deol, *Shaheed Bhagat Singh: A Biography,* 1985, p. 6.

19 Virender Sindhu, *Yugdrista Bhagat Singh Aur Unke Mritunjaya Purkhe,* op. cit., p. 71.

20 Ibid., p. 68.

21 N.A.I. Home Political File, 1907, 148-235.

22 Bhagat Singh's article in *Bandematram* published in 1931 under the title – '*Swadheenta Ki Ladai Mein Punjab Ka Pahla Ubhar,* Virender Sindhu, ed., *Patra Aur Dastavej,* 1996, p. 88.

23 *Abhyudaya,* 8 May 1931.

[24] Virender Sindhu, *Yugdrista Bhagat Singh Aur Unke Mritunjay Purkhe*, op. cit., p. 132.

[25] Harish K. Puri, "Bhagat Singh and the Ghadar Movement," *Mainstream*, 22 March 2008.

[26] Bhagat Singh's article on Kartar Singh Sarabha in *Chand* (*Phansi Number*, November 1928) reprinted in 2002, p. 270.

[27] A poster bearing the '*Message of Mata Vidyavati to Youth*', photograph in Malwinder Jit Singh Waraich, *Bhagat Singh: The Eternal Rebel*, 2007.

[28] Chaman Lal, *Ghadar Party Nayak Kartar Singh Sarabha*, 2007, p. 9.

[29] Transcript of interview of Jaidev Gupta, NMML, p. 14.

[30] Virender Sindhu, *Patra Aur Dastavej*, 1996, p. 18.

[31] *Why I am an Atheist*, op. cit., p. 122.

[32] Virender Sindhu, *Patra Aur Dastavej*, op.cit., p. 9.

[33] Yashpal, *Simhavalokan*, 2005, p. 53.

[34] Comrade Ramchandra, *Naujawan Bharat Sabha and HSRA*, 1986, p. 12.

[35] Transcript of interview of Lala Feroz Chand, NMNL, p. 34.

[36] Dharamvir, *Bhai Parmanad Aur Unka Yug*, 2005, pp. 231-239.

[37] Virender Sindhu, *Yugdrista Bhagat Singh Aur Unke Mritunjay Purkhe*, op. cit., p. 143.

[38] Jogesh Chandra Chatterjee, *In Search of Freedom*, 1967, p. 215.

[39] Satya Ketu Vidyalankar, *Arya Samaj Ka Itihas*, p. 56-57; Shanta Malhotra, *Shreya Marg Ke Pathik*, p. 50-51; Umakant Upadhyaya, "Sardar Bhagat Singh Calcutta Mein," *Jangyan*, New Delhi, August 2006, pp. 27-29.

5

Bhagat Singh in the Revolutionary Movement

Bhagat Singh's idea of self-sacrifice for the motherland was further developed when he became a member of the revolutionary party. His studies of the revolutionary movements in other countries also helped him in formulating definite plans to realise his goal along with popularising the ideals of the revolutionary movement and bringing about a surge of partiotic sentiments throughout the country through his martyrdom.

Bhagat Singh was initiated into the revolutionary movement while in National College, Lahore. There, he was spotted early by his history teacher, Jayachandra Vidyalankar who himself was a staunch believer in the ideology of armed rebellion as the only means of liberation from the British rule. While teaching history in the class, he used to direct the discussion towards the prevailing political circumstances and observe his students' reaction. Then, he used to talk individually with the chosen ones about their life's mission. Jayachandra Vidyalankar guided the students to essential readings like Dan Breen's '*My Fight for Irish Freedom*', biographies of Mazzini and Garibaldi, history of French Revolution, books on Voltaire, Vera Figner, Prince Kropotkin, and *Rowlet Committee Report* etc.[1] Such books helped in shaping the rebellious mind of young Bhagat Singh. This way Jayachandra Vidyalankar had selected a group of promising and committed boys like Bhagat Singh, Sukhdev, Yashpal and Bhagwati Charan

Vohra, who became the fulcrum of revolutionary movement in Punjab in the coming years.

In the beginning of 1923, Jayachandra Vidyalankar had become associated with Sachindra Nath Sanyal, the famous revolutionary. Sachindra Nath Sanyal was awarded life imprisonment in Benares Conspiracy Case in 1915 but was released in February 1920 as a result of the Royal amnesty. After the sudden suspension of Non-Cooperation Movement by Mahatma Gandhi in February 1922, Sachindra Nath Sanyal began to revive the revolutionary party in North India.[2] Originally a key member of the Dacca Anushilan Samiti, he drifted away on account of his differences with the new strategy adopted by Samiti. Anushilan Samiti, due to the heavy crackdown launched by the British authorities, had decided to avoid overt acts of violence and instead concentrate on fund raising. Secret report of the British Government elaborates on the stand adopted by Sanyal:

> "Sachindra Sanyal was a discordant element in the execution of this [Anushilan Samiti's] policy. He was bent on creating a sensation in the country, and advocated the immediate commission of dacoities, an extensive campaign of assassination and outrage against obnoxious police officers, and the issue of inflammatory revolutionary pamphlets."[3]

Sachindra Nath Sanyal was successful in associating with himself veterans like Ram Prasad Bismil and Jogesh Chandra Chatterji and some grey horns like Chandra Shekhar Azad. The newly formed group was named as Hindustan Republican Association. Sanyal endeavoured to expand his organisation in Punjab with the help of Jaya Chandra Vidyalankar. During one of his visits to Lahore in 1923, Sanyal was at Vidyalankar's home where Bhagat Singh met Sachindra Nath Sanyal for the first time and was initiated into the revolutionary party.

Some time later in the same year (1923), Bhagat Singh's family decided to tie him in matrimony as per the wishes of his grandmother, Smt. Jayakaur. This development shocked Bhagat Singh as he had already decided to devote his life for the cause of the nation. He tried to convince his father that he was too young for marriage but without any success. Bhagat Singh put this problem before Sanyal who happened to be at Lahore. Sanyal has described the developments in the following words:

"While talking to Bhagat Singh I learnt that his father Kishan Singh was preparing to get him married. I felt that since I myself had committed a blunder by getting married, I must tell Bhagat Singh that if he gets married he will not be able to do much in the revolutionary movement. Bhagat Singh himself did not want to get married. It was also my principle to make sure the extent to which every member could go when it came to sacrificing. We regarded only that person suitable for the party who was ever ready to leave his home and to jump into his field of work. With the same purpose in mind, I asked Bhagat Singh, "Are you ready to quit home? In case you get married, you would not be expected to work at a higher level in future. And in case you stay at home, your family will get you married. I do not want you to get married. This is why I desire that you should leave home and stay where I advise you to stay." Bhagat Singh agreed to do so. Following my advice Bhagat Singh went to United Province."[4]

Jaidev Gupta who was Bhagat Singh's intimate friend since school days, explained later Bhagat Singh's refusal to marry. When he asked Bhagat Singh as to why he was not ready to marry, Bhagat Singh answered that he had chosen a path which was full of many possibilities. His two uncles (Ajit Singh and Swarn Singh) had gone that way and they had left two widows. Should he leave another widow for weeping and wailing?[5]

Bhagat Singh secretly left home a few days before the date fixed for his engagement ceremony, leaving a letter for this father.

"Respected father,

Namaste,

My life has already been committed to a noble cause – the cause of freedom of India. For that reason comforts and worldly desires have no attraction in my life.

You kindly recall that at the time of my sacred thread ceremony, when I was just a child, Bapuji (grandfather) had bequeathed me for the service of the country. I am, therefore, honouring the pledge of that time. Hope you will excuse me.

Yours obediently,

Bhagat Singh"[6]

Sanyal asked Bhagat Singh to shift to Kanpur which was developing as a centre of newly organized revolutionary group. Jogesh Chandra Chatterjee, earlier a revolutionary of Anushilan group, was then in-charge of the Kanpur centre. Jogesh Chatterjee recalled receiving Bhagat Singh in Kanpur: "Sanyal Babu gave him a letter for me, sent him to Kanpur. It was in the day time that he arrived at our place and gave me that letter. We talked but I did not know where to put him in the night. I was staying in Bengali mess where all the members were Bengalis. The sudden presence of a Sikh youth might create suspicion with the police. However he had to be accommodated in the same mess."[7]

Kanpur group was also experiencing financial distress. But a remedy was soon worked out. Jogesh Chandra Chatterjee writes: "Jaya Chandra Vidyalankar happened to come to Kanpur for some work. He also saw the practical difficulties involved in Bhagat Singh's stay at the Patkapur Mess. He met [Ganesh Shankar] Vidyarthi and referred this matter to him. Vidyarthi agreed to give a room to Bhagat Singh in '*Pratap*' office. Bhagat Singh would learn journalism there and it was a place where so many persons came, his stay would not attract any suspicion. He gave Rs. 10/- per month to Bhagat Singh as scholarship to learn journalism. Bhagat Singh's room where he shifted from our mess was in the inner side of the building. So, this way the problem of his stay as well as of financial assistance were solved and we also felt relieved."[8]

Kanpur marks the beginning of the revolutionary career of Bhagat Singh. It was at Kanpur that Bhagat Singh met Ajoy Ghosh, Batukeshwar Dutt, Jogesh Chandra Chatterjee, Bejoy Kumar Sinha and Suresh Bhattacharya etc. for the first time. Ajoy Ghosh and Batukeshwar Dutt later became co-accused with Bhagat Singh in Lahore Conspiracy Case and underwent the hunger strike together. Again it was at Kanpur that Bhagat Singh started taking part in the party activities including armed actions. Probably the first 'action' in which Bhagat Singh took part was a dacoity. Revolutionaries were forced to commit dacoity in the times of grave financial crisis. Jogesh Chatterjee later recalled that apart from Bhagat Singh, party members who participated in a decoity in a village near Allahabad included Manmathnath Gupta, Rabindra Nath Kar and Pranabesh Chatterjee from Benaras, Banwari Lal from Rai Bareilley, Jagdish Chatterjee, Jung Bahadur Singh and Virbhadra Tiwari from Kanpur, Ram Prasad Bismil from Shahajanabad and J.N. Sanyal from Allahabad.[9] But this action was a disappointment as they failed to collect any money because unlike the professional dacoits, revolutionaries were not able to inflict the necessary torture on the inmates in order to locate the hidden money and jewellery.[10]

Meanwhile Kishan Singh, unaware of Bhagat Singh's whereabouts, was frantically searching for Bhagat Singh. At the same time, Bhagat Singh's grandmother became seriously ill and wanted to see Bhagat Singh at any cost. Luckily, Jaidev Gupta came to know that Ram Chand of village Jhadrake in district Montgomery, a common friend of Jaidev and Bhagat Singh, had received a letter from Bhagat Singh. Jaidev met Ram Chand and came to know that Bhagat Singh had also revealed his Kanpur address in this letter but with strict instructions to Ram Chand not to divulge it to any one. Jaidev was able to persuade Ramchand to accompany him to that address.[11] Thus both Jaidev and Ram Chand reached '*Pratap*' office in Kanpur.[12]

When Bhagat Singh came to know of Jaidev and Ram Chand's visit he avoided meeting them. Vidyarthi was also reluctant to let

Bhagat Singh go back to Punjab. Jaidev and Ram Chand came back empty handed and told the whole story to Kishan Singh. Kishan Singh then wrote a letter to Hasrat Mohani, his friend and a Congress colleague, to persuade Vidyarthi. He also wrote separate letters to Bhagat Singh and Vidyarthi. In these letters he promised not to press Bhagat Singh for marriage and also conveyed his grandmother's wish to see Bhagat Singh. As a result of this exercise, Bhagat Singh returned home six or seven months after he had left. Bhagat Singh's sweet presence and care nursed back his grandmother in a short time to good health. But soon, Bhagat Singh became involved in an incident as a consequence of which he was catapulted back to revolutionary movement.

In those days, Akali movement (to free Sikh gurdwaras and places of worship from the corrupt control of '*Mahants*' who had the support of British government) in Punjab was in full swing. Since September 1923 the movement had entered a new phase when Maharaja Ripudaman Singh, the ruler of Nabha state, was deposed and put under house arrest in Dehradun for showing sympathy towards the Akali movement. The Sikh community got incensed over this act of British and a new '*morcha*' (a site where passive resistance was demonstrated) was opened in Jaiton (Nabha). Sikh *jathas* (batches) started visiting Jaiton to show their solidarity with the abdicated ruler and protest against the British act.

One such *jatha* (fifth *Shaheedi jatha* which started from Lyallpur on 12 April 1924)[13] was to pass through Banga village in April 1924. As Kishan Singh was well known in the area for his patriotic outlook, some Sikh *jathedars* (Kartar Singh and Jwala Singh) met him and requested him to arrange a reception for the '*jatha*' in his village.[14] It was a very difficult task as the Government was against providing any sort of assistance to the Akali *jathas* who were in direct confrontation with the Government. Moreover, Kishan Singh had to be present in Bombay for an urgent business during the days when the *jatha* was scheduled to visit his village. But Kishan Singh had confidence in the organizing potential of

Bhagat Singh (then a boy of 17 years) and so he confidently assigned the arduous task to him.

The Government machinery, in thwarting any local help to the visiting *jatha*, was being led by Sardar Bahadur Dilbagh Singh, an honorary magistrate, who was also a cousin of Kishan Singh. Dilbagh Singh had made this issue a matter of prestige and issued strict orders in the area not to render any help to the visiting *jatha*. In such challenging conditions one gets a glimpse of Bhagat Singh's mettle. Bhagat Singh was aware of the great respect that the villagers had for the *shaheedi jatha*. He quietly motivated them to shed their fears and participate in the reception. At the same time he secretly organised the collection of the cooked food etc. To top it all, when the *jatha* came, he gave a rousing speech praising the Akali movement as well as the revolutionary martyrs and bursted fireworks. This brilliant performance as a whole roused the villagers and the *jatha* was given a thumping reception.

Successful reception of the Akali *jatha* in the face of Government opposition and more so inviting Dilbagh Singh's ire, focused police attention on Bhagat Singh. Punjab Government's intelligence report states that as a result of his role in welcoming the *jattha,* Bhagat Singh was booked under Criminal Law Amendment Act, section 17 (1).[15] As a result of these circumstances, Bhagat Singh immediately left Banga and went underground.

Bhagat Singh used this opportunity to rejoin the revolutionary work. The Punjab Government intelligence report mentions that during this period Bhagat Singh was in UP (United Province): "During this period, he was in UP. It is reported that having gone to UP, he stayed for a month at Kanpur…..He was stated to have gone to Aligarh from Kanpur and worked for 3 months as the headmaster of National Muslim University School."[16] Jogesh Chandra Chatterji, in his memoirs has also written about Bhagat Singh's appointment as headmaster of National School which was situated in village Shadipur, *Tehsil* Khair in the district of Aligarh. This school was established by Thakur Todar Singh, a prominent Congressman of the area, who had a soft heart for revolutionaries. Todar Singh was looking for a suitable person for the job of headmaster and Bhagat Singh's name was suggested by Ganesh Shankar Vidyarthi who was impressed by Bhagat Singh's studious nature. Jogesh Chandra Chatterjee readily permitted Bhagat Singh to work in the above mentioned school as it served two purposes: Bhagat Singh's salary will add to the party's meagre resources and secondly, national school could work as a centre of recruitment for the party.[17]

Some time afterwards Bhagat Singh shifted to Delhi. With the help of a recommendation letter from Jayachandra Vidyalankar, he got a job in '*Arjun*', a Hindi daily from Delhi, at a monthly salary of Rs. 25. While at '*Arjun*', Bhagat Singh shared the room of Satyaketu Vidyalankar, which was situated near Lahori Gate police station Lahori Gate in Delhi.[18] It was during this period that the Hindustan Republican Association (HRA) pamphlet '*The Revolutionary*' was circulated all over India. Bhagat Singh in his essay '*Why I am an Atheist*' gives the date of distribution of '*The Revolutionary*' as 28th January 1925. With the help of Satyaketu Vidyalankar and one Jayadev Vidyalankar Bhagat Singh helped dispatch and distribution of this pamphlet.[19] Manmathnath Gupta, a member of HRA who was convicted in Kakori Case has cited Sachindra Nath Bakshi, another Kakori convict that Bhagat Singh also participated in Bichpur's decoity (Pilibhit district in UP) on 9th March 1925 alongwith Ram Prasad Bismil, Ashfaqulla Khan, Manmathnath Gupta, Ramkrishna Khatri, S.N. Bakshi and Chandra Shekhar Azad.[20]

Besides journalism and revolutionary organization, Bhagat Singh also became active in organizing the youth movement. He started deliberations with like minded students, graduates and teachers of National College, Lahore, which had become a centre of enlightened youth. This brainstorming culminated in the formation of Naujawan Bharat Sabha in the beginning of 1925. Naujawan

Bharat Sabha has been dealt in detail in a separate chapter below. Here it would suffice to say that Naujawan Bharat Sabha was the public face of the revolutionary party.

The famous Kakori case, though not involving Bhagat Singh directly, occupies a special place in Bhagat Singh's career as a revolutionary. On 9th August 1925, a team of 10 revolutionaries, including Chandra Shekhar Azad, Ram Prasad Bismil, Rajendra Nath Lahiri, Roshan Singh and Ashfaq Ulla Khan successfully looted the government treasury worth about Rs. 4500 being carried in 8 Down Passenger train in Kakori near Lucknow. Government crackdown was unexpectedly quick and heavy. Most of the leaders were arrested by October 1925. Sachindra Nath Sanyal and Jogesh Chandra Chatterjee, both arrested before the incident, were also tried in the case. Chandra Shekhar Azad, could not be arrested until his death in an encounter with Police on 27th February 1931. In all 21 persons were tried, Ram Prasad Bismil, Rajendra Nath Lahiri, Roshan Singh and Ashfaq Ulla Khan were given capital punishment. Jogesh Chandra Chatterjee, Govind Charan Kar, Mukandi Lal and Sachindra Nath Sanyal were given transportation for life. Others were given stiff prison terms.

Kakori case dealt a severe blow to HRA. All its top leaders except Azad were locked in British prisons. Ajoy Ghosh, a member of HRA, recalled the impact of Kakori backlash:

"In 1925 like a bolt from the blue came the Kakori arrests. Most of our leaders were in prison within a few weeks....But what really shattered my dreams was the effect of these arrests. Men who had profound sympathy with our case would now avoid us... We tried to rebuild the party out of the shattered remnants of the Kakori round ups. It was an uphill task. Revolution it seemed now was far, very far."[21]

Even a revolutionary of the stature of Ram Prasad Bismil began to realize the futility of revolutionary actions. In his autobiography, written a couple of days before his scheduled hanging (19th December 1927), Bismil pleaded with his countrymen that unless the majority of Indians were educated and were aware of their duties, they must not take part in the revolutionary conspiracies or else their sacrifice will go waste.[22]

It is during such an hour of crisis that second rung leaders like Bhagat Singh, Sukhdev and Bejoy Kumar Sinha, under the leadership of Chandra Shekhar Azad, took up the reins of the organisation and worked for its revival. Until then they were junior functionaries in the party with no role in policy formulation. For Bhagat Singh, it was a very tough and frustrating time as he felt his dreams were on the verge of collapse. In the opinion of J.N. Sanyal, "the years 1926-27 and 1928 may be regarded as depicting a wandering and restless spirit of young Bhagat Singh."[23]

Bhagat Singh's first impulse to the Kakori crisis, according to J.N. Sanyal, was to take revenge.[24] He lent himself whole heartedly in developing plans to rescue his jailed comrades. For this purpose he made several rounds to Kanpur and Lucknow but he could not succeed.[25] Bhagat Singh wrote about the period following the Kakori event:

"Up till then we were to follow. Now came the time to shoulder the whole responsibility. Due to the inevitable reaction for some time the very existence of the party seemed impossible. Enthusiastic comrades- nay leaders- began to jeer at us. For some time I was afraid that some day I also might not be convinced of the futility of our own programme. That was a turning point in my revolutionary career."[26]

As in the past, well directed Government crackdown had been able to break the back of revolutionary party. In this hour of crisis, a realisation emerged among the younger members that the programmes and policies of revolutionary violence followed up till now, needed amendments. Ideological foundations of revolutionary work needed to be strengthened. The policy of violence against the state had its own limitations. Violence also alienated the public or the masses from the revolutionary party. Without the support of the masses a revolutionary party could not sustain itself – financially and politically. Decoities in the homes of rich or government treasuries had proved to be counterproductive. Revolutionaries enjoyed very little public support; people were not ready to come out in the streets in support of revolutionaries. Pamphlets and manifestos had proved to be ineffective.

Kakori backlash brought all these unpleasant facts out in the open. The revolutionary edifice erected by blood and toil seemed to be in shambles. Bhagat Singh's dream of taking on the British Empire through his sacrifice was in danger. A single minded pursuit of his ideal of martyrdom had brought him too far. He had reached the point of no return. The question that faced him was-what to do?

But Bhagat Singh's urge for studies, his capacity to learn and unlearn, and his ability to sway the leadership of the revolutionary group, rare for his age, stood him at this hour of crisis. What followed here onwards is best explained in his own words:

"Study" was the cry that reverberated in the corridors of my mind. Study to enable yourself with arguments in favour of your cult. I began to study. My previous faith and convictions underwent a remarkable modification. The romance of the violent methods alone, which was so prominent among our predecessors, was replaced by serious ideas. No more mysticism, no more blind faith. Realism became our cult. Use of force justifiable when resorted to as a matter of terrible necessity: non violence as policy indispensable for all mass movements. So much so about methods. The most important thing was the clear conception of the ideal for which we were to fight. As there were no important activities in the field of action I got ample opportunity to study various ideals of the world revolution."[27]

The main centre of Bhagat Singh's studies was the Dwarkadas Library, Lahore, established by Lala Lajpat Rai. Its librarian Raja Ram Shastri, reached Lahore in 1926 and began acquiring the latest books for the library. Shastri was a product of Kashi Vidyapith, a national university. He became a life member of Servants of the People Society of Lala Lajpat Rai and was assigned the librarian-ship of Dwarkadas library. A close friend of Bhagat Singh and Sukhdev, he has left behind detailed accounts of Bhagat

Singh's activities in the library. Bhagat Singh had by now begun serious studies of international revolutionary movements.

With new ideals and new hopes, Bhagat Singh began to reorganize the revolutionary party. For this purpose, a meeting of the important members of the party was held at Kanpur in 1927.[28] Here it was decided that Bhagat Singh and Bejoy Kumar Sinha would tour Punjab, United Province and Bihar and establish connections with the scattered groups. But before any substantial work could be done in this direction Bhagat Singh was unexpectedly arrested in Dussehra bomb incident case at Lahore.

Bhagat Singh was arrested on 29th May 1927 and was kept in custody till 4th July 1927.[29] The police took the stand that his arrest was in connection with a bomb blast in Lahore on 16th October 1926 during Dussehra celebrations.[30] Bhagat Singh was in the eyes of the Punjab police since 1924. They also had some information regarding his association with the revolutionary party in the U.P. Since 1926, his mail was censored by the Punjab C.I.D.[31] By linking Bhagat Singh with the Dussehra blast, police wanted to put pressure on him to divulge information about the revolutionary party. Bhagat Singh himself explained the situation further:

"After many days' conversation with the police officials, I guessed that they had some information regarding my connections with the revolutionary movement. They told me that I had been to Lucknow while the trial was going on there, that I had negotiated a certain scheme about their rescue, that after obtaining their approval, we had procured some bombs, that by way of test one of the bombs was thrown in the crowd on the occasion of Dussehra in 1926. They further informed me, in my interest, that if I could give any statement throwing some light on the activities of the revolutionary party, I was not to be imprisoned but on the contrary set free and rewarded, even without being produced as an approver in the court.... [And] if I did not give any statement as demanded by them, they would be forced to send me up for trial for conspiracy to wage war in connection with Kakori Case and for brutal murder in connection with Dussehra bomb outrage"[32]

Ultimately, police could gain nothing out of Bhagat Singh. He was released on bail from High Court on a surety of sixty thousand, a huge amount in those days, which was furnished by barrister Duni Chand and Shri Daulat Ram.[33] Heavy bail amount and moral obligation towards Duni Chand and Daulat Ram made Bhagat Singh sit idle for some time. Seeing it an opportune time, Kishan Singh engaged Bhagat Singh in setting up a dairy at village Khasaria near Lahore, but still the police did not withdraw the case for sometime. The case was withdrawn only after Shri Bodhraj asked a question in Legislative Assembly as to why the Government was not prosecuting Bhagat. Dr. Gopichand Bhargava, another member of Assembly also gave a notice for a similar question. Ultimately, the Government decided to forego the bail.[34] Bhagat Singh was a free man again. He lost interest in the dairy and again became absorbed in secret work and revival of Naujawan Bharat Sabha.[35] According to his niece Virendra Sindhu, Bhagat Singh lost all contact with his home after April – May 1928.[36]

Meanwhile, the work of making contact with the scattered revolutionaries and ultimately bringing them under one organization was speeded up. In this regard, a preliminary meeting was held in Kanpur in July 1928.[37] In accordance with the decisions taken in this meeting, preparations started for organising a meeting of the revolutionaries in Delhi in September. Bhagat Singh and Bejoy Kumar Sinha toured different places to convey the broad elements of a comprehensive plan which was to be given shape in Delhi. Shiv Varma was sent to Calcutta to contact the Bengal revolutionaries. Those who agreed were invited to Delhi for the meeting on 8-9 September 1928.

The scheduled meeting took place in the ruins of Feroz Shah Kotla in Delhi. In all, ten members participated: Bejoy Kumar Sinha, Shiv Varma, Jaidev Kapur, Surendra Pandey and Brahm

Datt Mishra from United Provinces (U.P.); Phanindra Nath Ghosh and Man Mohan Bannerji from Bihar; Bhagat singh and Sukhdev represented Punjab; and Kundan Lal (one of the absconders in the Kakori Case) represented Rajputana.[38] For reasons of security, Chandra Shekhar Azad was not brought to Delhi. He had already given his approval to decisions accepted by majority. The Bengal group was conspicuous by its absence. Shiv Varma, who was given the responsibility of briefing and inviting the Bengal Group, was unfortunately introduced to the wrong man and so he was not able to establish contact with the group led by Trailokya Nath Chakraborty and Pratul Ganguli.[39]

This small meeting at Delhi became monumental in the history of revolutionary movement by virtue of the decisions that were taken in it. More so, for Bhagat Singh it marked the emergence of an ideologue of the party as he took the lead in conceptualizing and transforming the new ideas into pragmatic programmes.[40] The meeting marked the coming together of various groups working separately in Punjab, UP, Bihar and Rajputana under one organization. The party was re-organised on democratic principle. A Central Committee was elected consisting of seven members, namely Bhagat Singh, Sukhdev, Bejoy Kumar Sinha, Shiv Varma, Phanindra Nath Ghosh, Kundan Lal and Chandra Shekhar Azad.[41] Chandra Shekhar Azad was elected as the Commander-in-Chief of the party. In-charges of the provinces were also appointed. – Sukhdev of the Punjab, Shiv Verma of U.P., Phanindra Nath of Bihar and Kundan Lal of Rajputana. Central office was established at Jhansi in charge of Kundan Lal. Bhagat Singh and Bejoy Kumar Sinha were appointed as links between various provinces.

Apart from revamping of the organizational structure of the party, Feroz Shah Kotla meeting also adopted a change in the policy regarding armed actions. Bhagat Singh advocated actions which were associated with the popular sentiments such as attacking the Simon Commission, and the oppressive government officials.[42] Bhagat Singh attributed earlier failures of party to the inability of revolutionaries to act for the popular causes. Moreover, public was not aware of the programmes and ideals of the revolutionaries and hence the question of public help did not arise.[43] This necessitated a public face of the revolutionary party whose function should be to organize its propaganda. Bhagat Singh also said: "Our actions must be planned on the basis of their political impact on the people of the country. They must give voice to the basic aspirations of the people. Only then shall we come closer to them. We must do something ... something that can arouse political awakening and self confidence among the people and bond them with the [revolutionary] party."[44]

The most debated question in the meeting involved Bhagat Singh's proposals for emphasis on socialistic ideals and changing the name of the party from Hindustan Republican Association to Hindustan Socialist Republican Association. Both Phanindra Nath Ghosh and Manmohan Bannerji opposed this proposal.[45] Their plea was that the name 'Hindustan Republican Army' was adopted by senior leaders like Sachindra Nath Sanyal, Ram Prasad Bismil and Jogesh Chandra Chatterji, and the name itself had acquired a good deal of prestige, hence it should not be changed.[46] Also, it must be kept in mind that constitution of Hindustan Republican Association prepared by Sachindra Nath Sanyal already contained some socialistic principles and HSRA had adopted that constitution without changing or adding a single word, the only change being the addition of word 'Socialist' in its name. Bhagat Singh took the position that the party should openly declare its socialistic ideals. So, difference between the stand taken by S.N. Sanyal and Bhagat Singh was that Bhagat Singh wanted to project the Socialistic ideals adopted by the party with greater rigour and for that purpose addition of the word 'Socialist' was an ideal proposition. Jaidev Kapur recalled Bhagat Singh speaking in the meeting: "It is important for us to tell ... and for this we must make a declaration that we wish to establish an egalitarian social order. There must not be any discrimination between the high and the low, the rich and the poor. We desire an end to the exploitation of the many by the few ... The time has now come for us to declare that our objective is to achieve complete independence and to establish a socialist order."[47]

The Delhi meeting also fixed the immediate tasks at hand. With a well defined and toned up organization, members of HSRA began their scheduled tasks. As decided in the meeting Bhagat Singh removed his hair and beard at Ferozpur in the middle of September 1928.[48] He also adopted a new party name – 'Ranjit' for himself. In October he ended his formal association with Naujawan Bharat Sabha as the General Secretary because due to his packed schedule of activities for HSRA work he could no longer devote sufficient time to the Sabha activities.[49]

Meanwhile the Simon Commission, which was on its visit to India since February 1928 was scheduled to visit Lahore on 30th October 1928. Its mission was to suggest future political reforms for India. Non-inclusion of any Indian in the seven member commission meant for deciding the future of India was seen as a national insult by all shades of political opinion in India. The Commission faced protests wherever it went. Sensing trouble, the Superintendent of Police in Lahore made it mandatory for protesters to take prior permission. But despite the danger of police repression all the parties in Lahore decided to organise a united protest against the visit of Simon Commission. Naujawan Bharat Sabha was playing a leading role in organizing a protest march. Bhagat Singh was in Lahore and was helping in preparations for the protest march while remaining in background.[50] On 30th October, Simon Commission was greeted by several thousand protesters led by Lala Lajpat Rai, Madan Mohan Malviya, Sardar Mangal Singh, Dr. Mohammad Alam, Sardul Singh Caveeshar, Lala Duni Chand, Lala Bodh Raj, Dr. Gopi Chand Bhargava, Maulana Jafar Ali and Abdul Qadir Kasuri. It was a peaceful and orderly protest march. The procession, stopped by barricades erected near Lahore Railway Station, was shouting slogans, *"Simon Commission Go Back, Go Back"*. Police under the orders of J.A. Scott, Police chief of Lahore, lathi-charged the slogan shouting people. It did not spare Lalaji's group. Lala Lajpat

Rai himself was stuck on his chest and had to be hospitalised. As a result of his injuries Lalaji died on 17th November 1928.

The whole country was drowned in grief at the news of Lalaji's death and the Government was held responsible for it. Strikes were organized all over the country. People in general felt very sore and humiliated; if the government could physically assault a leader of Lajpat Rai's stature what could be the treatment to general public. Reaction of Basanti Devi, widow of C.R. Das is worth mentioning:

"I quake with shame and disgrace that the lowly and violent hands have dared to touch the body of one so old, so revered and so loved by 300 million people of the land. Does the youth and manhood of the country still exist? Does it feel the burning shame and the disgrace of it? A woman of the land demands clear answer to it"[51]

The brutal attack on Lala Lajpat Rai and the strong public reaction generated by it laid the ground for HSRA's first 'action'. Bhagat Singh sensed the anger in the public. It struck immediately to him that HSRA should give expression to the prevalent feeling of revenge by attacking the police officials responsible for Lalaji's death. That way the masses will associate the revolutionary party with the popular desire and consequently the party will get sympathy and support of the general public. Such an action would show to the world that Lalaji's beating was not taken lying down by India. Moreover it would advertise the existence of a revolutionary party in India.[52]

Sukhdev, an excellent organiser, made ideal preparations for the coming action. He acquired on rent several premises in Lahore and other cities. Besides, he also recruited several efficient members in his group such as Jaigopal, Hansraj Vohra and Prem Dutt.

Bhagat Singh and Chandra Shekhar Azad were already present in Punjab in the early part of November 1928.[53] By 17th November, the day Lala Lajpat Rai died; some members of the party – Sukhdev, Bhagat Singh, Chandra Shekhar Azad, Mahabir Singh, Kundan Lal, Rajguru and Kishori Lal were present in Mozang House, a party hideout in Lahore. The Party was feeling acute shortage of money and to solve the problem a plan was formulated to raid Punjab National Bank on 4th December. But unfortunately, the plan had to be aborted at the last moment as a vehicle could not be arranged.

On 17th December HSRA created sensation throughout India by killing Saunders, Assistant Superintendent of Police, in front of police headquarters of Lahore in broad daylight. Incidentally, HSRA had planned to kill J.A. Scott. Saunders was no where in picture when the action was being planned. Details of Saunders' murder are provided in the statement of Jaigopal, who turned approver, in the court.

Murder of Scott, was discussed at a meeting in Mozang house on 9th or 10th December by Azad, Sukhdev, Bhagat Singh, Kishori Lal, Rajguru, Mahabir Singh and Jaigopal. Jaigopal later turned approver and revealed all details to the police. Jaigopal was asked to report the movement of Mr. Scott. Initially, 15th December was fixed as date of murder of Scott as 16th was to be celebrated as Kakori Day in the memory of Kakori martyrs. On the afternoon of 15th December Jaigopal reported that Scott had not turned up. As a result date of action was rescheduled to 17th December, 16th being Sunday. In the afternoon of 17th Jaigopal reported about Scott's presence in his office. At two O' clock Azad distributed weapons to Bhagat Singh, Rajguru and himself for the task of eliminating Scott. Cycles were arranged and hidden nearby. At about 4-15 PM, an English police officer whom Jaigopal believed to be Scott, came out of the office and started his motor cycle. Jaigopal made a signal to the waiting team. Rajguru who was the nearest, immediately rushed and shot the officer. Bhagat Singh also ran towards the fallen man and shot him five or six times. Hearing the sound of gun shots, a traffic inspector named Ferns and a constable named Chanan Singh rushed towards the assailants. Bhagat Singh fired at Ferns but he ducked and fell down in the process. Chanan Singh continued to give chase but was finally stopped by Azad who shot and wounded him mortally. The trio then returned safely to their hideout.

Jaigopal's statement leaves some questions unanswered: why Jaigopal failed to identify Scott even after a week long surveillance? Scott used to travel to his office in a car. On what basis Jaigopal presumed that Scott had come to office on a motorcycle? Was Saunders an occasional visitor to this office? Was he not noticed by Jaigopal earlier?

Sukhdev's remarks written on the margins of a copy of court proceedings provide a different version of Saunder's murder. This copy was brought to public light by Mathura Das Thapar, Sukhdev's younger brother. Sukh Dev has written:

"Bhagat Singh was to fire first, M [Rajguru] was sent only to guard Bhagat Singh. Pandit [Chandra Shekhar Azad] was to guard these both, while escaping. B.S. (Bhagat Singh) marked that Sahib is not Scott, as he turned towards P.Ji [Pandit Ji] to tell him so, meanwhile 'M' fired which he should not. He never recognized Scott. Then B.S. [Bhagat Singh] was duty bound to fire the wrong victim. Thus happened the murder of Mr. Saunders."[54]

Murder of a police official in a daring manner sent a chill down the British bureaucracy. Police made drastic efforts to find a clue about the attackers and a large number of persons were arrested on mere suspicion. But despite heavy police surveillance, revolutionaries were able to slip out of Lahore. Bhagat Singh disguised himself as a non- Sikh government official, in the company of wife (Durga Devi Vohra), son (Sachin, Durga Devi's son) and a servant (Rajguru). The family boarded 14 Down Express for Kanpur in the early hours of 20th December. Rajguru separated at Kanpur station while Bhagat Singh, Durga Devi and Sachin proceeded to Calcutta. Destination of Bhagat Singh was chosen after careful thought. Calcutta was the venue of Congress session and people from all over India were assembling there. Thus it was easier to hide. Bhagwati Charan Vohra and Sushila Didi were already in Calcutta. Most importantly, in Calcutta, Bhagat Singh could contact the Bengal revolutionaries and get their help in setting up a bomb factory.

Bhagat Singh was able to meet and exchange views with leaders of Bengal revolutionaries such as Trailokya Nath Chakraborty (leader of Anushilan Samiti), Pratul Ganguly and Prof. Jyoish Ghosh(leader of New Violence Party).[55] Bhagat Singh came to know that Bengal revolutionaries though agreeing on necessity of armed struggle did not agree with HSRA's newly adopted policies especially its stand on socialism and individual heroism.[56] The biggest achievement of Bhagat Singh's Calcutta trip was that HSRA was able to get the services of Jatindra Nath Das, the bomb expert, for training party members in the art of making bombs. Bombs were vital in HSRA's future scheme of things.

Jatin Das helped Bhagat Singh in collecting equipment and chemicals necessary for establishing a bomb factory. He gave some initial training to Bhagat Singh, Phanindra Nath Ghosh and Kanwal Nath Tiwari at Arya Samaj Mandir of Calcutta where Bhagat Singh was staying with Tiwari. In the beginning of February, Jatin Das was at Agra training Bhagat Singh, Chandra Shekhar Azad, Sukhdev, Bejoy Kumar Sinha, Shiv Varma, Sadashiv, Phanindra Ghosh, and Lalit kumar Mukherjee. The party had two houses in Agra, one at Hing Ki Mandi and other at Nai Ki Mandi.

By the middle of February, Jatin Das was able to assemble a few bombs which were to be used in the rescue operation of Jogesh Chatterjee. Party was aware that Jogesh Chatterjee's transfer from Agra to Lucknow Jail was scheduled for the evening of 16th February. But their information about the train which was to carry Jogesh Chatterjee proved to be incorrect. Revolutionaries had made preparations for rescue action at 10 PM but police escort with Chatterjee left earlier for Kanpur where he was to be kept for the night owing to the absence of a direct train to Lucknow from Agra. The revolutionary party also reached Kanpur in another train. But the rescue action could not take place because police lockup at Kanpur was found to be too difficult to be attacked successfully.[57]

Despite the failure of Jogesh Chatterjee's rescue operation, the bomb making at Agra continued. Party now wanted to attack Simon Commission which was touring different places in India. But after much thought this action was also cancelled due to tactical and logistical problems. Successive failures disheartened the party members. They were now desperate for a spectacular action. It was in these circumstances, in the last week of February or first week of March, that the Central Committee of HSRA decided to bomb the Central Assembly.[58]

The idea of attacking Assembly was not entirely a product of frustration. According to Raja Ram Shastri, the idea had originated in Bhagat Singh's mind when he first read about the French anarchist August Vallaint throwing bomb in the French Assembly.[59] Political conditions of the country also favoured such an action. The ongoing visit of Simon Commission had generated a wave of protests throughout India in the form of demonstrations and strikes. Government's reaction was in the form of police lathi charges, arrests and firing. Mahatma Gandhi had already started the boycott of foreign goods. His arrest in Calcutta on 4th March 1929 had given great impetus to the movement for the boycott of foreign cloth. Workers were also organising themselves and were able to stage several massive strikes.

On the other hand, the Government was bent upon resorting to harsh measures. On 20th March 1929 many office bearers connected with the labour movement throughout India were arrested. Government also introduced two bills in the Central Assembly namely the Trade Disputes Bill and the Public Safety Bill. The objective behind the first bill was to curtail the trade union rights of the workers. Shri C. S. Ranga Aiyar, member of the Swaraj Party, while discussing the bill said: "It is nothing short of strangling a child in its cradle; and, Sir, I charge the Honourable Labour Member with committing an act of that kind by bringing in legislation of this nature, strangling the young Trade Union Movement."[60]

The avowed object of the second Bill was to check the spread of communism and to deal with those who directly or indirectly advocated the overthrow of British Government by violent means. In the opinion of Madan Mohan Malaviya, bill was "a measure by the authority of which the executive Government will usurp the place of the judiciary, condemn a man without a trial and then give him the chance of a farce of an appeal before three judges."[61] Moti Lal Nehru had earlier called the measure the "Slavery of India Bill" and said: "I take this Bill as a direct attack on Indian Nationalism and the Indian National Congress"[62] The Bill was defeated in the Assembly in September 1928. Its re-introduction by Government in January 1929 created a furore. On April 2nd, Vithal Bhai Patel, President of the Assembly, stated in the House that fundamental basis of the Public Safety Bill was identical with the on-going Meerut Conspiracy Case. Hence the Bill could not be debated without violating the sub judice rule that forbids debate on pending court proceedings. He therefore, advised the Government to "postpone the Bill pending the Meerut trial, or if they attach greater importance to the passing of this Bill at this juncture, to withdraw the Meerut case and then proceed further with the Bill."[63] He promised to give his ruling on 8th April. Government refused to accept either of President's suggestions therefore hinting that it would enact the Bill using special powers against the mandate of the House, if necessary.

Taking cue from Valiant's example, the Central Committee of HSRA decided that harmless bombs should be exploded in the Central Assembly to issue a warning that any further humiliation and suppression of this country will not be tolerated. The main motive behind this daring action was to arouse public awakening and instil fear in the British bureaucracy. As Yashpal put it, the attack on Assembly had two aspects: Firstly, if foreign Government could override people's representatives by force then it was high time that its own existence should be challenged by use of force. Secondly, people's representatives should also get the message that constitutional protest in a slave country had no relevance. It was necessary to expose the real face of the imperialistic government and fight a full scale war against it.[64]

While discussing the modus operandi of the proposed attack, a hotly debated issue was whether the perpetrators of the act should escape after the action or give themselves up. The master strategist of the party, Chandra Shekhar Azad, was confident that it was possible to escape after the attack. He saw no point in surrendering.[65] This view was strongly opposed by Bhagat Singh and some other members of the party. Their contention was that mere throwing of pamphlets would not serve any purpose. People would see them merely as blood thirsty revolutionaries, contrary to the policy of mass oriented actions adopted by the party. The bomb throwers must not make any attempt to escape. At the same time they must not miss any opportunity to publicize their ideology and programmes during the trial and bear all hardships and punishments happily. This way they would be able to come nearer the masses and inspire them to make sacrifices for independence.[66]

Another issue before the Central Committee was to choose volunteers for the proposed action. Bhagat Singh was most keen to participate in this action because it would lead to the fulfilment of his long cherished desire i.e. martyrdom. But majority of the members considered Bhagat Singh too valuable to be lost in this action. Bhagat Singh had to unwillingly accept the verdict of the majority. Other names were discussed and committee finalised the names of Batukeshwar Dutt and Bejoy Kumar Sinha.[67] Sukhdev was not present in this meeting. As soon as he came to know that Bhagat Singh was not among the volunteers chosen for the task, he was livid with anger. He took the position that when Bhagat Singh knew that he himself was the best man for the task how could he be a party to the decision of sending some one else. He taunted Bhagat Singh bitterly, calling him an egoist and even a coward. Sukhdev's unsparing reproach caused Bhagat Singh to call another meeting of the Central Committee and virtually forced the Committee to agree to his participation in the Assembly action. Thus Sukhdev also had a role in making Bhagat Singh a legend as the events proved soon after this action.

The objective of the action and names of the volunteers having been decided, HSRA revolutionaries made final preparations for the D-day. Jaidev Kapur, posing as a student, befriended one of the staff members of Assembly's secretariat to make a detailed survey of the Assembly House. He was also able to arrange visitors' passes. By using these passes Bhagat Singh and Dutt were able to get entry in Assembly prior to the designated date for a preliminary reconnaissance. They also got themselves photographed for publicity sake. These photographs later appeared in various newspapers after the bomb incident.

On 8th April 1929, visitors' galleries in the Central Assembly had more than usual number of visitors. The President of the House, Vithalbhai Patel was expected to give his ruling on the controversial Public Safety Bill. At 12.30 p.m., the House passed the Trade Disputes Bill with a narrow majority among cheers from the official benches and sullen chagrin of the opposition. At 12.35 p.m., the President rose to give his ruling. He could hardly utter a sentence when the proceedings were interrupted by a loud explosion followed by another, accompanied by pistol shots and a bunch of red pamphlets thrown into the Chamber. After the smoke cleared and stampede halted, two youths could be seen shouting "Long Live Revolution".[68] They offered themselves for arrest. "I have done my duty to the country", one of them is reported to have explained adding "look, here is my revolver."[69] Before throwing the bomb, Bhagat Singh was heard by the visitors in the gallery to have shouted "*Bande Mataram.*"[70] Even at this tumultuous hour, both the accused, as the press reported, were absolutely calm and self-composed. Approached by a pressman, one of them (probably Bhagat Singh) smilingly said: "Don't cross-examine me. You will hear a lot of our army in court."[71]

Notes & References

[1] Yashpal, *Simhavlokan*, 2005, p. 58; Manmathnath Gupta, *Bhagat Singh and His Times*, 1977, p. 82.

[2] Sachindra Nath Sanyal, *Bandi Jeewan*, 2006, pp. 259–265.

[3] N.A.I. Home Political, 253, 1925, p. 13.

[4] Sachindra Nath Sanyal, op. cit., pp. 270-271.

[5] Oral transcript of Sh. Jaidev Gupta, NMML, p. 29.

[6] Translated from the Urdu original.

[7] J.C. Chatterjee, *In search of Freedom*, 1967, p. 220. Bhagat Singh's biographers have given different versions of Bhagat Singh's coming to Kanpur. According to G.S. Deol (*Shaheed Bhagat Singh, A Biography*, 1985, pp. 20-21), Sanyal gave a letter to Bhagat Singh for Ganesh Shankar Vidyarthi and on his advice Bhagat Singh adopted a pseudonym – 'Balwant.' Manmathnath Gupta (*Bhagat Singh and His Times*, 1977, pp. 86-87) has quoted Suresh Chandra Bhattacharya, one of the revolutionaries in Kanpur centre. Suresh Bhattacharya claims that he was asked to arrange for Bhagat Singh's stay in Kanpur. Suresh Bhattacharya's account has some discrepancies including the one that Bhagat Singh was already being sought by the police when he came to Kanpur.

[8] J.C. Chatterjee, op. cit., p. 226.

[9] Ibid., p. 228. This action must have been conducted before 18th October 1924, the date on which Jogesh Chatterjee was arrested in Calcutta.

[10] Ibid.

[11] Transcript of Jaidev Gupta, NMML, p. 30.

[12] According to Jaidev, Bhagat Singh never forgave Ram Chand for breach of faith. He never wrote or spoke to Ramchand after that incident. (Ibid.).

[13] Sohan Singh Josh, *Akali Morchon Ka Itihas*, 1974, pp. 417-418.

[14] G.S. Deol op. cit., p. 24; Virender Sindhu, *Yugdrista Bhagat Singh Aur Unke Mritunjay Purkhe*, op.cit., p. 148.

[15] Punjab Government report (Home Political Punjab, 67, 1924, pp. 211-212) cited by M. S. Waraich (*Bhagat Singh: The Eternal Rebel*, 2007, p. 27).

[16] Ibid.

[17] J.C. Chatterjee, op. cit., pp. 230-231.

[18] *Arya Samaj Ka Itihas*, Vol 6, 1987, p. 56.

[19] Ibid.

[20] Manmathnath Gupta, op. cit., p. 72.

[21] Ajoy Ghosh, *Bhagat Singh and His Comrades*, 1979, p. 18.

[22] Ram Prasad Bismil, *Atmakatha*, 1958, p. 141.

[23] J.N. Sanyal, *S. Bhagat Singh*, 1983, p. 19.

[24] Ibid.

[25] Shiv Varma, *Sansmritiyan*, 1974, p. 15; J.C.Chatterjee, op. cit., p. 324.

[26] *Why I am an Athiest*, cited in Shiv Varma, *Selected Writings of Bhagat Singh*, 1996, p. 123.

[27] *Why I am an Atheist*, op. cit.

[28] J.N. Sanyal, op. cit., p. 19.

[29] Bhagat Singh's 4 letters published in *Jansatta* of 25th March, 2007 and *The Tribune* of 8th April, 2007.

[30] N.A.I. Home Political, F. 254, 1926.

[31] Home, (Punjab), C.I.D 9349.S.B.C.

[32] *Why I am an Atheist*, op.cit.

[33] Virender Sindhu, op. cit., p. 157.

[34] Virender Sindhu, op. cit., p. 158, Yashpal, op. cit., p. 91. Ramchandra gives February 1928 as the date of quashing of bail order (*NBS & HSRA*, p. 38) but it could not be confirmed by any other source.

[35] Chronological sequence of events (judgement of Lahore Conspiracy Case) reports on Bhagat Singh's movement from January 1928 onwards. Malwinder Singh Waraich and Gurudev Singh Sidhu (MSW & GSS), eds., *The Hanging of Bhagat Singh, The Complete Judgement and Other Documents*, 2005. Punjab Government report on NBS states that NBS started its activities in March 1928 after a gap of one year. (N.A.I., Home pol. 130 & KW, 1930, p. 37).

36 Virender Sindhu, op. cit., p. 159.

37 J.N. Sanyal, *S. Bhagat Singh*, 1983, p. 24.

38 G.S. Deol, (*Shaheed Bhagat Singh: A Biography*, op. cit., pp. 28-29) puts the number of those who attended the meeting to 60 revolutioanries including 5 women. Kamlesh Mohan is also incorrect in saying that Bengal group attended the meeting which also was attended by Yashpal and Bhagwati Charan Vohra (*Militant Nationalism in Punjab*, p. 95).

39 Shiv Varma, *Selected Writings of Shaheed Bhagat Singh*, 1996, p. 34.

40 This opinion is shared by Shiv Varma and Jayadev Kapur who were present in the meeting and also J.N. Sanyal.

41 Judgement of the Lahore Conspiracy Case cited in MSW & GSS, op. cit., p. 100.

42 Saunders' murder and Assembly bombing were such kind of actions.

43 Oral Transcript of Jaidev Kapur, NMML, pp. 51-52.

44 Ibid.

45 Shiv Varma, Selected *writings of Bhagat Singh*, 1996, p. 35.

46 J.N. Sanyal, op. cit., 1983 , p. 26.

47 Transcript of Jaidev Kapur, NMML, pp. 54-55.

48 Judgement of the Lahore Conspiracy Case cited in MSW & GSS, p. 102.

49 Comrade Ramchandra, *NBS and HSRA*, p. 57.

50 Transcript of Jaidev Gupta's interview.

51 *The People* (Lahore), 22 November 1928.

52 J.N. Sanyal, *op. cit.,* p. 30; Also see Sukh Dev's letter cited in M.D. Thapar, *Mere Bhai Shaheed Sukh Dev*, 1998, p. 216.

53 Judgement of the Lahore Conspiracy Case cited in MSW & GSS, p. 103.

54 A. G. Noorani, *The Trial of Bhagat Singh,* 2005, p. 145; M.D. Thapar, *Mere Bhai Shaheed Sukh Dev*, 1992, pp. 74-76.

55 J.N. Sanyal, op. cit., pp. 36-37.

56 Ibid., p. 37.

57   Bhagwan Das Mahour, Sada Shiv Malkapurkar and Shiv Varma, *Yash Ki Dharohar*, 2006, p. 36. Also see judgement of the Lahore Conspiracy Case cited in MSW & GSS, pp. 112-113.

58   Judgement of Lahore Conspiracy Case, chronological account of facts, cited in MSW & GSS, p. 114; Shiv Varma, *Selected Writings of Bhagat Singh*, 1996, p. 36.

59   Raja Ram Shastri, *Amar Shaheedon Ke Samsamaran*, 1981, pp. 100-101.

60   L.A.Deb. Vol;. III, dated 8th April, 1929, p. 2973.

61   L.A.Deb. Vol;. III, dated 7th February, 1929, p. 588.

62   L.A.Deb. Vol;. III, dated 6th February, 1929, pp. 531 and 534.

63   L.A.Deb. 1929, Vol;. III, dated 2nd April, 1929, pp. 2653-54.

64   Yashpal, *Simhavalokan*, 2005, p. 122.

65   Azad had taken the vow that he will never get arrested.

66   Later events justified their line of thinking. Pamphlets thrown in the Assembly after the bomb attack failed to make any positive impact on the public opinion. Their act of bomb throwing was bitterly criticized from all quarters. It was only after Bhagat Singh and B.K. Dutt's statement was read out in the Sessions Court on 6th June 1929 that public perception changed and they were hailed as heroes fighting for a just cause.

67   Shiv Varma, *Selected Writings of Bhagat Singh*, (1996), p. 36. Shiv Varma was present in this meeting.

68   *Hindustan Times* of 8th April, 1929, cited in *The Bomb Incident*, June 1958, p. 31.

69   *The Hindu* of 8th April, 1929, op. cit., p. 35.

70   *The Times of India* of 8th April, 1929, op. cit., p. 38.

71   *The Statesman*, 8th April, 1929, op. cit. p. 41.

6

Bhagat Singh, The Naujawan Bharat Sabha and the Kirti Group: A Brief Encounter

The popular image of Bhagat Singh is that of a revolutionary involved secretly in the acts of violence against the British government. His open political work, though brief, is a lesser known aspect of his political career. Naujawan Bharat Sabha (hereafter NBS or Sabha) provided the necessary platform for constructive political work to Bhagat Singh and other youths of Punjab in the 1920's. Bhagat Singh was one of the founders of the Sabha, and remained actively associated with it as its General Secretary till October 1928.

NBS was a product of the circumstances that were created by the abrupt calling off of the Non-Cooperation Movement in 1922. A section of the youth in the Punjab, which had actively participated in the Non-Cooperation Movement, had become disillusioned with the Gandhian approach of non-violent struggle which the Congress was following. They were not satisfied with the Congress' goal of dominion status and defined their objective of 'Swaraj' as 'complete independence'. They were inspired by the youth movements in other countries such as Italy, Ireland and Turkey. Such youth were willing to adopt all possible means, violent and non-violent, which could lead to complete independence of the nation. In Yashpal's words, "The programme of Naujawan Bharat Sabha was to denounce the Congress Party's Gandhian policy of compromise, and motivate people towards a revolutionary political programme and to arouse public sympathy for the (revolutionary) movement."[1]

Confusion prevails about the year of founding of the NBS. All the recent works on Bhagat Singh have taken the position that NBS was founded in March 1926. Source of this information can be traced to two reports on NBS from the Punjab Government to Home Department dated 21st March 1929 and 2nd August 1929, respectively.[2] That these reports are not flawless is evident from the fact that they do not give the credit of establishing NBS to Bhagat Singh and his friends of National College Lahore but to Dr. Satya Pal. Absurdity of this fact was pointed out by R.B. Bhagwan Das, a senior intelligence officer. D. Petrie, the then Director of the Intelligence Bureau also upheld the opinion of Bhagwan Das.[3]

March 1926 as the date of formation of NBS is not acceptable to Bhagat Singh's colleagues in the Sabha. Comrade Ramchandra (1903-1997), who was the founder member of NBS as well as its second President, has dealt with the problem of the date of foundation of NBS in the following words:

"Some uninformed people have made many wrong statements about this. There is no record of the Sabha available too. From my memory and connected events of that time I say that it was formed towards the end of 1924. Chhabil Dass too agrees with this timing. I have come across a file in the... National Archives. ...... It is Home Political File No. 27/5 of 1931.

"This is a file in which the English translations of the speeches of political workers prosecuted under Section 124-A is given ...This is the speech I delivered on May 17, 1931 at Ganj Mandi, Rawalpindi, on return from Peshawar, I earned prosecution for it.

"In my speech I had said that Naujawan Bharat Sabha was established seven years back. This comes to 1924.[4]"

But at another place Ramchandra writes that NBS was founded in 1924-25.[5] Chhabil Das (1900-1988), who was also one of the founder members of NBS as well as the Principal of National

College, was also of the opinion that NBS was formed around 1924.[6] Though these statements do create some ambiguity but they definitely take the date of formation of NBS to well before 1926. It is more plausible to accept early 1925 as time when the NBS was created because Bhagat Singh in the last part of 1924 was in Delhi, working with the Hindi daily '*Arjun*' and in January 1925 he had helped the distribution of the pamphlet *Revolutionary*.[7] After that he was back in Punjab. Ajoy Ghosh, Gopal Thakur, Prithvi Singh Azad and Yashpal have also mentioned 1925 as the year of formation of NBS.[8]

Yashpal, a close associate of Bhagat Singh in the revolutionary party and also a member of the NBS, has written in his memoirs that though many young men were involved in the establishment of NBS but mainly it was the work of Bhagat Singh, Bhagwati Charan Vohra and Ramchandra.[9] Its first meeting was held in a small room over Parimahal Khaddar Bhandar in Lahore.[10] This meeting was attended by Principal Chhabil Das, Master Paras Ram, Master Gurudutt, Bhagwati Charan Vohra, Bhagat Singh, Sukhdev, Jai Dev, Babu Singh, Ganapati Rai, Jaswant Singh, Som Dev, Banarsi Das and Comrade Ram Chandra.[11]

The newly formed association was initially named "Young India Association" following similar movements in the West such as Young Ireland, Young Turkey and Young Italy. Members of the newly formed association decided that all meetings and proceedings of the association must be conducted in Hindustani. Comrade Ram Chandra pointed out that English name of the association must be dropped and instead its Hindustani equivalent be adopted. After a good deal of discussion, Bhagat Singh agreed to the new name proposed by Ram Chandra viz. Naujawan Bharat Sabha (NBS). The Sabha adopted its motto as 'Service, Sacrifice and Suffering'.[12]

Another prevalent misconception is about the first President of the *Sabha*. Most of the biographers of Bhagat Singh, including Gurdev Singh Deol[13], Virendra Sindhu[14] and Mamnathnath Gupta[15] have named Ramkrishna[16] as the first President of the *Sabha*. But

Punjab Government's letter to Home Department, dated 21st May 1929, very plainly gives the name of first President of the *NBS* as 'Gurudutt Singh'.[17] Gurudutt, who later became famous as a prolific writer, at that time was headmaster of the National School in Lahore. During the Non-Cooperation Movement he was expelled from Government College where he was a demonstrator in chemistry. Gurudutt has written about his tenure as the first President of NBS in his memoirs.[18] Comrade Ramchandra has also discussed Gurudutt's role in detail.[19] Gurudutt continued as President of NBS till 1926.[20] Gurudutt's place was taken by Comrade Ramchandra.[21] Ramchandra was arrested on 1st August 1927.[22] Thereafter Ramkrishna was elected as the President of NBS, Lahore.[23] Turning to the Provincial NBS (after April 1928, the Sabha was organized on Provincial and District levels. At both levels there were separate Presidents, Secretaries and working committees, propaganda committees etc.) Kedar Nath Sehgal was the first provincial President (since April 1928). Sohan Singh Josh was elected as the second President of the provincial NBS on 24th February 1929.[24] But he could work in that position for hardly a month when he was arrested on 20th March 1929 in Meerut Conspiracy Case.[25] It was only after the arrest of Josh that Ram Krishna was elected as the President of the provincial NBS, on 30th March 1929.[26] Since the foundation of the Sabha, Bhagat Singh and Bhagwati Charan Vohra were chosen as the first General Secretary and Treasurer respectively.

In its initial phase, programme of NBS comprised debates on moral, literary and social subjects, the popularization of *swadeshi* (indigenous) goods, the inculcation of a sense of brotherhood, stimulating interest in Indian languages and civilization, and encouragement to plain living and physical fitness.[27] Each member of the Sabha had to sign a pledge, before his enrolment, that he would place the interests of the country above those of his community.

Raja Ram Shastri, the librarian of Dwarka Das Library of Lahore, who was a close friend of Bhagat Singh as well as a member of NBS, recalled:

"In reality it was an open platform of the revolutionary party. Its doors were open to all who believed in the policies or the ideals of the Naujawan Bharat Sabha or had sympathy for its cause. Although the Sabha was critical of the Congress, yet the Congressmen who called themselves extremists sympathized with the Sabha and also helped the Sabha. One characteristic of the Sabha was that there was no division of labour between its leaders and activists. All joyfully shared every kind of work – spreading the *durees* (cotton mats), readying the stage, distributing pamphlets and making speeches ..."

"After the failure of the Non-Cooperation Movement, the country turned towards communal violence. Several parts of the country witnessed communal riots. The attention of the Naujawan Bharat Sabha turned towards this problem. The Sabha raised its voice for communal harmony. Through the speeches delivered from its platform, people were exhorted to shun bloodshed. Sometimes, the Sabha also organized collective public dining so that people from different communities could forget their mutual differences and move forward."

"One of the objectives of Naujawan Bharat Sabha was to also arouse the feeling of patriotism among the youth. The Sabha also aspired that Indian youth should always realize that India is one indivisible nation and the task of national reconstruction is to be performed by them only."[28]

NBS in its early days was a broad front of nationalist forces. Muzzaffar Ahmed, a veteran Communist leader, was invited to give a lecture at Sabha, when he visited Lahore in December 1926. He observed: "What I felt as an outsider was that it was a loosely knit organization and its leaders belonged to various shades. It contained nationalists, Communists and of course Bhagat Singh and his friends."[29]

Bhagat Singh's enthusiasm and organizing ability was a great asset to the Sabha. He used novel ways to reach out to the people. Once he acquired a magic lantern and used it to great effect to spread revolutionary ideas. J. N. Sanyal, one of the first biographers of Bhagat Singh, has described in detail the innovative use of such lantern shows and lectures in detail.

"While engaged in organizing the "Kakori Day" celebrations, an idea came into the mind of Bhagat Singh to deliver public lectures on the lives of the Indian youth who had laid their lives in the Lahore conspiracy case of 1915 and 1916. He set to work and collected photos from obscure places and got lantern slides made of them.... He had an idea of going on a lecture tour throughout northern India, accompanied with the lantern slides of the Panjabi martyrs. Though he could not carryout his plans as far as northern India was concerned, he organized very successful lectures at Lahore and nearby places. On the first day of the lantern lectures at Bradlaugh Hall, the whole hall was packed to suffocation, and lectures were listened with rapt attention. It should be noted however, that Bhagat Singh was prevented from delivering the lectures himself on account of the huge security. But he instructed his lieutenant Bhagwati Charan, gave him full material and provided him lecture notes. On account of the striking success of these lantern lectures they were soon prohibited by the Panjab Government."[30]

Through such innovative methods, NBS was able to create a favourable atmosphere for the spread and growth of revolutionary ideas. NBS continued to celebrate days of national importance like 'Kartar Singh Sarabha Day', 'Naujawan Sufferers' Day' and 'Jallianwala Bagh Day' every year. Through these celebrations, Naujawan Bharat Sabha tried to awaken the youth and to familiarise as well as inspire them with the saga of sacrifices and patriotism.

NBS also started a Tract Society to disseminate revolutionary literature in the form of low-priced pamphlets written in the language of the common man. The Society under the leadership of Principal Chhabil Das brought out several pamphlets such as translation of Agnes Smedley's '*India and the Next War*'. Principal Chhabildas himself wrote several tracts in Urdu- '*Inquilab-Jindabad*', '*Chingariyan*', '*Inqualabi Sharare*', '*Hum Swaraj Kyon Chahatein Hain*', '*Socialism*', '*Naujawano Se Do Batein*' and '*Bharat Mata Ka Darshan*'. Bhagat Singh liked these booklets very much and also gave his suggestions.[31]

An important milestone in the life of NBS was its association with the Kirti (meaning 'worker' in Punjabi) group. This association began in April 1928 and continued up to 1934. Kirti group, though it worked under the flag of NBS during this period, had a separate identity based on a different ideological approach, leading to friction and conflict between the two groups constituting the NBS. It must be stated at the outset that NBS was a forum of patriotic youth, committed to complete independence of the motherland with romantic inclination towards the ideal of equality preached by socialism, while the Kirti group was Soviet Russia controlled Communist group. For a proper understanding of the relationship between the two constituent groups, origins and evolution of the Kirti group need to be explored.

Origins of the Kirti group (named as Kirti- Kisan Party since the middle of 1928) lay in what was left of the Ghadar movement after it lost its steam. Some former Ghadarites living in United States of America were attracted towards Bolshevik Russia in the hope of getting assistance for resuming their struggle for the liberation of their motherland. In 1921, Jagat Singh, the editor of Ghadar Party newspaper *Independent India* met Trotsky.[32] Santokh Singh (1892-1927), another prominent leader of the Ghadar party, came in contact of Marxism in jail in United States while serving sentence under San Francisco Conspiracy Case in which some Ghadarites were tried.[33] He along with Rattan Singh, another Ghadarite, attended the Fourth Congress of the Communist International[34] in Moscow in the first week of November 1922. According to a secret Government report they were promised help by the Indian Communist Party in Berlin also on the condition of carrying out its plans in India.[35] Santokh Singh was also believed to have addressed the Second Congress of the Red Labour International.[36]

Though the original Ghadar movement had envisaged an armed revolt against the British throughout the India, its new offshoot (Kirti group), with the Comintern's help, focussed upon spreading Communism and launching anti – colonial struggle in Punjab only. Surprisingly, M.N.Roy, who was Comintern's main representative in India, was kept aloof from this project, perhaps on the insistence of the former Ghadarites. A British intelligence report outlines the initial plan of the Ghadarite- Comintern intrigue:

"Comintern have sought to revive the main Ghadar movement in America and its "home" branch in India, contact between the two being maintained by a number of disaffected Sikhs in Moscow, Tashkent, Kabul and Amritsar. To begin the story at the Indian end, the first move was apparently made as far back as May 1923, when Santokh Singh and Rattan Singh were commissioned to visit India. The moment was opportune, for the Akali Sikh movement was at its greatest intensity and feeling everywhere was at a high pitch. In Kabul there was a nucleus of dangerous Sikhs, comprising three particularly important men, Harnam Singh, Gurmukh Singh and Udham Singh, all of them convicted Ghadarites who had broken jail in India and escaped to Afghanistan. Representatives of the Kabul Party are believed to have approached the Shiromani Gurdwara Parbandhak Committee of Amritsar, and to have placed before them a scheme including, *inter alia*, the formation of secret societies for revolutionary work cloaked as communal organisations, the bringing of the Sikh temples in Afghanistan..., the fomenting of trouble among the independent frontier tribes, the assassination of British officers with the help of Bengal revolutionaries, and the training of young Sikhs in foreign military schools."[37]

This ambitious plan apart, the movement soon drifted towards organisation of masses through propaganda. Ghadarite-Comintern combine, from the beginning attached great importance to propaganda and strived towards establishing a separate organ of the Ghadar Party in Punjab. Rattan Singh, while in America in 1925, in a letter impressed upon the necessity of starting a newspaper: "A Gurumukhi newspaper, under the name of 'Kirti' ought to be published... I settled with my companions at the time of my departure that the business could only be successful only if the 'Kirti' was successful. We are trying to send money soon for this paper."[38] During the last part of the year 1925, Santokh Singh (on his arrival in India in the middle of 1923, was arrested on North-West Frontier and put under house arrest for two years), started preparations for bringing out a monthly magazine "Kirti" in Punjabi in association with two of his Ghadar Party comrades-Bhag Singh Canadian and Karan Singh Cheema. British intelligence reports maintain that Kirti continued to receive large sums of money from Indian emigrants abroad and Bolshevik sources.[39]

The real purpose behind the launching of Kirti monthly was to organise the Communist movement in Punjab by making use of the local sympathy for the Ghadar heroes. In January 1926, the Kirti Party advertised its objectives as follows: "This journal will be the voice of Indian workers in America and Canada and will be dedicated to the sacred memory of those heroes and martyrs who awakened sleeping India.... The journal will sympathise with all the workers throughout the world... the subjugated, weak, and oppressed nations and subjugated India." The first issue of Kirti as a Punjabi monthly appeared in February 1926 with Santokh Singh as its editor.[40] Sohan Singh Josh has also observed that "the Kirti was not only a propaganda journal but a mobiliser and organiser too."[41]

Armed with a mouthpiece, the Kirti group began preparations
to organise a cadre based organisation. After careful deliberations,
the group put the organisation of the workers and peasants on a
backseat and decided to focus on the youth movement which had
greater potential in Punjab at that time. Sohan Singh Josh, who
following the death of Santokh Singh became the editor of the
Kirti on 21st January 1927[42] recalled: "The *Kirti* management had
decided to build an organisation of the youth. They had brought
out a poster signed by Bhag Singh Canadian and Sohan Singh
Josh for that purpose in March 1928 and they were making
preparations to hold a youth conference in Jallianwala Bagh,
Amritsar on 11, 12 and 13 April 1928. The Punjab Congress was
also holding a political conference on those dates at the same
place."[43]

By that time Naujawan Bharat Sabha had caught the attention
of the young men throughout Punjab. Sabha's leadership also saw
Punjab Political Conference as a good opportunity to expand and
therefore sent Bhagat Singh to open dialogue with the Amritsar
based 'Kirti' group led by Sohan Singh Josh. As a result of Bhagat
Singh's talks with Sohan Singh Josh of Kirti, both the groups
participated in the Conference. Punjab CID's report on Naujawan
Bharat Sabha gives a brief description of the proceedings:

"During the Punjab Political Conference at Amritsar in April
1928, a Young Men's Conference was also held and was
presided over by Kedar Nath Sehgal who delivered a most
objectionable Presidential address. A number of seditious and
subversive resolutions were passed including inter alia
resolutions appreciating the sacrifices of certain convicts hanged
in the Kakori Train Dacoity case, advising young men to prevent
the people from taking any part in a war of the future and
appealing to the country to start a regular agitation for the repeal
of the Arms Act. At the same time great stress was laid on the
necessity for the subjection of religion to politics in the cause of
nationalism. A resolution proposing that no young man who

desired the complete independence of his country should become a member of any political communal organisation was however, opposed by several Muslims and had to be shelved. During the conference it was also decided to organize the youth of the Punjab in a central body called the Nau Jawan Bharat Sabha with head quarters at Amritsar and branches in every district and to associate the Sabha with the Kirti group of Amritsar."[44]

At the same venue, on 12th April 1928, Kirtis formally launched their political party namely Kirti Kisan Party with the objective of organising the peasants and workers.[45] Sohan Singh Josh was elected as the General Secretary and M.A. Mazid as the Joint Secretary of the Party.

The British Government was very much apprehensive of the Conference. Fortnightly Report of April 1928 said that recent events "have definitely increased the chances of trouble from a comparatively small but very virulent group, the members of which are in favour of methods of violence.......... It is now clear that a combination had been formed among certain extreme members of the Congress, the Akali irreconcilables, the 'Kirti' and 'Kisan' group of Sikh community and the students' revolutionary association. The object is to reproduce the conditions of 1919 by any means and attempts will be made to stir up the masses."[46]

According to Sohan Singh Josh, Bhagat Singh met him for the first time in context of the above mentioned youth conference, a few days before the conference. From the account of this meeting given by Sohan Singh Josh, the following points emerge which need to be examined closely.

1. Naujawan Bharat Sabha was unknown outside Lahore (in April 1928). Sohan Singh Josh was not aware of its existence until Bhagat Singh met him.

2. *Kirti* group was the real organiser of the Conference. Naujawan Bharat Sabha was just a small group participating in it.

3. On Bhagat Singh's request, the 'Kirti' group decided to consider the adoption of the name of the conference to Naujawan Bharat Sabha Conference.

4. In Sohan Singh Josh's words "We had selected K.N. Sehgal as President of the conference". Moreover 'Kirti' group was not aware of the fact that Sehgal was also a member of the Lahore Naujawan Bharat Sabha.

Looking at the first point, it is difficult to digest the claim of Sohan Singh Josh that Naujawan Bharat Sabha was unknown outside Lahore. In reality, Naujawan Bharat Sabha was well known in the Punjab as newspapers such as *'The Tribune'* regularly carried news related to the activities of the Sabha. Sabha had openly started celebrating days of national significance. It had opposed Lala Lajpat Rai and his Independent Congress Party in September 1926 in elections to Provincial Council and Central Assembly.[47] In March 1927, Sabha had invited Dr. Bhupendra Nath Dutta, a well known Bengal revolutionary and brother of Swami Vivekananda, who lectured on the youth movement in the West.[48] In the last week of March 1928, Sabha had organised "National Week" with much fan fare in Lahore. During this week public meetings were held.

About the second issue, as to who was the real force behind organisation of the conference, it is necessary to quote Comrade Ramchandra, one of the founders of Naujawan Bharat Sabha and a leading political activist and journalist of that time:

"In 1928 Punjab Congress had decided to hold a Congress Political Conference during *Baisakhi* at Amritsar. I told Bhagat Singh it was time that we also hold a provincial conference at Amritsar. Bhagat Singh agreed with me but asked who would arrange it for us. I replied 'you'. He asked how? I told him that Naujawan Bharat Sabha had caught the attention of the young men. So if two three people came out to announce our conference it would be held. Young men, Hindus and Muslims have already met us. You should go to Amritsar and contact them. Further on account of our socialist views 'Kirti' people are also near us........ Thereupon Bhagat Singh visited Amritsar met 'Kirti' leaders and others and it was finally announced that a provincial Naujawan Bharat Sabha Conference shall be held on April 13 and 14 in Jallianwala Bagh, Amritsar along side the Congress Conference."[49]

Sohan Singh Josh's assertion that "we had selected Kedar Nath Sehgal as the President" of the youth conference, also appears to be wrong. He indeed has chosen not to mention the controversy involving President-ship of the conference. As Ram Chandra has written, earlier someone had proposed the name of Dev Das Gandhi, son of Gandhiji for President and Dev Das Gandhi had accepted the proposal. Naujawan Bharat Sabha was surprised by this proposal because in their view political views of Dev Das Gandhi did not match with the aims, objects and policies of the Sabha.[50] Having got some inkling of the resistance to his name, Dev Das Gandhi then promptly issued a statement to express his inability to preside over the conference. His statement appeared in *The Tribune* and *Hindustan Times* of April 5, 1928. Ram Chandra than proposed names of Kedar Nath Sehgal, Ram Saran Das[51] and Bhagat Singh as President of the Conference.[52] Ram Saran Das and Bhagat Singh refused the offer and hence Kedar Nath Sehgal presided over the Conference. Kedar Nath Sehgal was well known for being one of the accused in the first Lahore Conspiracy Case (1915) for his participation in the Ghadar movement. Hence Kirti wanted to use his Ghadarite legacy to make their programme popular. Kedar Nath was the eldest as well as the most known among members of NBS and also he was associated with the Sabha since its early days.

Interestingly, during the trial of Meerut Conspiracy Case (Sohan Singh Josh was among the accused), prosecution also charged Josh with capturing the existing youth organisations including the NBS. In his statement in the court, Josh made a blatant lie: "As regards the allegation of the prosecution of 'capturing of all the known existing youth organisations' it is false on the face of it. With regard to Naujawan Bharat Sabha I can definitely say that the question of its 'capturing' cannot arise, because *it was not existing before at all, but was brought into existence by us.*"[53] (Emphasis added)

From the above discussion it becomes quite obvious that Sohan Singh Josh has attempted to belittle NBS. At the same time, he has tried to project 'Kirti' group as a force to reckon with. But the reality is that Naujawan Bharat Sabha had definite aims, objectives and policies. It had an experienced and committed leadership. On the other hand 'Kirti', as a foreign tool was incapable of launching a youth movement of its own. Bhagwan Josh has aptly presented Kirti's incapacity in the following words:

"Kirti asserted an urgent need to have some kind of militant organisation based on mass movement. But what should be the nature of the organisation, what kind of programmes should it put forward and towards what (which) social classes should it orientate its political activities? Not to speak of any attempt to answer such questions, they were not even being posed during that period (1926-27). The new vision was more like a dream rather than a concrete perspective suggesting ways and means to launch anti-imperialist struggles."[54]

Thus, contrary to Sohan Singh Josh's claims, Kirti group was very eager to be associated with the Sabha which had a large following of dedicated patriotic youth. The fact that Kirtis chose not to function in the youth movement under their own name but under the name of NBS speaks for itself. Kirti group wanted to use the platform painstakingly created by the Sabha over the last three years. On the other hand, association with 'Kirti' (for the time being) suited the Sabha too, Naujawan Bharat Sabha was short of funds and also it did not have a mouth piece. 'Kirti' group was receiving money from abroad and it already had a Punjabi monthly with plans to start an Urdu newspaper also. So the coming together of Amritsar based Kirtis and Lahore based NBS can be termed as a marriage of convenience.

However, due to inherent fundamental differences between the two groups, the relationship between the NBS and Kirti group was not smooth. Soon after the Amritsar Conference, Second Fortnightly Report of the Government of Punjab for the month of June 1928 remarked: "It was originally expected that Naujawan Sabha would be financed by the Kirti funds, but Kirti party has hesitated to finance the Sabha."[55] A report by Chief Secretary of Punjab to the Home Department, dated 21st May 1929, summed up the relations between the Kirti Group and Sabha:

"The Kirti group showed some reluctance at first to finance or trust the Sabha unless the Kirti group could assume complete control of it and these differences took expression in the successive moves of the headquarters from Amritsar to Lahore and back to Amritsar. This phase ended with the election of the new executive of the Sabha on the 24th February, 1929 when the Kirti group came to the top with predominance on the executive, S.S. Josh becoming President, M.A. Mazid Vice President and Hari Singh Chakwalia, Secretary."[56]

Bhagat Singh and his group representing the Naujawan Sabha maintained a separate identity. They were not carried away with the dictates of Communist International. Sohan Singh Josh has himself admitted the ideological differences between Bhagat Singh group and Kirti party.

"After some time two main political trends emerged in the Sabha. One represented our Kirti group - the majority Marxist trend which laid stress on organising the workers and peasants, fighting for the agrarian and economical demands and making them conscious of their political role in the freedom struggle... The other trend was represented by Bhagat Singh and his comrades. It was a minority trend, which became clear after my discussions with him. Bhagat Singh wanted to do something very quick, through the use of bombs and pistols, in order to politically awaken the slumbering youth and students who had forgotten their duty towards their motherland, something spectacular that would make them sit up and do some thinking about the soul- crushing British enslavement of India and come forward to make sacrifices for the cause of freedom."[57]

Sohan Singh Josh went on to point out the limitations of the ideology of Bhagat Singh and his group:

"Such thoughts and line of action immensely appealed to the immature youth. But these are bookish revolutionary knowledge, which can become helpful tools only if it becomes the yardstick for properly measuring all aspects of a given situation and is thoughtfully and flexibly applied to solve the problems of a country. Transplanting of revolutionary conditions of one country to another with different situation generally results in disaster.[58]

Surprisingly, despite the ideological differences, management of the *Kirti* approached Bhagat Singh to join the editorial staff of the Urdu *Kirti* which had come into existence in April 1928.[59] They also paid him about Rs 1100 to use as he liked over and above his payment for his work on the staff for about three months.[60] Earlier also, as Sachindra Nath Sanyal has written, Bhagat Singh had refused to join Sardar Gurumukh Singh's organisation being run on the Bolshevik lines.[61] Gurmukh Singh was working under the guidance of Santokh Singh, the founder of the Kirti group.[62] Sanyal was very disappointed at the communal nature of Gurmukh Singh's organisation, as only the Sikhs could become its members.[63]

Bhagat Singh chose to resign from the NBS in October 1928 to dedicate full time and energy to the underground revolutionary work. Ideological differences apart, Kirti group took advantage of the popular image of Bhagat Singh and his revolutionary colleagues in Lahore Conspiracy Case as the national youth icons. As a result of the sacrifices of Bhagat Singh and his comrades of HSRA, the collection of funds on behalf of *Kirti* in America, swelled.[64]

Though the Kirtis distanced themselves from the activities of the revolutionary group in the NBS, the Sabha, with the active support of its original nucleus, was able to remain the public front of the revolutionary party. Ramchandra explained the arrangement:

"After long discussions we decided that the secret organisation keeping its separate existence would recruit its members from Naujawan Bharat Sabha...... (and) carry propaganda for violent actions separately and not involve Naujawan Sabha openly. The action party would take advantage of political occasions and resort to violent propaganda and actions with a view to arouse the people. Naujawan Bharat Sabha would give shelter to such comrades and help in their defence. But it would keep itself on the fringe, help defend the violent actions, keeping its separate existence, so as to escape police action and in the guise of separate independent constitutional structure, carry on the organisation of the youths, the peasants and workers and propaganda for socialism, all the time closely cooperating with violent actions."[65]

Sabha helped in organising defence of the accused in Lahore Conspiracy Case. When the under trial revolutionaries in Lahore Conspiracy Case went on hunger strike, the NBS, by organising protest marches and public meetings built pressure on the Government from outside. To stop the Sabha in its efforts in popularising the revolutionaries' cause, Government banned NBS on 23rd June, 1930.[66] Sabha had some prior inkling of eventuality of the Government's action and thus was able to withdraw its funds from the bank earlier. According to Ramchandra, these funds were passed to HSRA to organise action for the proposed rescue of Bhagat Singh from the jail.[67] Unfortunately, the HSRA's plans did not succeed and it lost Bhagwati Charan Vohra, an intellectual as well as a very committed revolutionary, while testing a bomb for the proposed action. After the ban, Sabha operated under the name of 'Bhagat Singh Appeal Committee'[68] and started a vibrant signature campaign to save the lives of Bhagat Singh, Sukhdev and Rajguru, when Privy Council dismissed the appeal on their behalf on 11th February 1931. Ban on the NBS was revoked on 5th March 1931 (as a result of the Gandhi- Irwin Pact) and Sabha began to function under its own name again. After the hanging of Bhagat Singh, Sukhdev and Rajguru on 23rd March, Naujawans organised strikes, and appealed to erect a memorial in the memory of Bhagat Singh, Raj Guru and Sukhdev.

Meanwhile, inherent differences between the Communist controlled Kirti group and Naujawan Bharat Sabha took a turn for the worse during the Karachi session of Congress in last week of March 1931. Karachi session of Congress was being held six days after the hanging of Bhagat Singh, Sukhdev and Rajguru. Gandhiji was under fire from youth leaders for having failed to save the lives of Bhagat Singh, Sukhdev, and Rajguru. Kirti group used this occasion to create disturbances during the proceedings and to denounce the Congress leadership. Real reason behind Kirti group's irresponsible behaviour was the instruction from the Communist International. Sixth Congress of the Communist International (July 1928) had taken a decision that there should be no joint front with any bourgeoisie party in the liberation struggles, as it held the possibility of betrayal at a crucial stage. Guided by these resolutions of Communist International, Indian Communists declared Indian National Congress to be a class party of the bourgeoisie and broke all connections with it.[69] Kirti group persuaded a number of Sabha workers at Karachi to present black flowers to Gandhiji. They were also able to circulate a manifesto on behalf of the Sabha, by clandestine methods, which used intemperate language against national leaders.[70] Kirti elements also did not permit Madan Mohan Malviya to speak who was invited on behalf the Naujawan Bharat Sabha. Subhas Bose, who was chairing the meeting, condemned the ugly incident and declared that foreign rowdy elements had disrupted the meeting.[71]

Kirti group's attempts to capture Naujawan Bharat Sabha and latter's desperate attempts to survive with its nationalist programme, independent of Comintern's dictates, while battling acute shortage of funds till 1934 (when Sabha amalgamated with Congress Socialist Party) has been well documented by Comrade Ramchandra,[72] but is out side the scope of this chapter.

Notes & References

[1]   Yashpal, *Simhavalokan*, 2005, p. 66.

[2]   N.A.I. Home Political File, 130 & K.W., 1930.

[3]   Ibid.

[4]   Comrade Ramchandra, *Naujawan Bharat Sabha and HSRA*, 2003, pp. 18-19.

[5]   Comrade Ramchandra, *Ideology and Battle Cries of Indian Revolutionaries*, 1989, p. i & 228.

[6]   Transcript of Chhabil Das's interview, NMML, New Delhi, p. 21.

[7]   Satya Ketu Vidyalankar (ed.), *Arya Samaj Ka Itihas*, Vol. VI, 1987, pp.56-57. The pamphlet '*Revolutionary*' dated 1 January, 1925 was distributed all over India.(H.W.Hale, *Political Trouble in India 1917-37*, p. 196).

[8]   Gopal Thakur, *Bhagat Singh: Man and His Ideas*, 1953, p.4; S.P. Sen (ed.), *Dictionary of National Biography*, p. 155.

[9]   Yashpal, op. cit., p. 66.

[10]   Gurudutt, *Bhav Aur Bhawana*, 2000, p. 80.

[11]   Ramchandra, *NBS & HSRA*, op. cit., p. 14.

[12]   Ibid, p. 17.

[13]   Gurudev Singh Deol, *Shaheed Bhagat Singh A Biography*, 1985, p. 25.

[14]   Virender Sindhu, *Yugdrista Bhagat Singh Aur Unke Mritunjayay Purkhe*, 2004, p. 151.

[15]   Manmathnath Gupta, *Bhagat Singh and His Times*, 1977, p. 103.

[16]   Born in 1901, in District Jhang (now in Pakistan), graduated from National College, Lahore. He became a Communist er. He died in early 1930s in Central Asia.

[17]   N.A.I. Home Political File, 130 & K.W., 1930.

[18]   Gurudutt, op. cit., p. 81.

19   Comrade Ram Chandra, *Naujawan Bharat Sabha and HSRA*, 2003, p. 20.

20   According to Gurudutt, he resigned from Presidentship a little before the closure of National School. National School was closed in 1926.

21   Comrade Ram Chandra, *Naujawan Bharat Sabha and HSRA*, p. 20; N.A.I. Home Political File, 130 & K.W., 1930.

22   Comrade Ram Chandra, *Naujawan Bharat Sabha and HSRA*, op. cit., p. 37.

23   Ibid., p.186.

24   N.A.I. Home Political File, 130 & K.W., 1930.

25   *Challenge: A Saga of India's Struggle For Freedom*, 1984, p. 337.

26   N.A.I. Home Political File, 130&K.W., 1930.

27   Ibid.

28   Raja Ram Shastri, *Amar Shaheedon Ke Sansmaran*, 1981, pp. 91-95.

29   Manmath Nath Gupta, *Krantidoot Bhagat Singh Aur Unka Yug*, 1972, pp. 97-98.

30   J.N. Sanyal, *S. Bhagat Singh*, 1983, p. 21.

31   Manorama Diwan, *Inqulabi Yatra*, 2006, p. 39.

32   N.A.I. Home Political, 287, 1921 cited in by Bhagwan Josh, *Communist Movement in The Punjab (1926-1947)*, 1979, p. 43.

33   Ibid. Other conspiracy cases to try the Ghadarites in foreign lands were Chicago Conspiracy Case in U.S.A. and Mandley Conspiracy Case in Burma.

34   See below chapter: *Was Bhagat Singh a Marxist*.

35   N.A.I. Home Political, 21/I, 1924.

36   N.A.I. Home Political 7, 1924.

37   David Patrie, *Communism in India, 1924-1927*, 1972, p. 139.

38   Bhagwan Josh, op. cit., p. 66.

39   Santokh Singh received a sum of ten thousand rupees from Kabul Party and three thousand from America. (N.A.I. Home Political, 235, 1926).

40   Sohan Singh Josh, *My Meetings with Bhagat Singh and on Other Early Revolutionaries*, 1976, p. 11.

41   Ibid.

[42] *Documents of the History of the Communist Party of India, vol. III-C,* 1982, p. 4.

[43] Sohan Singh Josh, *My Meetings with Bhagat Singh and on Other Early Revolutionaries*, op. cit.

[44] N.A.I. Home Political, 130 & KW, 1930.

[45] *Kirti* (Urdu) of May 1928 cited in *Documents of the History of the Communist Party of India, vol. III-C,* 1982, p. 297.

[46] Ramchandra, *NBS & HSRA*, op. cit., p. 44.

[47] N.A.I. Home Political, 130 & KW, 1930.

[48] Ibid.

[49] Comrade Ram Chandra, *Naujawan Bharat Sabha and HSRA*, p. 39.

[50] Ibid., pp. 39-40.

[51] An associate of Ajit Singh, Ram Saran Das was convicted for life in 1915 in the First Lahore Conspiracy Case. After his release he became s member of NBS.

[52] Ibid., p. 40.

[53] *Documents of the History of the Communist Party of India, vol. III-C,* op. cit., p. 292.

[54] Bhagwan Josh, op. cit., p. 42.

[55] Comrade Ram Chandra, op. cit., p. 230.

[56] N.A.I. Home Political, 130 & KW, 1930.

[57] Sohan Singh Josh, *My Tryst with Secularism* ,1991, p. 133.

[58] Ibid.

[59] Sohan Singh Josh, *My Meetings with Bhagat Singh and on Other Early Revolutionaries*, 1976, p. 18.

[60] Ibid.

[61] Sachindra Nath Sanyal, *Bandi Jeewan*, 2006, p. 270, 289.

[62] Ibid., p. 289.

[63] Ibid., p. 270.

[64] David Patrie, op. cit., p. 253.

[65] Comrade Ramchandra, op. cit., pp. 53-54.

[66] Ibid., p. 129.

[67] Ibid.

[68] This fact was admitted by Government in a Fortnightly Report on Political Situation for February 1931 (N.A.I. Home Political File 18/I/31, 1931, cited in G.S. Deol, *Shaheed Bhagat Singh: A Biography*, 1985, p. 82).

[69] Bipan Chandra, *India's struggle for Independence*, 1989, p. 302.

[70] Ramchandra, op. cit., pp. 171-72.

[71] Ibid., p. 172.

[72] Ibid., pp. 228-248.

7

Making of the Legend: Jail Life

The last one year, eleven months and fifteen days of his life (8th April 1929 to 23rd March 1931), which Bhagat Singh spent in British Indian Jails, were the most glorious and visible part of his revolutionary career. During this period, he shone the brightest in the most trying conditions- facing trials, police brutalities, a 113 days long hunger strike, and awaiting execution. It was during this period that his sterling qualities of grit, courage, intelligence and resourcefulness came to the fore. He achieved more than what he or his revolutionary colleagues could have hoped for, when he, along with Batukeshwar Dutt courted arrest after bombing the Central Assembly on 8th April 1929. The distribution of the red pamphlet in the Assembly followed by their arrest announced to the whole world the fact of their heroic deed. While in jail, he was able to spread the message of revolution far and wide. The great patriotic impulse that he was able to generate, even among those who were against the use of violent methods in the struggle for freedom, was the contribution of his jail days. He planned his martyrdom, extracted the maximum price for his life from the colonial rulers and became the most popular martyr in India, adoringly referred to as *Shaheed- i- Azam* or the 'prince among martyrs'.

Before the Assembly bomb incident, Bhagat Singh was virtually unknown outside the circle of his revolutionary friends. The very nature of his underground activities made him shun publicity. But after 8th April, 1929, his rise to fame was surprisingly sudden. In a very short time his popularity rivalled that of Mahatma Gandhi, a fact which is admitted by British intelligence as well as the official chronicler of Indian National Congress- Pattabhi Sitaramayya. Sitaramayya recalled that Bhagat Singh, just before his execution, was "as widely known all over India and was as popular as Gandhiji".[1] In the assessment of H.W. Hale, Assistant Director of Intelligence Bureau, for some time, Bhagat Singh was more popular than Mahatma Gandhi:

"Bhagat Singh ...... became a national hero and his exploits were freely lauded in the nationalist press, so that, for a time, he bade fair to oust Mr. Gandhi as the foremost political figure of the day. His photograph was to be met with in many homes, and his plaster bust found a large market"[2]

In this connection, observations of *The Tribune*, three days after his execution are also worth noting:

"The name of Bhagat Singh, of which no one outside his immediate neighbourhood had heard before he emerged into prominence in the Assembly Bomb Case, became a household word all over the province and over a large part of the country, and for months, '*Bhagat Singh Zindabad*' became as common a cry in the mouths of tens of thousands of people, including even small children who had just stepped out of the cradle, as 'Wilkes and Liberty' became in London in the days following the imprisonment of Wilkes,"[3]

Trial in Assembly Case

The tale of Bhagat Singh's trial and execution is the saga of his becoming a legend in the public eye. It started with his arrest in the Central Assembly's visitors' gallery on 8th April, 1929 and reached its climax on 23rd March, 1931 with his execution.

It may surprise many but the immediate response of press as well as the political leaders to the incident of bomb throwing in the Central Assembly was of condemnation and shock. General tenor of the press was that of outright condemnation of the incident.

Writing under the heading, *"Bomb Argument"*, *The Statesman* wrote:

"It is a crime of a type which by no stretch of language can be called political. It should excite the indignation of every man of every party, for the intention is simply indiscriminate murder. The whole thing is as cowardly as it is wanton......It may prove that the Government is faced by a new and formidable conspiracy relying on violent measures. If so, it can be met and crushed. The assassins will not be allowed to prevail."[4]

The Tribune too was scathing in its condemnation of the act. It pointed to the similarities in the pamphlets pasted on the walls of Lahore after Saunders' murder and the pamphlets thrown in the Assembly. Declaring it as the work of Hindustan Socialist Republican Army (HSRA), editorial went on to write:

"There can be little room for doubt that that body (HSRA)..... is working for the indefinite prolongation if not perpetuation of India's subjection. That such outrages can have no other effect except that of strengthening the forces of reaction and making the task of the party of constitutional independence more difficult."[5]

About the red pamphlet thrown after the blasts, *The Tribune* ridiculed the author of the pamphlet.

"The man who thinks that he is going to uproot either the bureaucratic rule in India or Government through the Assembly by throwing bombs into the Legislative Chamber is not only devoid of political sanity and common sense but entirely ignorant of history, however glibly he may talk of the Bourbons and the Czars."[6]

Mrs. Annie Besant called it "as one of those foolish attempts which can only discredit those who are working for reforms in legitimate ways." She further added that "a mad act like throwing bombs is a symptom that attempts are being made to provoke a conflict between Asia and Europe and all persons who consider peace necessary to progress should definitely and openly express their condemnation of such crimes."[7]

Naivety of such hasty reactions was exposed by the later developments. As the strategy during the prison life of Bhagat Singh and Batukeshwar Dutt unfolded itself they became the darling of the masses. In less than two months, public perception towards the men in question took an about turn. Their statement in the Sessions Court made them popular overnight.

The trial started in Delhi in the court of Additional District Magistrate, Mr. F.B. Pool on 7th May 1929. Mr. Asaf Ali was appointed the counsel for the accused through the efforts of Kishan Singh in spite of Bhagat Singh's wish that he had no special requirement for a counsel as he wanted advice only on one or two trivial matters.[8] Entering the court room, both Bhagat Singh and B.K. Dutt shouted in loud voice – 'Down with Imperialism'; and 'Long Live Revolution', thus setting a trend which continued throughout their trials. Another new trend they set was that of showing indifference to the trial proceedings. *The Tribune* of 9th May 1929 reported: "they kept smiling laughing all the while the trial was in progress."[9] Both of them also declined to make any statement. They were then committed to Sessions for trial.

Trial in Sessions Court started on 6th June 1929. Highlight of the trial in the Sessions Court was the reading out of the statement on behalf of Bhagat Singh and B.K. Dutt by their counsel Asaf Ali on the first day (6th June). The statement was a bomb-shell in itself for nobody had expected such a brilliant exposition of the ideology of revolutionaries from these two youths. The statement started with openly admitting the charges of throwing the bombs into the Assembly chamber. Statement called the Assembly action as a "practical protest" against the sham parliament, which "exists only to demonstrate to the world India's humiliation and helplessness, and it symbolises the overriding domination of an irresponsible and autocratic rule."[10]

The statement referred to the imposition of Trade Disputes Bill as "inhuman and barbarous measure" by which "the starving and struggling millions were deprived of their primary rights and sole means of their economic welfare." The purpose of their act of throwing bombs in the Assembly was only to give "a timely warning" and not to kill. The statement declared that revolutionaries were inspired by Guru Govind Singh, Shivaji, Kamal Pasha, Rija Khan, Washington, Garibaldi, Lafayette and Lenin. It justified the use of violence by pointing out that "force when aggressively used is 'violence' and is therefore morally unjustifiable, but when it is used in furtherance of a legitimate cause, it has its moral justification". Moreover the revolutionaries "hold human life sacred beyond words, and would sooner lay down their own lives than injure any one else". Explaining the meaning of revolution in the slogans they raised, statement explained:

> "Revolution does not necessarily involve sanguinary strife nor is there any place in it for individual vendetta. It is not cult of the bomb and the pistol. By "revolution" we mean that the present order of things, which is based on manifest injustice, must change....... Revolution is an inalienable right of mankind. Freedom is an imperishable birth right of all. Labour is the real sustainer of society. The sovereignty of the people is the ultimate destiny of the workers."

Bhagat Singh and B.K. Dutt, in their statement boldly asserted that for their ideals, they "welcome any suffering for which they may be condemned. At the altar of this revolution we have brought our youth as an incense, for no sacrifice is too great for so magnificent a cause."

The statement in Sessions Court was very carefully planned and circulated in advance. According to Jitendra Nath Sanyal, who himself was a co-accused in the Lahore Conspiracy Case, typed copies of the statement were sent to all the important newspapers even before the statement was made in the court. Sanyal writes that important extracts of the statement were also published is some foreign newspapers such as *La Humanite* of

Paris, *Pravda* of Soviet Union and some newspapers of Ireland.[11] Many leading papers in India published the full statement. *The Tribune* carried the full statement under bold headings:

"Bhagat Singh and Dutt explain why they threw bombs"

"We wanted to make deaf hear"

"No faith in utopian non-violence"

"Assembly is a hollow show."

"We could have ambushed Simon but that was not our intent"[12]

Besides published by newspapers, the statement was also distributed on mass scale. Naujawan Bharat Sabha took up the work of printing and distributing the statement along with the photographs of Bhagat Singh and Dutt. In U.P., Punjab and North West Frontier Province (N.W.F.P.) Naujawan Bharat Sabha took the lead in organising meetings in praise of the brave patriotic act of Bhagat Singh and Dutt. First of such meeting was held at Amritsar on 7th June 1929, the very next day of the reading out of statement in Sessions Court and a day before it was published by leading newspapers on 8th June 1929. A report of the Punjab CID forwarded to Home Department of Government of India noted that this meeting "was important, however, from the fact that it was on this occasion that the names of Bhagat Singh and Dutt .... were brought into prominence. Their action in throwing bombs was held up to admiration and portions of their defence statement were quoted to show that they had no intention of taking life but had merely wished to warn Government to change their policy of repression."[13] Statement was also distributed in Bengal through the efforts of Jatin Das and his emissary Dhiren Mukherji. While transporting the pamphlets containing the statement from Delhi to Calcutta, Dhiren Mukherji left copies of statement with Jatindera Nath Sanyal to be distributed in Banaras and Allahabad.[14]

The statement had a profound impact. Bhagat Singh and B.K. Dutt became a popular news item and began to be hailed as patriots suffering for the cause of the country. Attitude of the political leaders also underwent a marked turnaround. Leaders, who had condemned the bombs incident in harsh words, suddenly began to appreciate the motives of Bhagat Singh and Dutt. Jawaharlal Nehru in a public meeting at Meerut on 13th June said: "at first he (Jawaharlal Nehru) had been shocked but everything has been made clear by the statement of the accused. They (accused) could not be called cowards."[15] Now onwards, Jawaharlal Nehru began to take an avid interest in Bhagat Singh. He as General Secretary of the Congress also got published the joint statement of Bhagat Singh and Dutt in the Congress Bulletin of July 1, 1929. Gandhiji objected to the publication on two grounds. First, that it was "out of place" in a publication which was meant to record the activities of Congress, and, second, it was prepared by the counsel of the accused (Asaf Ali). Nehru apologetically defended its publication, saying that there was general appreciation of the statement in Congress circles. He also made it clear that the counsel of the accused (Asaf Ali was also a close friend of Nehru) only touched up or polished the language of the statement, otherwise it was a genuine statement.[16]

Meanwhile, Sessions Court pronounced the judgment in the Assembly Case on 12 June 1929, and found Bhagat Singh and B.K. Dutt guilty under section 307 of C.R.P.C. and section 308 of Indian Explosive Act and sentenced them to transportation for life. *Abhyudaya,* Hindi weekly of Allahabad, in its issue of 15th June reported that both accused accepted the judgement laughingly and raised slogans.[17] *The Tribune* carried the excerpts of the Judgment. Its sympathy with the accused was expressed in its disapproval of the life sentences: "Neither the facts of the case as they transpired during the trial nor the judgment of the Sessions judge, so far as the press reports go, can be held to justify the sentence of transportation of life"[18]

Later, Bhagat Singh and Dutt appealed to High Court against the judgment of the Session Court not because they hoped to escape with lesser sentence but because they did not want to miss any opportunity to publicise their views and awaken the masses. Their joint statement in the Lahore High Court brilliantly challenged the basis of the Session Court judgment. Citing examples from the lives of Jesus Christ, General Dyer and other cases, they questioned the "laws which do not stand the test of reason and which are against the principles of justice."[19] They asked to be judged on the basis of motive of their action, which was "to give a timely warning that the unrest of the people is increasing and that the malady may take a serious turn, if not treated in time and properly."[20] They added "we have come here to clarify our position.…. the question of punishment is of secondary importance before us."[21] But the court was not moved. It up held the life sentences in its judgment on 13th January 1930.

The public response to the Assembly action went beyond the original expectation of the HSRA. Revolutionaries' isolation from the mainstream politics ended as political leaders began to openly show sympathy for them. Their public image was also transformed—earlier they were regarded as misguided patriots. Now Bhagat Singh and Dutt were being appreciated for their high purpose, courage, intellect and clarity of thought. All this was made possible by the revolutionary vision displayed by Bhagat Singh who had prevailed upon his colleagues in the Central Council of HSRA to organise an action in which the motive was not to hit and run but to get oneself arrested and present the ideas and ideals of the party before the public. Thus by the time court proceedings in the Assembly case were over, Bhagat Singh had already become a hero.[22] For the first time, in full public view, an individual was challenging the British Government openly and boldly, without any fear of the consequences. It is no wonder that Bhagat Singh and B.K. Dutt caught the public imagination as no revolutionary had done before.

Trial by Special Magistrate and Hunger Strike

Assembly case proved to be just a trailer, for the real episodes of 'the Bhagat Singh show' were to follow. Next move of Bhagat Singh and Dutt was to go on hunger strike to improve the conditions of political prisoners in jail. Bhagat Singh was already aware of the harsh and insulting conditions faced by political prisoners and particularly those who were accused of revolutionary activities. Bhagat Singh and Dutt were shifted to Mianwali jail and Lahore Central jail respectively soon after their conviction in Assembly case to face trial in Saunders Murder Case. Even before the start of trial in Saunders' murder, Bhagat Singh had no doubts about his getting the death sentence. In order to make his death more expensive and more extracting, Bhagat Singh did not want to waste any opportunity. The hunger strike started on 15th June but the decision to go on hunger strike was taken in Delhi itself. [23] This epic hunger strike captivated the interest of million of Indians for the next four months.

On 17th June 1929, Bhagat Singh wrote two letters to Inspector General of Jails, Punjab. First was a request to be transferred to Lahore Central Jail as the Mianwali was quite far from Lahore, where the trial proceedings in the Lahore Conspiracy Case were to start. In the second letter he demanded the status of political prisoner which was denied to him. "I am being treated as an ordinary criminal. Therefore I have gone on hunger strike since the morning of 15th June 1929."[24] He also put forward his demands: to be treated as a political prisoner, special diet, no forcible labour, availability of toilet requisites and 'literature of all kinds'. Bhagat Singh and Dutt were also able to communicate the news of their hunger strike to the nationalist press which whole heartedly came forward to help them by publicising it on a country wide scale.

'*Abhyudaya*' of 29th June was at pains to explain that hunger strike of Bhagat Singh and Dutt was not for selfish reasons but to improve the lot of all political prisoners.[25] 30th June was observed all over India as 'Bhagat Singh Day' in order to express sympathy with the hunger striking prisoners.[26] Call for this day was given by several political organisations.[27] People kept fasts and in the evening held meetings. Among those who kept fast were the undertrials of Lahore Conspiracy Case. A note prepared by the Punjab Government (dated 7th July 1929) reveals that growing popularity of Bhagat Singh and Dutt was a matter of concern for the Government:

"Meetings were held at Lahore and Amritsar respectively on the 18th of June, and they were followed by the meeting at Amritsar on the 30th. There was a large attendance at the Lahore meeting and a fairly large attendance at the Amritsar meeting of the 30th. The chief feature of these meetings was the casting aside of all restraint; Bhagat Singh and Dutt were eulogized as heroes and martyrs, direct incitements were made to violence, inflammatory appeals were made to youth...."[28]

The concern was not limited to the Punjab government. In a telegram to the Secretary of State, the Viceroy of India, Lord Irwin described the situation:

"A recent feature of the extreme side of the political agitation is public glorification of Bhagat Singh and B.K. Dutt, the two convicts in the Delhi Assembly bombing. It was from the first a tendency in certain quarters to regard them as patriots and martyrs and this was encouraged by their line of defence, which was that their action had been in the nature of a demonstration and a warning. Their written defence statement was an elaborate justification of their act, which they described as making "the end of the era of utopian non-violence" and a prophecy of the advent of era of revolution. Public meetings were held to congratulate them on their convictions, and on the 19th of June two such meetings were held at Lahore and Amritsar under the auspices of the Naujawan Bharat Sabha. At these meetings the general trend of the speeches was to eulogize Bhagat Singh and Dutt and to exhort youths to follow their example."

"Subsequently the two convicts went on hunger strike on the pretext that their object was to improve the treatment of political prisoners ……... *The object is most probably to attract popular sympathy. In this they appear to have succeeded* (emphasis added), and a meeting of congratulation and sympathy, which was well attended, was held at Amritsar on the 30th June under the joint auspices of the Provincial Congress Committee and the Naujawan Bharat Sabha …… The speeches at this meeting were very inflammatory and contained direct incitation to violence. There was open praise of Bhagat Singh and Dutt, and their portraits were distributed to members of the audience with copies of their statement in court.….. A feature of this and similar meetings was the shouting by some members of audience of "long live revolution" and "down with imperialism." [29]

Nationalist press was playing a courageous role in hailing Bhagat Singh and Dutt as patriots and the 'brave ones'. *Abhyudaya* of 29 June quoted B.K. Dutt as saying: "My death will lead to betterment of the lot of the political prisoners". *Abhyudaya* led the Hindi newspapers in reporting on Bhagat Singh and Dutt. It repeatedly published their photographs on 20th April, 6th July, 20th July, 12th October, 1929; 15th September, 9th October 1930; and 25th March 1931. To counter the nationalist press in popularising Bhagat Singh and Dutt, Government backed Anglo-Indian newspapers published article such as '*Miscreants or Martyrs*' and described the meetings in their support as: 'propaganda to instil anarchical or revolutionary tenets among the youth of India'.[30] The appellation of Bhagat Singh and Dutt as miscreants raised a storm of protest in the vernacular and Indian-edited English press.

Efforts of the nationalist press were bolstered by the periodic bold statements by prominent national leaders. Jawaharlal Nehru, then General Secretary of the Congress, declared himself to be in full support of the huger striking revolutionaries. In a statement issued on 5th July 1929 he said:

"I have learnt with deep grief of the hunger strike of Bhagat Singh and Dutt. For 20 days or more they have refrained from all food and I am told that forcible feeding is being resorted to. The two young men may have done wrong, but no Indian can refrain from admiring their great courage and our hearts must go out to them now in their great and voluntary suffering. They are fasting not for any selfish ends but to improve the lot of all political prisoners. As days go by, we shall watch with deep anxiety this hard trial and shall earnestly hope that the two gallant brothers of ours may triumph in the ordeal."[31]

Bhagat Singh and Dutt were in their twenty fifth day of hunger strike when the trial proceedings in the Lahore Conspiracy Case opened in the court of Special Magistrate, Rai Saheb Pandit Shri Kishen, on 10th July 1929. Apart from Bhagat Singh and Dutt there were 23 other accused charged with murder of J.P. Saunders and Chanan Singh; throwing of the bombs in the Assembly; establishment of bomb factories in Lahore, Agra and Saharanpur; the commission of a decoity in Bihar in the course of which a murder was committed; and attempt to loot Punjab National Bank in Lahore. Six out of the twenty five who were declared absconders were: Chandra Shekhar Azad alias Pandit Ji, Bhagwati Charan Vohra, Kailashpati alias Kali Charan, Yashpal, Sat Gurudyal and Kailash. The nineteen who faced the trial were Sukhdev, Kishori Lal, Agya Ram, Deshraj, Prem Dutt, Surendra Nath Pandey, Jaidev Kapur, Shiv Varma, Gaya Prasad alias Dr. B.S. Nigam, Jatindra Nath Das, Mahabir Singh, Bhagat Singh, Batukeshvar Dutt, Ajoy Kumar Ghosh, Jitendra Nath Sanyal, Kamal Nath Trivedi alias Tiwari, B.K. Sinha, Shivram Rajguru and Kundan Lal. Bhagat Singh and Dutt were lodged in Lahore Central Jail while the rest of the under trials were in Borstal Jail, also in Lahore.

The first issue before the accused was to chalk out their strategy for the trial. Bhagat Singh also had the task of motivating his colleagues who were demoralized after the spate of arrests and the news of former colleagues turning approvers. Recalling the first few days of the trial, Ajoy Ghosh wrote in 1945:

"For three days we paid no attention to the proceedings but held prolonged discussions which Bhagat Singh, though so weak that he had to recline in an easy chair all the time, took the leading part...The first thing, he emphasised, was the need to get rid of the idea that all was over. Ours was not to be a defence in the legal sense of the word. While every effort must be made to save those who could be saved, the case as a whole was to be conducted with a definite political purpose. Revolutionary use was to be made of the trial, of every opportunity to expose the sham justice of the British government and to demonstrate the unconquerable will of revolutionists. Not merely by our statements when the time came but even more by our actions inside the court and prisons we were to fight for the cause of all political prisoners, hurl defiance at the government and show the contempt we had for its courts and its police. Thus we were to continue the work we had begun outside - the work of rousing our people by our actions."[32]

To chalk out a detailed strategy Bhagat Singh formed a small group consisting of Sukhdev, Bijoy Kumar Sinha and himself.[33] He himself declined to be represented by a lawyer and only asked for a legal advisor. After detailed discussions revolutionaries facing trial decided the programme of action to be adopted during the trial: to fight for the primary rights of the undertrials such as comfortable chairs, tables, newspapers and lunch tents; to fight the government's efforts to restrict the entry of visitors in the courtroom; to cross-examine the important witnesses like approvers in such a way as to bring on record and thereby before the public, the aims and objectives of the party, heroic side of the struggle; to demonstrate in the court room and send messages on days like Kakori Day, Lala Lajpat Rai Day, First May Day, Lenin Day, and events like death of Shyamji Krishna Verma.[34]

Meanwhile an influential defence committee consisting of 14 members was formed even before the case proceedings started. Lajjawati and Feroz Chand were its secretaries.[35] Others included Pandit K. Santhanam (treasurer) , Gopichand Bhargava, Lala Duli Chand, Saifuddin Kichlew, and Kishan Singh. As Lajjawati was to reveal later, Committee received massive public support, it was able to collect funds in excess of ten thousand, mainly from poorer classes.[36] As a result of the world wide publicity, which the case was getting, donations were also received from Poland, Japan, Canada, and South America.[37]

After three days of the trial's opening, 11 undertrials of the Lahore Conspiracy case lodged at Borstal jail also joined the hunger strike of Bhagat Singh and B.K. Dutt. This new development increased the troubles of the Government many fold, as the court proceedings facilitated full media coverage which could lead to strong public sentiments in favour of the hunger striking accused. Government was already nervous about the prospect of Bhagat Singh's death due to prolonged hunger strike. Government report on Bhagat Singh's hunger strike had already expressed the fear that "his death might, and probably would be followed by a more violent and more widely spread agitation than has yet taken place."[38]

Government's apprehensions about the sympathetic publicity provided to the hunger strikers by the newspapers was correct. *The Tribune* published the following story on Bhagat Singh and Dutt on 14th July:

> "Both these prisoners looked very weak. It is understood that yesterday evening eight Pathans were employed in each case to forcibly feed them. They were forcibly laid on ground, their neck, legs, hands and chest being violently pressed to the floor by the Pathans while a rubber tube was inserted into the nose and throat for the passage of milk. Both the prisoners suffered considerably as a result of their struggle with the Pathans and Bhagat Singh bore marks of violence on his body"

Such reports were part of daily news as the press representatives were a regular part of the audience in the trial court. Newspapers such as *The Tribune* published detailed accounts of slogans raised, songs sung, evidence of important witnesses like approvers and exchanges between the under trials and the magistrate. Such reporting usually projected the magistrate and authorities in a poor light. Court proceedings used to begin with shouts of 'Long Live Revolution', and 'Down with Imperialism', then national song - *'Vande Matram'* was sung. Other patriotic songs such as *"sar farioshi ki tammanna ab hamare dil mein hai"*, *"kabhi voh din bhi ayega ki jab azaad ham honge"* were sung daily. All these activities used to fill the courtroom with patriotic flavour and visitors' chests used to swell up. All such scenes had made the venue of the trial most sought after place in Lahore. Despite the discouraging behaviour of police, courtroom used to be full. People used to stand even outside the courtroom so as to hear Bhagat Singh speaking and he deliberately used to 'roar' loudly to carry his voice outside the courtroom.

Their calculated court room performances along with the gallant steadfastness of Bhagat Singh and his group highlighted by media coverage were creating a strong impression on public mind. Public image of Bhagat Singh was in the process of transformation from 'Bhagat Singh the revolutionary' to 'Bhagat Singh the phenomenon'. *Abhyudaya* while reporting the court proceedings of 16th July wrote that slogans of 'Long Live Bhagat Singh' and 'Long Live Dutt' were raised with usual shouts of 'Long Live Revolution' in the courtroom.[39] 'Bhagat Singh Day' celebrations in Lahore organised by Naujawan Bharat Sabha on 21st July 1929 were attended by about ten thousand people. Government report conceded that it was "the largest gathering that has attended any political meeting for some considerable time past."[40]

Meanwhile the undertrials of Lahore Conspiracy Case were fighting a grim battle with hunger, forced feeding and resultant complicaitons. Horrors of the forcible feeding of Bhagat Singh and Dutt had already become known to the people through the press even before the hearing of the case proceedings started in Lahore. For the other undertrials, Government waited for ten days after their hunger strike began and on eleventh day (23rd July), their forcible feeding started. Shiv Varma and Ajoy Ghosh, both of whom were among the hunger strikers, later wrote moving accounts of the stiff resistance put up by the hunger striking revolutionaries to the brutal ways of forcible feeding by the jail doctors, in their memoirs.[41] It was a situation in which a message went around that while the strikers wanted to die for their cause but the authorities were hell bent to keep them alive.

During forced feeding, milk was forced by a rubber tube inserted through nostrils to the stomach of the hunger striker while eight to ten people pinned him down in an immovable condition. Hunger strikers employed novel ways to prevent feeding by this method-such as biting the tube with teeth, or damaging the throat with boiling water and chillies to make such feeding impossible (as Kishori Lal did). Even if the milk reached the stomach of the hunger striker he used to vomit it. Ajoy Ghosh used to swallow flies to induce vomiting. During the struggle, sometimes the tube instead of going to the stomach moved into the lungs thereby flooding lungs with milk, leading to severe pneumonic infection. Several hunger strikers underwent this situation but all except Jatin Das recovered. His condition continued to deteriorate progressively. Hunger strikers were also adamant in refusing to take any medication in any circumstances. Media attention was focussed on the day to day condition of the hunger strikers and it was talked about in every home.

Heroic struggle of the Lahore Conspiracy Case hunger strikers attracted the attention of the whole country. Many political prisoners lodged in different jails of India joined the hunger strike in sympathy. Many eminent political leaders openly came out in support of Bhagat Singh and his comrades. Motilal Nehru while giving a speech on 4th August 1929, at Allahabad to celebrate 'Political Sufferers Day', issued a bold statement:

"Remember, they have not gone on hunger strike to benefit their own selves but in order to see that all the political prisoners were accorded special treatment in jail and were not treated like ordinary prisoners. They have not committed an act of which they should feel ashamed. They did a certain act, which they thought was in the interest of the country. If that act happened to be against any law of the state, the government might punish them for it. But their treatment in jail should not be like the treatment of ordinary prisoners or convicts."[42]

Jawaharlal Nehru visited the prisoners on 9th August and issued a forthright statement about their condition, their cause and their resolve.[43] *Abhyudaya* reported this statement under the heading – '*Kurbani Rang Layegi*' (Their sacrifice will bear fruit). Same issue carried news on the hunger strikers under the title – '*Aan Par Mar Jayenge*' (They will lay down their lives for their cause).[44] By the end of August, it seemed certain that Jatin Das may die any day. Condition of others was also quite bad. Their condition (reported by the national press on a day to day basis) flared up public feelings and protests were organised across the country.

The pressure of countrywide protests was increasing day by day on the Government for whom the issue of hunger strike had become a matter of prestige. Ultimately, fearing the worst, the Government appointed a Punjab Jail Enquiry Committee on 2nd September 1929. In response to this gesture by the Government, all the strikers except Jatin Das abandoned the strike. Bhagat Singh and Dutt had by then completed 81 days of their hunger strike. But the promises made by the members of the Jail Enquiry Committee were not fulfilled. Jatin Das, despite his critical health, was not released unconditionally and Bhagat Singh and Dutt were not allowed to associate with their fellow accused. Hence on 5th September, the hunger strike was resumed by Bhagat Singh and Dutt. Three others joined them the next day. Reasons for not releasing Jatin Das were spelled out in a note by H.W. Emerson, the Home Secretary, written on 7th September, 1929:

"The reasons why the Punjab Government were unable to release Jatindra Das unconditionally are his past record, the seriousness of the part he is alleged too have played in the conspiracy and the fact that, if he had been released unconditionally it would have been a direct incentive to other accused in this case and also to accused in other cases to adopt hunger-strike as a means of evading justice".[45]

Hunger striking revolutionaries, by playing with their lives, besides rousing the public sympathy and the patriotic sentiments across the country, were causing anxiety in the government circles for other reasons as well. Government was deeply worried by the fact that the trial itself was brought to a stand still by the absence of the accused in the court due to their serious health conditions. Moreover, there was danger of such tactics being followed in other cases in different parts of the country. Emerson wrote in his note:

"So far... the tactics followed by the accused have brought the process of the law to a deadlock. Moreover, the accused have shown that a deadlock can be created in similar conspiracy cases where the witnesses are numerous; and further that even where the accused and the witnesses are comparative few in number and it is possible for an accused indefinitely to delay justice so far as he himself is concerned. ... Apart from the importance of the Lahore Case, the situation created by the accused is of general concern, since the device adopted by them is capable of imitation in other cases. In fact, since the example has been set by the Lahore accused, there have been several cases of under trial prisoners going on hunger strike."[46]

To deal with the situation, in the opinion of Home Secretary, the most suitable remedy was to bring a Bill to give "a judge or magistrate discretion to proceed against an accused in his absence."[47]

Meanwhile, Jatin Das passed away on 13th September after 64 days of his heroic battle. His martyrdom took the public discontent across the country to a new height. His body was taken to Calcutta by train. At every station where the train halted, thousands paid their last respects to him with tearful eyes and patriotic fire in their hearts. His funeral in Calcutta was attended by lakhs of people. Throughout the country, people of all political shades condemned Government's attitude towards the hunger strike. The issue was also discussed in the Central Assembly while discussing the 'Hunger Strike Bill'. The Bill proposed to do away with the presence of an accused in the court in a situation when he voluntarily rendered himself incapable of appearing before the court. During the debate, members of the House including M. A. Jinnah, Motilal Nehru and M. R. Jayakar bitterly criticised the Government for sacrificing fundamental principles of jurisprudence and for discriminating Indians on racial grounds. Jatin Das and his comrades received high accolades for commitment to their cause. In the course of his long speech Jinnah lambasted the Government for its policy and admired the hunger strikers:

"I ask the Hon'ble Law Member to realise that it is not every body who can go on starving himself to death. Try it for a little while and you will see….. The man who goes on hunger strike has a soul. He is moved by that soul and he believes in the justice of his cause, he is not an ordinary criminal……. It is the system, this damnable system of Government which is resented by the people…… Is there today in any part of the globe a civilised government that is engaged, day in and day out….. in prosecuting their people?.... Do you realise, if you open your eyes, that there is resentment, universal resentment, against your policy, against your programme?"[48]

Motilal Nehru, referring to Bhagat Singh during the debate said, "He has acted under the best of impulses and in the fullest belief that he was acting for, and in the cause of, his country."[49] Jayakar made the point, "If India today were a self-governing country these intrepid and brave men would have been the material out of which were created captains of ships and commanders of armies".[50]

On 5th October 1929 Bhagat Singh and his comrades suspended their 113 days long hunger strike when Jail Enquiry Committee submitted its recommendations but the Government still dilly - dallied in implementing the recommendations. Bhagat Singh and other strikers again had to go on strike for two weeks in February 1930 before the government was finally forced to frame rules in implementing the main recommendations of the enquiry committee.

On 19th October, 1929 Bhagat Singh and Dutt were able to send message to the Punjab Students' Conference at Lahore. This message was published in *The Tribune* of 22nd October 1929 which for its source quoted Subhash Chandra Bose, the president of the conference, as saying that message was received on *wireless*. The message received a thunderous applause from the students with the slogans of 'Bhagat Singh Zindabad'.[51]

As a result of the patriotic and brave campaign by the nationalist press, Bhagat Singh had become a popular national figure by the time the hunger strike ended. Print media succeeded in generating waves of sympathy in favour of hunger striking revolutionaries across the country and also outside India. Motilal Bhargava, a keen observer of the role of press in the freedom movement, has rightly observed that "nationalist newspapers and the press in general carried harrowing tales of jail rigours and the tribulations of the fasting prisoners. Hundreds of leaflets, books, posters enlisting and idolising the revolutionaries appeared in all parts of the country. Bhagat Singh became a national hero."[52]

Trial by the Tribunal

After the battle of hunger strike was won the focus shifted back to the trial. Here too, the Government was in a disadvantageous position. Case itself was moving painstakingly slow, only a fraction of the total of 607 witnesses was examined as yet. Hunger strike had already delayed the proceeding. As mentioned earlier, Bhagat Singh's strategy had converted the courtroom into a platform of revolutionary propaganda. With the undertrials having become household names, prominent leaders were paying visits to them in the court. They included Subhash Chandra Bose, Jawaharlal Nehru, Baba Gurdit Singh, Motilal Nehru, Rafi Ahmed Kidwai and K.F. Nariman. It was an ironic situation: accused had become heroes while the magistrate and the Government officials were reduced to objects of hate and ridicule. Many a time, in the debates between the accused and the magistrate, the magistrate's helplessness as a puppet of British bureaucracy was thoroughly exposed and often he became the laughing stock of all present in the court. Vindictive reactions by the magistrate only proved to be counterproductive. In one such incident on 23rd October 1929, a scuffle broke out between police and the accused on the issue of forcible handcuffing. The accused were mercilessly beaten in full view of the visitors. This led to a tremendous furore in the media and created great public effect all over India. Action of the police was vehemently deplored in the press and the meetings.

Net result of the above mentioned developments was that the trial itself was becoming counter productive for the Government. Trial had become quite prolonged and there was no end in sight. Moreover the case itself faced the danger of weakening up. In Ajoy Ghosh's words: "due to tremendous popular enthusiasm that the case had evoked, a number of key witnesses had turned hostile, more were likely to follow suit, and two of the approvers had retracted their confessions" Mr. Ferne, the only official present at the time of Saunders' murder had failed to identify Bhagat Singh. Ghosh added, "the whole case was in danger of ending in a fiasco if ordinary legal procedures were followed and ordinary legal facilities allowed us."[53]

The impact of press reporting in heightening the Government's frustrations and anxieties while dealing with the difficulty in proceeding with the Lahore Conspiracy Case is best represented in a note written by D. Patrie, Director Intelligence Bureau. *The Tribune* of 21st December and *Hindustan Times* of 23rd December had carried detailed reports of Lahore Conspiracy prisoners glorifying the Kakori heroes while celebrating 'Kakori Day' in the court room. This event drew an immediate response from the Director of Intelligence Bureau. In a note dated 24th December, he recorded:

"The appearance of this report has led me to give definite expression to the growing feeling of uneasiness created in my mind by the long drawn out proceedings in which they are being conducted….. I can not but feel that the impression produced on the public mind is far from every point of view deplorable. The proceedings are reported at great length day by day in the press, and they show undignified wrangles between the Magistrate and the accused with victory generally inclining to the side of latter. …. The press accounts invariably depict him as getting the worst of the exchanges, and anyone accepting such accounts at their face value could hardly have a vestige of respect left either for the Magistrate, the Court he presides over, or to the law he administers. Not only this, but the whole proceedings, as conducted and reported, are a skilfully staged drama for the glorification of the accused and their associates in the revolutionary movement… It seems to me invariable that unless something is done, both to shorten the proceedings… and to ensure that they are conducted with proper decorum, they will inevitably do more to stir up revolutionary activity than the conclusion of the case, if successful, can do to suppress it."[54]

British Government was coming round to the view that under ordinary law revolutionaries were able to use trial proceedings to their advantage. An extraordinary measure like special tribunal was necessary to deal with the situation. Government's fears were aggravated by the incident of revolutionaries' attempt to blow up the Viceroy's special train near Delhi on 23rd December. Immediately after this event, H.G. Haig, Home Member of the

Government, in his note of 24th December 1929, prepared the ground for a special ordinance to speed up the trial proceedings:

"The latest manifestation of revolutionary activity in the shape of the bomb outrage against His Excellency's Special Train brought very forcibly to my mind again the dangers of permitting this Lahore Case to drag on with its increasing advertisement of revolutionary criminals ...I am myself very definitely of opinion that if any action is to be taken, secure by ordinance of the more rapid disposal of the Lahore Case, this is the time to act, while the impression of the dastardly bomb outrage is still fresh in men's mind both in India and in England."[55]

Lord Irwin (Viceroy) himself was in full agreement with the opinion quoted above. He wrote on 27th December 1929: "I fully concur in every thing that is said in notes as to the deplorable effect created by the Lahore proceedings- and think no time should be lost in getting into touch with the Punjab Government."[56] Consequently, the Governor General decided to use his extraordinary powers to set up a special tribunal on 1st May 1930 to try the Lahore Conspiracy Case. Tribunal was to consist of three High Court judges. It had the power to proceed with the trial in the absence of the accused. The judgement of the Tribunal was to be final and conclusive and there could not be any appeal against its judgement. An important aspect which was not mentioned in the text of ordinance but was very much implicit was that the tribunal could not operate a day after six months of its formation. In short, the objective behind the formation of tribunal was to complete trial proceedings within six months, without being affected by any stratagem that the accused might apply to prolong or disrupt the trial proceedings.

In the statement accompanying the ordinance Irwin put the onus of delays and obstruction in trial on the hunger strike and "defiant and disorderly conduct by some of the accused or demonstrations by members of the public".[57] Bhagat Singh promptly wrote a letter next day (2nd May 1930) demolishing the Governor General's arguments. In his letter Bhagat Singh also pointed out that revolutionaries had not resorted to hunger strike to protract the trial but for the cause of fighting for the rights of the political prisoners. They were not afraid of the trial or the sentences which they considered as trivial. Ordinance itself was a moral victory for the accused as the sham justice of the government had been exposed. Government itself had now thrown off its veil and admitted that fair chances for defence could not be given to the political accused.[58]

Bhagat Singh was right; ordinance was a victory for the accused and defeat for the government. Sir Horace Williamson, who was the Director of Intelligence Bureau from 1931 to 1936, regarded the ordinance as a personal victory for Bhagat Singh:

"Bhagat Singh made no mistake. The prisoners' dock became a political forum and the countryside rang with his heroics. His photograph was on sale in every city and township and for a time rivalled in popularity even that of Mr. Gandhi himself. His antics and those of his confederates eventually succeeded in bringing the ordinary law to a standstill and in reducing the courts to a state of impotence and it became necessary in 1930 for the Governor General to promulgate a special ordinance, without which their trial might never have been brought to a conclusion."[59]

Trial proceedings under the Tribunal started on 5th May 1930. The accused repeated their earlier ritual in the courtroom like slogan shouting and revolutionary songs which was resented by the two European judges John Coldstream and G.C. Hilton. On 12th May things took a turn for worse when the judges ordered that accused should be handcuffed and sent back to the jail. Policemen jumped into the dock and began implementing the order with brute force. Most of the accused received injuries. The only Indian judge of the tribunal, Syed Agha Haider, could not tolerate this barbaric spectacle in the court. He dissociated himself from that order and its consequences. He was later removed from the Tribunal for his pro-accused stand. This incident helped the accused to get more public sympathy and popularity. All the accused agreed to follow a new strategy that from now on they will not attend the court i.e. refuse to take cognizance of the court. They agreed to follow the Bhagat Singh's line of action – to show utter unconcern for brute force, so as to produce a moral impact on the rest of the country and specially the young. Trial in the absence of the accused i.e. *ex-parte* trial would further expose the judicial process in the eyes of the civilized world. Government soon realised the trap in which it was struck. It tried unsuccessfully to induce the accused to attend the court and changed the president of the Tribunal who was responsible for that humiliating order. But the accused were adamant on a *volte-face* from the tribunal- they demanded the new President Justice Hilton, who was also a party to that order, to go as well.

So the trial proceeded in the absence of the accused as well as their counsels who could cross-examine the witness. The Government was in a hurry to send Bhagat Singh and his comrades to the gallows before the expiry of the term of Tribunal. But in the process, it fully exposed itself and thus the purpose of Bhagat Singh and his group was fulfilled.

The judgement of the case was a foregone conclusion. Attitude of the Tribunal and behaviour of the accused had left no doubts whatsoever. Sensing the fate of his son, Kishan Singh made a last moment effort to save the life of Bhagat Singh. In a petition to the Tribunal, dated 20th September 1930, he produced an alibi that Bhagat Singh was in Calcutta at the time of Saunders' murder.[60] Bhagat Singh's response to this move was more than that of an enraged son. In a strongly worded letter to his father, Bhagat Singh accused his father of showing "a weakness of the worst type." He used this opportunity to publicise the revolutionary strategy adopted during the trial:

"I had only one idea before me throughout the trial i.e. to show complete indifference towards the trial in spite of serious nature of the charges against us. I have always been of opinion that all the political workers should be indifferent and should never bother about the legal fight in the court of law and should boldly bear the heaviest possible sentences inflicted upon them. They may defend themselves but always from purely political considerations and never from a personal point of view....My life is not so precious, at least to me, as you may probably think it to be. It is not at all worth buying at the cost of my principles"[61]

Bhagat Singh also insisted that his letter should be published. The purpose was to guide the political workers facing charges accused across the country. Kishan Singh promptly sent this letter for publication in several newspapers of Hindi, Urdu and English languages.[62]

On 7th October 1930, 15 months after the trial began; the judgement was announced on the expected lines. Bhagat Singh, Sukhdev and Rajguru were sentenced to death. Tribunal fixed 27th October as the date for their hanging. Shiv Varma, Bejoy Kumar Sinha, Kishori Lal, Mahabir Singh, Gaya Prasad, Jai Dev and Kamal Nath Tiwari were sentenced to transportation for life. Kundan Lal and Prem Dutt were sentenced to seven and five years of rigorous imprisonment respectively. Ajoy Ghosh, Jitendra Nath Sanyal and Des Raj were aquitted.

From Judgement to Execution

This judgement raised a storm all over the country. Newspapers published the news under bold headings on front page – "BHAGAT SINGH SENTENCED TO DEATH." Several newspapers including *Abhyudaya* published special editions for several days to cope with the flood of news regarding countrywide agitation. Newspapers reported strikes, public demonstrations and meetings in all major cities. Highest pitch of the protests was heard in Lahore. Most of the schools and colleges in Lahore were closed and the few which remained open were picketed. *The Tribune* of 9th October reported 'two arrests every five minutes' in Lahore. Arrested persons included many women. A big procession attended by thousands of persons started from Pari Mahal and passed through the city shouting 'Inquilab Zindabad' and 'Bhagat Singh Zindabad'. Later, a public meeting was addressed outside Mori Gate by Mehta Anand Kishore, Kishan Singh, Shrimati Parbati Devi (daughter of Lala Lajpat Rai) and Arjun Singh (grandfather of Bhagat Singh). Ajoy Kumar Ghosh, Jatin Sanyal and Des Raj attended the meeting.[63] On 9th October women political prisoners observed fast in jail against the sentences.[64]

Ajoy Ghosh has written about Bhagat Singh's impact on public mind, soon after the death sentence was announced: "What Bhagat Singh had come to mean to our countrymen I realised only when I was out. "Bhagat Singh Zindabad" was the slogan that rent the air whenever a meeting was held…. His name was on the lips of millions, his image in every young man's heart."[65]

Jawahar Lal Nehru, while speaking at Allahabad on 12th October 1930 expressed his feelings about the death sentences of Bhagat Singh and his comrades:

> "Whether I agree with him or not, my heart is full of admiration for the courage and self sacrifice of a man like Bhagat Singh. Courage of the Bhagat Singh type is exceedingly rare. If Viceroy expects us to refrain from admiring his wonderful courage and the high purpose behind it, he is mistaken. Let him ask his own heart what he would have felt if Bhagat Singh had been an Englishman and acted for England."[66]

As soon as the initial rush of anger over the sentences subsided, the Defence Committee started legal efforts to save Bhagat Singh and an appeal to the Privy Council (highest court of appeal in British Empire) were planned. Moti Lal Nehru also sent a strong request for appeal in the Privy Council so as to buy some time for saving the lives of Bhagat Singh and his comrades. Bhagat Singh had the least interest in saving himself but was persuaded through the logic of political advantages that the appeal could bring. Appeal in Privy Council, he was told, would focus international attention on political misuse of judiciary, deplorable conditions of political prisoners in Indian jails and the gallant struggle of Lahore Conspiracy Case undertrials. Another important aspect was that such appeals would postpone the execution until the time when the movement to save Bhagat Singh, Sukhdev and Rajguru would be at its peak, for maximum mass awakening.[67] According to J.N. Sanyal, major role in persuading Bhagat Singh to appeal was played by Bejoy Kumar Sinha who had an astute political sense. Bejoy Kumar Sinha recalled later, "I argued that delayed executions would mean a much higher pitch of revolutionary propaganda in view of the nation wide campaign for commutation of the death sentence. He finally agreed but somewhat reluctantly."[68] The sole issue in the appeal to the Privy Council (16 October 1930) was the technical ground that Lahore Conspiracy Case Ordinance was *ultra vires.* Privy Council dismissed the appeal on 11th February 1931 without admitting it to a regular hearing. Rejection of appeal by the Privy Council came as a big blow to all interested in saving Bhagat Singh, Rajguru and Sukhdev. But legal efforts to save Bhagat Singh continued even after the rejection of the appeal, to the last hour.

After the failure of Privy Council appeal, the focus of efforts to save Bhagat Singh and others shifted to a mass signature campaign to force the Viceroy to commute the sentences. This campaign was organized by "Bhagat Singh Appeal Committees' formed throughout Punjab and also outside the province. The campaign attracted immense public interest. During 'Bhagat Singh Day' celebration in Lahore on February 17, huge demonstration took place. A mile long procession shouting 'Bhagat Singh Zindabad' and 'Inquilab Zindabad' passed through various places in Lahore.[69] *The Tribune* of 20th February, 1931 reported one lakh signatures in Lahore itself. Reports from smaller towns were also encouraging. Young boys and ladies in groups were going from street to street to collect signatures. Key feature of the movement for commutation was its universality. Even moderate newspapers like *The Tribune* had openly stated that they had 'no hesitation' in associating themselves with the demand for commutation of the sentence.[70] Akalis and representatives of several Muslim localities had also sent their own appeals to the Viceroy.

Movement was also strong in Bengal and Bombay. According to J.N. Sanyal, detenue revolutionaries in Buxa Camp in Bengal requested the Viceroy for commutation of the death sentence of Bhagat Singh, Rajguru and Sukhdev, failing which, they said, reprisals would follow. It was not an empty threat. After execution of the trio, District Magistrate of Midnapore and Tippera were murdered and some other violent actions were conducted in repraisal.[71] *Tribune*'s correspondent from Bombay reported: "the news of Bhagat Singh's impending execution has cast a gloom over the city. A move has been set afoot to present a clemency petition signed by more than five lakh people. For this purpose volunteers have been going round the city beating *batakis* and inviting people to sign the petition."[72]

Demands for commutation of the sentences were also raised in England. London correspondent of *The Tribune* wrote – " A storm of indignation has broken out in the Indian and Labour circles at the reports from India that to all intents and purposes the Government of India propose to carry out the death sentences awarded to Bhagat Singh and his two associates….. Labour circles demand that the least that Government can do is to extend to the prisoners a proper judicial trial with the help of a jury."[73] Some members of the House of Commons also urged the Viceroy to commute the sentences through a telegram dated 6th March 1931: "House of Commons Independent Labour Party group earnestly urges you in view of truce pardon Lahore Conspiracy Case prisoners"[74]

It must be noted here that after the rejection of the appeal by the Privy Council, Bhagat Singh, Sukhdev and Rajguru were given time till the 21st February, to file their mercy petition.[75] But the trio did not submit any petition. By the middle of March, the movement for commutation had reached its pinnacle. It was at this moment, Bhagat Singh the strategist, played his master stroke. He was waiting for this critical moment. By now hope of commutation had become strong. Countrywide agitation, supported by a majority of Congressmen, also put pressure on Gandhiji to enter into negotiations with the Viceroy over the question of commutation. Though Mahatma Gandhi did not make the commutation of Bhagat Singh and his comrades' death sentence a precondition for any settlement or pact with the Viceroy, nevertheless, Gandhiji was quite optimistic about Bhagat Singh's life being saved. (See below, Chapter: *Gandhi vs. Bhagat Singh: Myths and Facts*). There were also some legal complications in the execution of warrant of death sentence as the Tribunal which had ordered the death sentence as well as the Ordinance which had created the Tribunal had ceased to exist. To strengthen the chances of saving Bhagat Singh and his comrades, Bhagat Singh Defence Committee and the team of lawyers associated with it wanted to submit a mercy petition. Pran Nath Mehta, representing the Defence Committee, who also acted as a lawyer to the trio wanted to convince them that petition would be drafted in such a way as not to compromise with their honour. Pran Nath Mehta met Bhagat Singh in jail with this proposal. Bhagat Singh asked him to come next day with his proposed draft. Next day, before Pran Nath could show the draft to him, Bhagat Singh in his usual relaxed and jovial manner told him, "*Are Yaar*, we have already sent our mercy petition to the Government". Pran Nath was simply bewildered to read the text of Bhagat Singh's letter to the Punjab Governor dated 20th March: "What we wanted to point out was that according to the verdict of your court we had waged war and we are therefore war prisoners. And we claim to be treated as such, i.e., we claim to be shot dead instead of being hanged."[76] They also warned the British Government that the war shall continue unless every sort of exploitation is put to an end. Thus they demolished all chances of any mercy on part of the Government and cleared the way for their martyrdom though Mahatma Gandhi's efforts to save their lives continued till the day of their hanging, as will be narrated later.

The three heroes were hanged at 7 pm on 23rd March 1931. Elaborate security arrangements were planned in advance by the Government to deal with the possibility of public outburst to the news of execution. The Punjab Government in a secret telegram to the Central Government dated 18th March had confirmed that "Bhagat Singh, Rajguru and Sukhdev will be executed at 7 on the evening of March 23rd. The news will be made known in Lahore on early morning of March 24th."[77] But the general public was under the impression that hangings will take place on the morning of 24th March because Kishan Singh had been informed by the jail authorities to bring all blood relations for the last interview with Bhagat Singh on 23rd March.[78] But the interview could not take place because authorities were adamant that only blood relations will be allowed to interview and no body else like Bhagat Singh's aunts. The three were hanged the same evening contrary to the established practice that the hangings were done in the morning. Bodies of the three martyrs were not given to their relatives and were secretly and hurriedly put through last rites on the bank of river Sutluj in Hussainiwala near Firozpur. The news about the hangings and the last rites were made public in the early hours of 24th March 1931. The news appeared in the newspapers on 25th March only.

The Legend

News about the execution sent the whole country in shock. Entire nation mourned its heroes. Throughout the length and breadth of the country there were strikes, processions and meetings. *The Tribune* expressed the feelings of the general public in these words:

> "Indeed few events in our history at least in recent years have made such a tremendous sensation in the country and so widened the gulf between the Government and hundred of thousands of people all over the country as the execution of

the three prisoners…Everywhere the feeling manifested by the large numbers of people is one of profound indignation and by the people as a whole one of deep distress and dissatisfaction."[79]

Mahatma Gandhi in the course of his statement on martyrdom of Bhagat Singh candidly observed, "There never has been within living memory so much romance around any life as had surrounded that of Bhagat Singh."[80] Bhagat Singh became a legend in his life time and that legend has only grown further after he was no more. Its evidence is provided by the amount of literature that has been produced on him after his execution and continues to be produced 76 years later.

Execution of Bhagat Singh, Sukhdev and Rajguru led to a flood of adulatory articles in the press in praise of the three martyrs. Many newspapers like '*Abhyudaya*' and '*Bhavisya*' brought out special numbers on Bhagat Singh. Most of these publications were banned by the government immediately. From the British point of view, more damaging than the newspaper articles were the publications, mostly in verse, which were clandestinely circulated in public gatherings, religious functions, cattle fairs etc. Such publications in form of booklets, pamphlets, folders, tracts, and posters openly glorified the slain heroes and exhorted people to follow their examples. As soon as these publications came to the notice of the Government they were banned. Number of such proscribed writings ran into hundreds. A recent work- *'The Hanging of Bhagat Singh: The Banned Literature'*, has traced 153 such publications out of which 35 are miscellaneous items such as pictures and posters. These publications were spread over 11 languages including Bengali, Gujarati, Kanaɔse, Marathi, Sindhi, Tamil, and Telgu besides Hindi, English, Urdu and Punjabi. Surprisingly, largest number of writings after Hindi (54) is in Tamil (19). Learned author of the above mentioned book has concluded: "These publications are an indisputable proof that Bhagat Singh, within a short span of time, emerged as a national hero and his sacrifice kindled patriotic feelings in the hearts of the Indian masses living not only in northern parts of the country but living in the far flung areas too."[81]

Notes & References

[1] Pattabhi Sitaramaiyya, *The History of Indian National Congress*, Vol. I, 1946, p. 456.

[2] H.W Hale, *Political Trouble in India, 1917-37*, 1974, p. 64.

[3] *The Tribune*, 26 March, 1931.

[4] *The Bomb Incident*, 1958, pp. 44-45.

[5] Ibid.

[6] Ibid.

[7] *The Tribune*, 11 April, 1929.

[8] Bhagat Singh's letter to his father, 26 April, 1929.

[9] *The Tribune*, 9 May, 1929. Also reported by *Abhyudaya* of 18 May, 1929.

[10] All citations from the statement are sourced from Shiv Varma, *Selected Writing of Bhagat Singh*, 1996, pp. 66-70.

[11] J.N. Sanyal, *Amar Shahid Sardar Bhagat Singh*, translated by Sneh Lata Sehgal, (first published in 1947), 1999, p. 49.

[12] *The Tribune*, 8 June, 1929.

[13] N.A.I. Home Political, 1930, 130 & KW.

[14] J.N.Sanyal, *S. Bhagat* Singh, 1983, op. cit., p. 48.

[15] *The Tribune*, 15 June, 1929.

[16] S.Gopal (ed.,) *Selected Works of Jawaharlal* Nehru, Vol. 4, 1973, p. 8 cited in A.G. Noorani, *The Trial of Bhagat Singh*, 1996, p. 67.

[17] *Ahhyudaya*, 15 June, 1929, Similar observation was made by *The Tribune*, 14 June, 1929.

[18] *The Tribune*, 14 June, 1929.

[19] Shiv Verma, *Selected Writings of Bhagat Singh*, 1996, p. 86.

[20] Ibid.

[21] Ibid., p. 87.

[22] His younger brother Kultar Singh also agreed with this fact. Oral transcript of Kultar Singh, NMML, p. 61.

23 B.K.Dutt cited in Virender Sindhu, *Yugdrista Bhagat Singh Aur Unke Mritunjay Purkhe,* op. cit., p.196; J.N. Sanyal, (Hindi version of 1931 by Snehlata Sehgal, op. cit., p. 51).

24 N.A.I. Home Political, 244 & K.W., 1930.

25 *Abhyudaya,* 29 June, 1929.

26 Manmath Nath Gupta, op. cit., p. 169.

27 *Abhyudaya,* 29 June, 1929.

28 N.A.I. Home Political, 130&KW,1930.

29 Ibid.

30 Ibid.

31 S. Gopal (ed.), *Selected Works of Jawaharlal Nehru, Vol. IV*, 1957, pp. 8-9.

32 Ajoy Ghosh, *Bhopal Singh and his Comrades*, 1979, pp. 23-24.

33 J. N. Sanyal, *S. Bhagat Singh*, 1983, p. 62.

34 Ibid., pp. 62-64.

35 Oral Transcript of Lajjawati, NMML, p. 117.

36 Ibid.

37 J.N. Sanyal, 1983, op. cit., p. 65.

38 N.A.I. Home Political, 130 & KW, 1930.

39 *Abhyudaya*, 20th July 1929.

40 Home Political, 130 & KW, 1930.

41 Ajoy Ghosh, *Bhagat Singh and His Comrades,* 1979, pp. 24-28; Shiv Varma, *Sansmritiyan,* 1974, pp. 43-44, 99-101.

42 *Selected Works of Motilal Nehru*, Vol.VII, 1998, p. 479.

43 S. Gopal, (ed.), *Selected Works of Jawahar Lal Nehru*, Vol.4, 1957, p. 13.

44 *Abhyudaya*, 17th August 1929.

45 N.A.I., Home Political File, 244 & K.W., 1930.

46 Ibid.

47 Ibid.

48 A. G. Noorani, *The Trial of Bhagat Singh,* 1996, pp. 84 – 89.

49 Ibid, p. 93.

50 Ibid, p. 94.

51. *The Tribune,* 22nd October 1929 and Shiv Verma *Selected Writings of Shaheed Bhagat Singh,* 1996, p. 74.

52. Motilal Bhargava, *Role of Press in the Freedom Movement,* 1987, p. 101.

53. Ajoy Ghosh, op. cit., p. 30.

54. N.A.I. Home Political, 172/30, 1930.

55. Ibid.

56. Ibid.

57. A.G. Noorani, op.cit., p. 296.

58. Shiv Varma, *Selected Writings of Shaheed Bhagat Singh,* 1996, pp. 88-89.

59. Sir Horace Williamson, *India and Communism,* 1976, p. 275.

60. A.G. Noorani, op. cit., pp. 173-74.

61. *The Tribune,* 4th October, 1930. *Abhyudaya* of 5th October 1930 published excerpts from Bhagat Singh's letter under the heading – *"Adarsh Ke Aage Jeewan Ka Koi Mulya Nahi"* (Ideals are more valuable than life).

62. Virender Sindhu, *Yugdrista Bhagat Singh Aur Unke Mritunjay Purkhe,* op.cit., p. 222.

63. *The Tribune,* 9th October, 1930. The newspaper ran a long editorial in Lahore Conspiracy Case lasting 5 days, 9th October 1930 – 14th October 1930.

64. *The Tribune* 11th Oct 1930; *Abhyudaya,* 11th October, 1930.

65. Ajoy Ghosh, *Bhagat Singh and his Comrades,* 1979, p. 31.

66. S. Gopal, *Selected works of Jawahar Lal Nehru,* Vol IV, pp. 394 – 395.

67. J.N. Sanyal, *S.Bhagat* Singh, 1983, p. 71.

68. Srirajyam Sinha, *Bejoy Kumar Sinha: A Revolutionary's Quest for Sacrifice,* 1993, p. 63.

69. *The Tribune,* 19th February 1931.

70. *The Tribune,* 18th February 1931.

71. J.N. Sanyal, op. cit., 1983, pp. 69-70.

72. *The Tribune,* 5th March, 1931.

73. *The Tribune,* 6th March, 1931.

74 N.A.I. Home Political, 11/28/31 & KW, 1932 cited in G.S. Deol, op. cit., p. 92.

75 N.A.I. Home Political, 4/21/1931, 1931.

76 Shiv Varma, *Selected Writings of Bhagat Singh,* op. cit., 1996, pp. 132 –133.

77 N.A.I. Home Political, 4/21/31, 1931.

78 *The Tribune*, 20ᵗʰ March, 1931.

79 *The Tribune*, 27ᵗʰ March, 1931.

80 *The Tribune*, 29ᵗʰ March, 1931.

81 Gurudev S. Sidhu, *The Hanging of Bhagat Singh: The Banned Literature*, 2007, p. vii.

8

Bhagat Singh:

The Man in the Eyes of his Comrades

In the popular imagination, Bhagat Singh is established as a great martyr who terrorized the British Government and inspired many with his bravery and courage. But the persona of Bhagat Singh, the man, is best expressed in the opinion of his friends, colleagues and contemporaries. Some of them have left behind their reminiscences and memoirs, which put together, bring to light various facets of Bhagat Singh's personality. What emerges is a multifaceted personality - lovable, studious, romantic and yet the bravest of braves. In Asaf Ali's words, "I had numerous occasions...to interview them, and I found Bhagat Singh a most lovable person, and B.K. Dutt one of the most affectionate, and both of them were certainly two of the bravest young men I had ever come across. Bhagat Singh was very handsome and was perhaps one of the gentlest and the most affectionate in temperament - the very antithesis of hard and blood-thirsty revolutionary. He showed brilliant intelligence almost beyond his years, and had he been spared, he would have been an outstanding personality in any field of life"[1]

Narrating his first meeting with Bhagat Singh, Ajay Ghosh wrote: "I believe it was some time in 1923 that I met Bhagat Singh for the first time. A young boy of about my age ...I was fifteen at that time. Tall and thin, rather shabbily dressed, very quite, he seemed a typical village lad lacking smartness and self- confidence. I did not think very highly of him at that time and told Dutt so when he was gone"[2]

However, this picture of Bhagat Singh had changed completely by 1928. Ajoy Ghosh continues: "One day in 1928 I was surprised when a young man walked into my room and greeted me. It was Bhagat Singh but not Bhagat Singh that I had met two years ago. Tall and magnificently propositioned, with a keen intelligent face and gleaming eyes, he looked a different man altogether. And as he talked I realised that he had grown not merely in years."[3]

Writing about the physical strength of Bhagat Singh, Bhagwan Das Mahaur has narrated a wrestling bout between Bhagat Singh and Chandra Shekhar Azad that took place in their Agra centre in 1928:

"After this, the bathing session began. Bhagat Singh put oil on Azad's back and Azad on Bhagat Singh's. Then they massaged each other's arms. Then they began to warm up which eventually ended in a wrestling bout. Bhagat Singh lifted Azad in his both hands and threw him on the ground, which bruised Azad's knees. I considered Azad to be a very powerful man. But now it was Bhagat Singh's prowess which had made a deep impact on me."[4]

His physique and physical strength apart, what struck the people most who met him for the first time was his disarming and friendly demeanure. Ajoy Ghosh noted: "Of affectionate nature, tender towards ailing comrades, frank and open hearted, with no trace of pettiness in his make up, he was a man who claimed the love of all who were even acquainted with him."[5] Shiv Varma has also left an account of his first meeting with Bhagat Singh in Kanpur in the last part of the year 1926:

"One morning when I was doing my college work in my room, I heard someone outside enquiring about my address from my neighbor. On hearing my name I came out to find a young Sikh, wearing dirty Salwar Kameej, his body wrapped in a blanket, standing in front of me. Tall in stature, fair complexioned, small piercing eyes, downy beard on a handsome face, long hair and a turban. 'He is Shiv Varma', the neighbor said on seeing me.

"The stranger enthusiastically embraced me as if he was an old friend. Pulling my hand, he entered the room as if the room belonged to him and not me... Ranjit's (Bhagat Singh's) easy manners, guileless laughter and smiling eyes had disarmed me in the very first meeting, and now it was impossible for me to disbelieve him."[6]

Open and frank nature of Bhagat Singh, which used to shock people at first sight, later became a part of his loving memory. Chatursen Shastri, the celebrated litterateur and editor of the *Phansi* number of '*Chand*' (1928) remembered Bhagat Singh in the following manner:

"A strange man! Sometimes talks non-sense like a child, sometimes becomes very serious, and sometimes, when he becomes furious, he does not spare any one, whether young or old ... No courtesies, no love of food or clothing. He is so outspoken that sometimes he scolds even me. But talks to me as if he is talking to his father. Calls me 'Babuji' – whether in anger or in a cheerful mood ... Out and out an eccentric ... comes to me only for two things, either to scold me or to ask for money ... In both cases without any embarrassment or hesitation. Very straightforward. Scolds me by calling me a coward – 'You don't do anything, despite being such a big literary figure.' This is what he says. When he needs money, he says, 'Give me some money Babuji.'"[7]

A striking aspect of Bhagat Singh's personality was his keen sense of humour. Bhagwan Das Mahaur was one of those who had to bear the brunt of Bhagat Singh's practical jokes the most. Peculiar facial features of Mahaur had caused Bhagat Singh to refer to him as 'Darwin's missing link' (between men and the monkey).[8] Rajaram Shastri narrates a similar incident in detail:

"One day Bhagat Singh came to me and asked me whether I would do him a favour? "Yes, what is that"? I said. "I will do if I could". He took out a picture from his pocket. He had, I think, torn it from some magazine. It was a picture of an ape. A good friend of ours was somewhat like an ape. Bhagat singh also used to call him 'ape' in his lighter talks. He wanted me to send this picture to him. Not only that, he also wanted me to convey his reaction on seeing it.

I laughed on seeing the picture and said, "You are really a naughty man, Bhagat Singh. If he comes to know that it is your work, he will be angry with you. You shouldn't do such things". "Brother, do it", he pleaded. "I want to enjoy his reaction. If you won't do it, I will send by post under your signatures". "If you do this", I said, "I will tell the whole thing and convince him that you are the villain of the piece". I don't know whether Bhagat Singh sent that picture to him or not!..." [9]

Bhagat Singh's friendly banter was at his best during meal times. His friends in Lahore recalled him sharing their meal almost forcefully. In those days, Bhagat Singh was usually short of money. Moreover, he avoided going to his village, as his father did not approve of his activities and long absence from home. Yashpal narrated the usual scene at the hotel :

"Bhagat Singh was always reluctant to go to home. Ramkrishna, after graduation, had opened a neat and clean hotel on Mohanlal Road. All of us had started going there for food. Whenever any of us was having food in the hotel and if Bhagat Singh with both ends of his turban dangling on his shoulders happened to pass by, he would enter the hotel, and taking a chair would join us without any formality, fold one chapatti into a bowl and siphon out all the ghee in the dal bowl and swallow it in one go. If Bhagat Singh spotted Raja Ram Shastri in the hotel, he would, hungry or not, leaving aside all essential work, drink all the ghee out of Shastri's bowl. "See, see what he is doing. See this Jat." Shastri would be calling for help in vain."

Rajaram Sastri has also described such incidents–

"In fact, Bhagat Singh full of humour as he was, would never lose a chance to make the atmosphere pleasantly light. He would often come to the Ramakrishna hotel to tease me. No matter whether it was noontime or in the evening, he would act the same way. He would sit opposite to me, tell some interesting story and start sharing my food. This, I used to mind, and in anger, I would inveriably scold him: "What is this? These dirty hands and all that? Why this encroachment without even a formality of seeking my permission? I donot like this. If you are hungry, say so. I will get you a plate". "No, no, it is not that", Bhagat Singh would retort innocently. "I am not that hungry. But if you insist what can I do? Order for a plate". Moreover, once the plate came, his next demand would be there, "How about a little *ghee*?" And then after some time he would say: "If you take something sweet after a meal, it adds up to its taste", and he would order for two plates (*katoris*) of *kheer*....

If some day the duo – Bhagat Singh and Sukhdev – were there, then it would be a bigger crisis. Sittings on my either sides, they would order plenty of things. One would say, "Raja Ram likes this thing". Another would complete the phrase: "Why don't you ask for it then? Raja Ram is not going to say no". "You eat whatever you like", I would say, and with a touch of anger, "Why do you drag my name?" Bhagat Singh liked *rasgullas* very much. He was crazy for them and would not rest unless he had put a lot of them in his belly. What wonderful days those were!"[10]

As is clear from the above incident, Bhagat Singh's jocularity was at it's peak while in the company of Sukhdev. Rajaram Shastri narrates, another incident:

"Bhagat Singh and Sukhdev used to come to my room in the dead of night. On most of the occasions, they found me in deep sleep. They would, however bang my door three to four times. On my opening the door, they would rush in. I would rush to my cot for there was only one cot and I did not want to lose it. Anyway, after taking off their shirts, etc. they would speak in a low tone, though meant for me to be heard? "Let Raja Ram sleep. We will sit and talk something".

"After a while, they would come and sit on my cot-one on its one side and the other on the other. Then they would slowly spread themselves on the cot and push me from both sides. Fearing being crushed between them, I would get up to sleep on the floor.

"The matter wouldn't end there. Bhagat Singh would then say to Sukhdev: "Sukhdev, we have to admit that Raja Ram is a thorough gentleman. He couldn't tolerate our inconvenience and left his comfortable bed for us." Sukhdev would reply in almost the same tone : "Yes, indeed he is a true friend. He cares a lot for us. See, he did't utter a word and took to the floor bed". This was too much to tolerate and breaking down a little, I would say angrily: "Stop this nonsense. First, you snatched my cot and then you are making a fool of me. Sleep on or else I will thrash you and throw you out". Bhagat Singh would, then speak: "Raja Ram's anger is justified. Socialism says that we should also get down from the cot, and sleep on the floor. Discomfort should be shared equally". And the next moment, placing the cot against the wall, they would also sleep on the floor by my side. What next ? A lot of laughter and deep sleep!

"This was not one-time occurrence. Whenever they came together in the night, the drama would be enacted in, by and large, the same manner."[11]

Besides being a funloving and lively youth Bhagat Singh was also attracted towards beauty, music and art.[12] Bejoy Kumar Sinha has observed that Bhagat Singh had the temperament of an artist.[13] Bhagat Singh was quite crazy for movies and shortage of money did not come in the way of watching the movie that he wished to see, even if it meant missing a meal. Mahaur writes about such an incident in Lahore :

"After emerging from hall, we came to know from posters that a film 'Uncle Tom's Cabin' was being shown in Lahore. Bhagat Singh proposed that this revolutionary film, which shows the Blacks' fight for their freedom in America, must be seen. However, there was no money. We used to get four annas daily for our meals... I had with me one and a half rupees for the evening meals, and next day's noon meals of three comrades. Bhagat Singh asked me to give that money to him. But I was given this money by Azad for meals. How could I give it to him? Bhagat Singh got angry and delivered a long lecture on the uses of art.

"These developments were taking place, and feet of all of us were moving towards the cinema Hall. At last, Bhagat Singh put the last proposal: "If you don't give me money, I will snatch it". I also wanted to see the film so I told him not to misbehave on the road. "Take this money", I said, "but mind you it is not being given to you. You are forcibly snatching it from me". "Ok, let it be that", he said.... Eventually, we saw the movie. It was just excellent.

"Bhagat Singh gave a very impressive lecture on the film and underlined the usefulness of it for the revolutionaries before Azad in such a way that the question of money being returned did not arise. Next day, we received our money for the noon meals all right. Bhagat Singh winked at me and smiled." [14]

Yashpal has also written about a funny incident related to Bhagat Singh's craze for movies:

"Jaidev Gupta had promised to take Bhagat Singh along to the cinema in the evening. Bhagat Singh, from wherever he was, came back in the evening, not willing to miss the cinema. He found Jaidev lying on the bed, relaxing with a novel. Bhagat Singh gave a kick on Jaidev's legs and shouted "Get up, have you forgotten the promise about cinema?" Jaidev, still lying, scolded him in an irritated tone, "What a strange rustic, I am unwell and you are thinking of the cinema. I have just returned from the doctor's. See that medicine.' He pointed towards the bottle lying on the table.

"Bhagat Singh asked sympathetically, 'What's wrong with you?' Jaidev replied in a serious tone, 'The doctor has diagnosed dyspepsia.'

"On hearing this English word, Bhagat Singh became silent. The inability to go to the cinema had irritated him. Picking up a dictionary he sat quietly on a chair and started searching for the meaning of 'dyspepsia.' Having found the meaning he threw the dictionary on the table. He once again kicked Jaidev's on his back and made him stand up by pulling his hand. 'You scoundrel, by overeating you have invited indigestion. And are sleeping like a lazy man, and will now stuff yourself with medicine. You want to scare me by calling it dyspepsia.'

"Jaidev kept on pleading unsuccessfully that he was not feeling well. But Bhagat Singh's argument was, 'You have indigestion. You should not eat anything in the evening. So whatever money you have, give it to me for the cinema. If you don't want to go, then don't go.'"[15]

Bhagat Singh was also fond of singing and had a good voice. He used to break into singing whenever he was in the company of friends and sometimes even when alone. Aruna Asaf Ali was once surprised to hear Bhagat Singh singing in a melodious voice in his solitary cell.[16]

Like a normal boy of his age, Bhagat Singh was also attracted toward the opposite sex. Yashpal has written that while in Lahore, Bhagat Singh also had a crush on a college going girl:

"Bhagat Singh, in his imagination, had made a thin and pale looking girl studying in a college, the 'Mansi' of 'Mewar Patan'. I don't remember now the story of 'Mewar Patan' but I still remember the Mansi of Bhagat Singh. This Mansi too had not made any promises to Bhagat Singh. It was merely Bhagat Singh's spontaneous attraction towards an educated, cultured-looking girl. So, when this Mansi did not find patriotism her cup of tea and got engaged to a well-dressed and well-behaved rich young man, Bhagat Singh's tower of ideals also collapsed."[17]

Apart from this temporary and obviously one sided romance, there in no other incident of this kind. It is true that, when HSRA had decided against sending Bhagat Singh for the Assembly action, Sukhdev had blamed Bhagat Singh's attraction towards a girl responsible for erosion in Bhagat Singh's commitment toward revolutionary objective of self sacrifice. But Bhagat Singh's letter to Sukhdev is a sufficient evidence to clear him of the blemish.[18] Rajaram Shastri in his memoirs has also thrown light on Bhagat Singh's views on love:

"Sometimes we also used to discuss love affairs, especially when Yashpal was around. Bhagat Singh never initiated such discussions. Nevertheless, when it was there somehow, he would intervene in his own way. Sometimes Sukhdev will say that Yashpal was doing a lot of physical exercise. However, not in an *akhara* or in a field but on the rooftop of his house. He also used to exhibit his well-developed muscles on such occasions.

"Bhagat Singh used to tease him, "Tell me the truth Yashpal, you are doing exercise or attracting some girl?" Yashpal would reply in still lighter vein, "I take my exercise. But if some girl looks at me what can I do?" This would lead to a light debate on the science of love.

"One day I asked Bhagat Singh, "Will you ever think of marriage or remain busy only with your revolution all the while"? His reply was, "Brother, for real love you have to have free atmosphere in the society so that the young couple may enjoy a love life without any objection from any side. We have been born in a slavish atmosphere. Our society doesn't permit real, true love. True love, not lust, lifts a person very high, it gives solace, it inculcates the spirit to die for one another".

"Once while discussion this topic, he became very serious. "What has happened, Brother", I asked him. Bhagat Singh said, "We are young men of a slave country. Our first and foremost task is to destroy these shackles of bondage. In this birth, we have to sacrifice our life for the motherland we may have to kiss the death-rope too. How can we get to love (somebody) in such circumstances?

"In this birth I will mount the gallows. However, when I will be born again in free India, I will play in some beloved's lap and bathe myself in her love to the best of my ability. Brother, I will not get married in this birth. I am a young man. There is hot blood flowing in my veins. The feeling of love is also alive in my heart. But it is not as strong as to lead me astray from my path of duty". We discussed this matter for pretty long time that day."[19]

But all those who knew Bhagat Singh agree that if there was a permanent love in his life, apart from his love for the motherland, it was for books. Shiv Varma has written that "though neary all our comrades involved in the case (Lahore Conspiracy Case) had good interest in reading and writing, Bhagat Singh was ahead of all in this field".[20] One of his demands for which he went on hungerstrike in Jail was 'literature of all kinds' which he himself elaborated as "history, economics, political science, poetry, drama or fiction, newspapers".[21] When he was a student at National College, his love for books had been noticed by his teachers, especially Principal Chhabildas. Chhabildas's daughter, Manorama Diwan, in a biography of her parents has written: "Our father used to say that Bhagat Singh was both a passionate revolutionary and a brilliant student. Being his teacher, I can certainly assert that he was very fond of studies … Whenever the name of any book was mentioned to Bhagat Singh, he at once expressed his wish to read it."[22]

His craving for books made him a regular visitor to Dwarka Das Library in Lahore where he met its librarian Rajaram Shastri and the two became good friends. About the type of books that Bhagat Singh used to study, Rajaram Shastri writes :

"A long time has elapsed, so I cannot recall the titles of all those books that Bhagat Singh used to read and circulate among his friends, but I still remember the name of some of the books. In the beginning, Bhagat Singh used to read more of the books that were about underground revolutionaries and fighting heroically against tyrannical rulers and men in power. *'My Fight for Irish Freedom'*, by the Irish revolutionary Dan Breen, was Bhagat Singh's favourite book. A small biography of Vir Savarkar in English was available in Dwarkadas Library. It was written in a simple yet forceful manner. Specially, one event in Savarkar's life, in which he jumped from the ship into the sea and swam to the shores of France, was very thrilling. Bhagat Singh was greatly impressed by this event. He got the book issued in his name many times and passed it onto other young men to read. A book titled *'Revolution in Italy and Biographies of Mazzini and Garibaldi'* was also among his favourite books. Another of his favourite books was *'Cry for Justice'*. This book was a collection of thoughts of those who had raised their voice for justice and suffered for their convictions ... Bhagat Singh got this book issued frequently and recommended other young men to read it."[23]

Rajaram Shastri makes a special mention of Bhagat Singh's liking for revolutionary novels:

"Sometimes he used to complain to me about the unavailability of revolutionary novels in the library. I used to search these novels for him. I still remember the titles of some of them : Gorky's *'Mother'*; Victor Hugo's *'Ninety-Three'* and *'Les Miserables'*; *'A Tale of Two Cities'* (by Charles Dickens) ... (Upton) Sinclair's *'Boston'* and *'King Cole'* etc. Another book was *'Heroes and Heroines of Russia'*."[24]

Central to Bhagat Singh's deep love for books was his inquisitive nature. According to Jogesh Chandra Chatterjee- "his inquistiveness was insatiable, and he was no blind follower. His youthful mind was ever alert to assess and grasp any new idea".[25]

Because of his intensive studies, at a young age of 20-22 years, Bhagat Singh was able to leave a lasting impression on all who met him. Besides being a good reader, Bhagat Singh was also a good speaker. His colleagues were impressed by the way he talked. Shiv Varma descibed Bhagat Singh's manner of speech when in a serious discussion as 'slow, steady and measured tone'. Ajoy Ghosh observed:

"Those who met Bhagat Singh ... have testified to his remarkable intelligence and to the powerful impression he made when talking. Not that he was a brilliant speaker. But he spoke with such force, passion and earnestness that one could not help being impressed".[26]

By virtue of his qualities, Bhagat Singh had emerged as a leader of the revolutionary party. Like an ideal leader, he led from the front and did not impose his leadership which came naturally to him. Mahaur reminisced:

"Bhagat Singh was, no doubt, one of the leaders of the party; in fact in terms of his involvement in the party work he was the biggest leader but he always took care not to put on the airs of a leader. He always kept on bridging the gap between the leader and the follower through his sense of humour. He always took care of this in the day to day activities. He never believed that the leader should sit idle and the followers do all the hard work. At times he would wash my clothes but without giving the least impression that he was trying to show off that a leader was doing the washing for a follower...."

"In case of any dangerous work, he insisted on leading from the front. Bhagat Singh believed that as a leade. he must expose himself to the maximum danger, otherwise the followers will lose confidence in the leader ... Throwing bombs in the Assembly and killing of Saunders involved some fame, but Bhagat Singh was also in the forefront of actions that involved imminent danger and no fame. For example, there was the question of testing a new bomb ..... Azad, Bhagat Singh and Sadashiv proceeded with the task. When the bomb was finally ready to be tested, Bhagat Singh himself held the bomb in his hands and threw it but only after he had made sure that Azad and Sadashiv stood well behind at a safe distance." [27]

Bhagwan Das Mahaur has thus painted an idealistic picture of Bhagat Singh as a leader. In contrast, Shiv Varma while discussing Sukhdev has given a different assessment of Bhagat Singh as a leader vis a vis Sukhdev. To quote Shiv Varma, "Compared to his own tastes and preferences in food and dress, Bhagat Singh was less concerned about the needs of his comrades; on the other hand, Sukhdev gave priority to the needs and tastes of his comrades and neglected his own." [28]

Despite being a leader of revolutionary party and believing in efficacy of all possible means to fight the British government, Bhagat Singh was a man full of emotions. In the words of J.N. Sanyal, "he had a heart full of emotion. Even in the characters of fiction, he used to take extraordinary interest, and used to suffer and enjoy with them." [29] Dinanath Siddhantalankar, with whom Bhagat Singh worked in *Arjun* during 1924-25 has written in his memoirs:

"Often at night he would sit all alone on the roof top and keep crying. For many days, I thought it was because of some family problems. One night, when I woke at around twelve o' clock, I found him sobbing loudly. I consoled him. Then I asked the reason behind his distress. After remaining silent for some time he told me that his heart was shattered because of the plight of the nation. On the one hand there was the tyranny of the foreigner, and on the other the countrymen were bent upon cutting each others' throats. In such a situation how shall the motherland win its freedom." [30]

Sensitivity of Bhagat Singh came to the fore after he participated in Saunders' murder. Shiv Varma made the following observation after the event:

"It was Bhagat Singh's own proposal to kill Lalaji's killer in order to avenge the national insult. Yet, for several days after

Saunders was shot dead, his mind remained agitated. He was a revolutionary but not blood thirsty. His objective was to make the entire humanity happy and for this reason his concern for human life was obvious."[31]

Bhagwan Das Mahaur has described the same situation in the following words:

"His face that I saw that day is fixed forever in my mind's eye. There was some emotion written on his broad forehead which I cannot describe. He had unlimited respect for human life and its importance and above all its beauty.

"Bhagat Singh had participated in the killing of two persons. He was so agitated that his restrained voice could not hide his perturbation. While talking, he frequently became silent and then remaining quiet for some time he resumed talking. At the same time he also tried to smile. Value of human life, its significance and above all its beauty occupied the highest place in his heart."[32]

Bhagat Singh considered human life as sacred, but when it came to sacrifice his own life for the cause of the nation, this very idea invigorated him. Inevitibility of the death sentence did not let him lose his cheerfulness in the court. Satyadev Vidyalankar in his memoirs gave an account of the court proceedings:

"During the long course of his trial, the Sardar was not even once seen gloomy. His cheerfulness never allowed others to become sad. Occasionally, during the court proceedings, he used to crack jokes with the prosecution witnesses, police officials, and even the Magistrate. Sometimes, his sarcastic humour used to make the entire courtroom reverberate with laughter. His liveliness kept the courtroom environment live."[33]

According to J.N.Sanyal, "From the moment of his arrest till the twilight on the evening of the 23rd March, when Bhagat Singh stepped out of his cell to commence his glorious and final journey, there was not a moment in his life when any gloomy thought entered his mind."[34]

Bhagat Singh was at his best at the hour of his death. His counsel, Pran Nath Mehta, who was the last one to meet Bhagat Singh from outside the jail, writes :

"On that day I was privileged to stay near Sirdar Bhagat Singh's condemned cell for nearly an hour… I had witnessed him as a hungerstriker, and had seen him in action in the courts, but I had never felt that he was that courageous and so great … In that atmosphere of death, I felt shaken, but he seemed to be entrenched firmly in the faith that looks through death. He seemed to be so much at peace with himself; he was so free from fear and unattached that he appeared to be divine".[35]

Bhagat Singh's exceptional qualities earned him a place in the heart of every Indian. It would be educative to see him from the eyes of Jayachandra Vidyalankar, a person who spotted him, groomed him as a revolutionary and then followed his entire career. Soon after the martyrdom of Bhagat Singh, Jayachandra Vidyalankar wrote:

"The young man (Bhagat Singh) who was suspected to be the murderer of Saunders could have easily committed, had he wished, many such actions by remaining underground, beyond the reach of the authorities; and that could have caused a sort of terror in the hearts of the enemies of the country and given solace and strength to the sufferers at their hands. I don't know how far was it correct for such a young man to have got himself arrested for doing such a small job (throwing bomb in the Assembly). But as far as I am concerned, I wouldn't have been happy even seeing Bhagat Singh doing the former job - that is leading a band of some 10 to 20 guerrillas and doing daring deeds (to frighten the rulers and encouraging his countrymen)- for I have always visualized a different Bhagat Singh. He had infinite potential to be one who could, after receiving proper education in warfare, lead, at an appropriate moment, the armies for the liberation of India and be arbiter to decide the fate of the battles fought for changing her history.

That Bhagat Singh had capacity and capabilities to play such roles would't be known to the persons who are full of him only after seeing a small part played by him."[36]

Notes & References

[1] Asaf Ali, "An Outstanding Maker of History," published in *Commonwealth* (Pune) on 23rd March 1949. This article was republished in M.M. Juneja, ed., *Selected Collections on Bhagat Singh*, 2007, pp. 125-132.

[2] Ajoy Ghosh, *Bhagat Singh and his Comrades*, 1979, p. 17.

[3] Ibid., p. 20.

[4] Bhagwan Das Mahour and others, *Yash Ki Dharohar*, 2006, p. 30.

[5] Ajoy Ghosh, op. cit., p. 28.

[6] Shiv Varma, *Samsmritiyan*, 1974, pp. 13-14.

[7] Chatursen Shastri, *Meri Atmakahani*, 1963, pp. 155-156.

[8] *Yash Ki Dharohar*, op.cit. p. 29.

[9] Rajaram Shastri, *Amar Shaheedon ke Sanamaran*, 1981, pp. 76-77.

[10] Rajaram Shastri, op. cit., pp. 72-74.

[11] Ibid., pp. 70-72.

[12] Shiv Varma, op.cit., p. 24.

[13] Bejoy Kumar Sinha, *The Tribune*, 23rd March 1967, cited in G.S.Deol, *Shaheed-i-Azam Sardar Bhagat Singh: Man and His Ideiology*, 1978, p. 102.

[14] *Yash Ki Dharohar*, op. cit., p. 39.

[15] Yashpal, *Simhavalokan*, p. 70.

[16] Virender Sindhu, *Yugdrista Bhagat Singh Aur Unke Mritunjay Purkhe*, 2004, p. 266.

[17] Yashpal, op. cit., p. 94.

[18] Virender Sindhu, *Patra Aur Dastavej*, 1996, pp. 25-27.

[19] Rajaram Shastri, op. cit., pp. 81-83.

[20] Shiv Varma, op. cit., p. 44.

[21] N.A.I. Home Political, 244 & K.W., 1930, p. 5.

[22] Manorama Diwan, *Inqlabi Yatra*, 2006, p. 39.

23 Rajaram Shastri, op. cit., pp. 97-98.

24 Ibid., p. 11.

25 Jogesh Chandra Chatterji, *In Search of Freedom,* 1967, p. 221.

26 Ajoy Ghosh, op. cit., p. 20.

27 *Yash Ki Dharohar*, op. cit., pp. 41-43.

28 Shiv Varma, op. cit., pp. 94-95.

29 J.N.Sanyal, *S. Bhagat Singh*, 1983, p. 80.

30 Virender Sindhu, *Yugdrista Bhagat Singh Aur Unke Mritunjay Purkhe,* op.cit., p. 262.

31 Shiv Varma, op. cit., p. 31.

32 *Yash Ki Dharohar*, op.cit., p. 40.

33 Virender Sindhu, *Yugdrista Bhagat Singh Aur Unke Mritunjay Purkhe,* op.cit., pp. 267-268.

34 J.N. Sanyal, op. cit., p. 83.

35 Manmathnath Gupta, *Bhagat Singh and His Times*, 1977, pp. 193-194.

36 *Abhyudaya,* 8th May 1931, p. 7.

Ideology

G.S. Deol, K.K. Khullar; 28th September 1907 - Virender Sindhu; 5th October 1907 - Mathura Das Thapar, Shiv Verma; 19th October 1907 - K.C. Yadav; 27th October 1907 - J.N. Sanyal; and 28th December 1907 - Ram Chandra, Manmath Nath Gupta. Apart from these dates there is a date of birth based on Hindu calendar – *Bishwin Trivada di Shukla Vikrami Samvat* (964, Saturday)*. This date of birth appeared in the short biographies of Bhagat Singh which appeared in *Bhawishya* of 4th April 1931 and *Abhudaya* of 8th May 1931 (Bhagat Singh number) and some authors have also mentioned it. Lack of consensus on Bhagat Singh's date of birth justifies the opinion of Prithvi Singh Azad, a noted revolutionary himself, in his write up on Bhagat Singh in *Dictionary of National Biography* that exact date of birth of Bhagat Singh is not known.

Bhagat Singh completed his primary school education in his village Banga. Later, he was admitted to D.A.V. school, Lahore. Bhagat Singh left D.A.V. School in 1921 during the Non-Cooperation movement. He also worked as a Congress volunteer and actively participated in the boycott of foreign goods during the Non-Cooperation movement. To enroll the non-cooperating students, Congress had planned to establish national schools and colleges throughout the country. Consequently the Punjab Provincial Congress formed a Board of National Education in early 1921. As a result, a national university under the name of 'Punjab Qaumi Vidyapeeth' was established with Lala Lajpat Rai as its Chancellor and Bhai Parmanand as its Vice-Chancellor. Lala Lajpat Rai had earlier established the "Tilak School of Politics' in December 1920 with the objective of evolving a band of life members to be trained in different departments of national work. With the starting of Non-Cooperation movement, Tilak School of Politics was practically suspended in favour of National College, Lahore (under the auspices of Punjab Qaumi Vidyapeeth). National College, Lahore was formally started on 16 May 1921.

Bhagat Singh was in ninth class when he left D.A.V. School to join National College where the students could take admission

9

Patriotic Quest for Martyrdom

(1)

At the age of hardly sixteen years when Bhagat Singh left home in 1923 to join the revolutionary party, the very first line of the letter that he had left behind for his father revealed his life's mission: "My life has already been dedicated to a noble cause - the cause of freedom of India."[1] Seven stormy years passed by and Bhagat Singh became the 'symbol of revolution'. While awaiting death sentence in the prison cell in October 1930, Bhagat Singh pondered over his life in an essay titled *'Why I am an Atheist'*: "With no selfish motive or desire to be awarded here or hereafter, quite disinterestedly, have I devoted my life to the cause of independence, because I could not do otherwise."[2] Patriotism thus remained the guiding spirit of Bhagat Singh throughout his revolutionary career.

Man is the product of his heredity and social environment. Bhagat Singh had inherited the legacy of patriotism, and sacrifice from his family. Ingrained in his inherited values was the Arya Samaj's message of patriotism and nationalism. Arya Samaj was the nursery of patriotism in the early 20th century Punjab. Bhagat Singh's formative influences included the martyrdom of Kartar Singh Sarabha and other Ghadar heroes, the tragedy of Jallianwala Bagh, the valour of Babbar Akalis and a cumulative impact of his close contacts with die hard patriots like Jai Chandra Vidyalankar, Bhai Parmanand, and Sachindra Nath Sanyal. (See above chapter: *Background and the Formative Phase)*. As a result of his early influences he nursed the highest form of patriotism i.e. martyrdom or the ideal of supreme sacrifice for the nation, so as to awaken and inspire the people to rise against the colonial rulers. The ideal of martyrdom remained the foremost quest throughout his revolutionary career.

Bhagat Singh's revolutionary career started in Kanpur in the illustrious company of revolutionaries like Sachindra Nath Sanyal, Jogesh Chandra Chatterji, and Chandra Shekhar Azad. The revolutionary party had firm belief in the dictum: *"The food on which the tender plant of liberty thrives is the blood of the martyr."*[3] The romance of sacrificing his life for the nation remained with Bhagat Singh throughout his short life. A few months before his death, while in the condemned cell, he came across the original citation of Thomas Jefferson and promptly noted it down in his notebook: "The tree of liberty must be refreshed from time to time with the blood of patriots and tyrants. It is its natural manure."[4]

Bhagat Singh's ideas on patriotism and self sacrifice were further strengthened and refined by his study of patriotic literature. He was particularly fond of revolutionary novels like Gorky's '*Mother*'; Victor Hugo's '*Ninety Three*' and '*Les Miserables*'; '*Tale of Two Cities*'; and Sinclair's '*Jungle*', '*Boston*' and '*King Kol*'.[5] Such novels must have added to the romance of martyrdom present in Bhagat Singh's mind. Some of these books also had a deep role in shaping his personality and viewpoint. Jaidev recalled about *Ninty Three*, Victor Hugo's classic on French revolution: "this book inspired Bhagat Singh very much, it made his character, what sort of man one should be, what is good, what is bad and in what circumstances how one should behave." Dan Breen's *My Fight for Irish Freedom*, in the opinion of Jaidev, was 'his gospel'.[6] Raja Ram Shastri, the librarian of Dwarka Das Library in Lahore, adds to the list of favourite books of Bhagat Singh the biographies of V.D. Savarkar, Mazzini, and Garibaldi and Upton Sinclair's *The Cry for Justice*.[7] He got reprinted Savarkar's *War of Indian Independence* clandestinely and secretly circulated it.[8]

Rajaram Shastri's memoirs provide us an idea of the chronology of Bhagat Singh's ideological journey through the books he read and the thoughts he shared with Shastri. As Shastri recalled, initially, Bhagat Singh was obsessed with the heroic accounts of the revolutionaries. His studies of the international revolutionary movements brought him in contact with Anarchism. Anarchism attracted him because it advocated daring acts to awaken the society and frighten the despotic rulers. Anarchists believed in propagating their views through self sacrifice. They also used court proceedings as a means to publicize their revolutionary thoughts. Anarchism was thus closer to the ideal of martyrdom. Among the Anarchist thinkers Prince Peter Kropatkin, Bakunin, and August Valliant made deep impact on Bhagat Singh. Sohan Singh Josh who first came into contact with Bhagat Singh in April 1928, recalled Bhagat Singh often quoting Prince Kropatkin (1842-1921): "Single deed makes more propaganda in a few days than a thousand pamphlets......One human being in revolt with torch or dynamite was able to instruct the world."[9] Bakunin's (1814-1876) book *God and the State* was one of the favorite books of Bhagat Singh. This book helped in providing a rational basis to Bhagat Singh's atheism which itself was a manifestation of deep humanism of Bhagat Singh. He read the book many times over and also gave it to his revolutionary colleagues to read.

French anarchist August Vaillant (1861–1894) also made lasting impressions on Bhagat Singh's mind. Shastri has written in detail about Bhagat Singh's first encounter with Valliant through the book *Anarchism and Other Essays*. Vaillant had thrown a bomb in the Chamber of Deputies inside the French parliament on December 8th, 1893. When asked in the court, Vaillant gave a long statement in the court and asserted that he did not wish to be defended.[10] Bhagat Singh learnt this statement by heart. Bhagat Singh followed his idol by throwing bombs in the Central Assembly. The red pamphlet thrown in the Assembly by Bhagat Singh and Dutt on 8th April 1929 began by quoting Vaillant's famous sentence- "*It takes a loud voice to make a deaf hear*". The fact that impact of Valliant on Bhagat Singh remained till the end is also evident in the way he followed his idol in displaying astonishingly carefree attitude during trial and even the dialogue with the magistrate near the scaffold, whom he is supposed to have addressed, "Well Mr. Magistrate, you are fortunate to be able to see today how Indian revolutionaries can embrace death with pleasure for the sake of their supreme ideal".[11]

Bhagat Singh's devotion to the ideal of patriotism and his veneration for martyrs is apparent in most of his writings for the various magazines and journals. He considered such writings as the most potent means of mass awakening. "Vishwaprem" (published in November 1924 in *Matwala*) and "Yuvak" (May 1925, *Matwala)* are soaked in the spirit of sacrifice for the greater good of nation and humanity. In "Vishwaprem," he exhorted the fellow Indians in the following words:

"The first task is to raise the fallen India. Shackles of slavery have to be broken. Tyranny must be ended. So must the slavery, because it tempts mankind, whom God has created in his own image, to wander away from the path of justice ..... You have to descend into the battlefield of action like Govind Singh, the true son of the Motherland ..... You will have to struggle throughout your life like Rana Pratap ..... Sacrifice yourselves to liberate your Motherland. Get ready to spend your whole life in the Andamans to free your captive Mother. Get ready to die to keep the sobbing Mother alive. Then our country will be free. We will become powerful."[12]

In "Yuvak" Bhagat Singh asked the Indian youth to awake, rise and offer themselves for the motherland:

"Your Mother, your Morning Prayer, your Highest Reverence, your 'Jagadamba', your 'Annapurna', your 'Trishuldharni', your 'Singhvahani', your 'Shasyashmlanchala' is in tears. Doesn't her sorrow move you even a little bit? Curse on your listlessness. You are shaming even your forefathers, with your lack of manliness. Even if there is still a trace of self respect in you, rise and prove worthy of your mother's milk; swear to raise her up; swear by every drop of her tears; steer her to victory and speak out in a clear voice: Vande Matram."[13]

His writing, "Holi Ke Din Rakt Ke Chheetain" (March 1926, *Pratap*) glorifies the martyrdom of a group of Babbar Akalis. "Kakori Ke Veeron Se Parichay" (May 1927, *Kirti)* and "Kakori Ke Shaheedon Ki Phansi Ke Halaat" (January 1928, *Kirti*) bring to light the outstanding qualities of the revolutionary heroes convicted in the Kakori case. Bhagat Singh also translated Dan Breen's classic '*My Fight for Irish Freedom*'into Hindi for greater dissemination of Irish revolutionary's exploits. He also contributed in the preparation of a compendium of biographies of martyrs in the special issue (*Phansi* number) of '*Chand*' (November 1928).

Bhagat Singh's essay, "Punjab Ki Bhasa Aur Lipi Ki Samasya" (1925) was a brilliant exposition of the role of language in nation building. In this essay, he cited with reverence, names of Guru Govind Singh, Swami Vivekananda, Swami Dayananda, Swami Ram Tirtha, and Guru Teg Bahadur among others for their nationalistic message. His greatest concern, in this writing was the unity of the nation:

> "The most important question before us at this juncture is to make India a unified nation. It is necessary to have one language for a unified nation, but this can not be done all at once. For this we have to move step by step. If we can not adopt one language for the whole of India at the moment, we should at least adopt one script.... We have to adopt one language, one script, one literature, one idea and one nation, but the adoption of a single language precedes all the other unities, so that we can communicate with and comprehend each other..... And this should be done in our own language, Hindi, rather than in an alien language like English."[14]

Other journalistic writings of Bhagat Singh were also drenched in the patriotism. Most of them were dedicated to the martyrs who laid down their lives for the cause of the nation. His article in *Kirti*, "Shri Madan Lal Dhingra" (March 1928) concluded with the following words:

"So much love for the Mother ! On the scaffold, the martyr is asked: 'You want to say something?' The answer comes promptly: 'Vande Matram, Mother! Salutation to you, Mother India!' The hero embraced the gallows…Blessed was that hero! Blessed is his memory! I bow again and again to the priceless gem in a lifeless country."[15]

Bhagat Singh's greatest veneration was reserved for his childhood idol Kartar Singh Sarabha. He wrote about him as his role model:

"Kartar Singh, the perfect devotee of the goddess of war, had not attained even the age of twenty, when he offered his life on the sacrificial altar of the Goddess of Freedom. He appeared suddenly like a storm, lit up the fire, tried to awaken the sleeping goddess of war, performed the sacrifice of revolt, and in the end was consumed by it. Who he was? Where did he come from? And where did he vanish? We just could not understand a thing. That he should have performed such great deeds just at the age of nineteen is truly astonishing. So much valour, such self confidence, such renunciation, such devotion, such dedication … all this is rare. Revolt flowed in every blood vessel in his body. This revolt was the sole ideal, the sole ambition and the sole hope of his life. He lived for it and, in the end, died for it."[16]

Bhagat Singh internalized the qualities of his idol so completely and got identified with him so much that any later writer would have used the same language to describe Bhagat Singh too.

(2)

Tujhe zabaah karne ki khushi, mujhe marne ka shauq,

Meri bhi marji wohi hai, jo mere sayyad ki hai [17]

(You delight in slaughter, I have a craving for death,

I have the same wish as my executioner!)

This Urdu couplet recorded in the jail note book of Bhagat Singh, speaks aloud his smouldering passion for death for the cause of the country while the British Government was desperate to execute him. Bhagat Singh expressed similar sentiments in his last letter to his younger brother Kultar Singh:

"Usey yeh fikr hai hardam naya tarze-e-jafa kya hai,

Hamen yeh shauq hai dekhen ki intiha kya hai" [18]

(They are ever anxious to devise new forms of treachery,

We are eager to see what limits there are to oppression.)

Since the time when he joined the revolutionary party, Bhagat Singh was eager to embrace the ideal of martyrdom. The first real opportunity of self-sacrifice came during the killing of Saunders, Assistant Superintendent of Police in Lahore, on 17th December 1928. Despite been advised to stay away, Bhagat Singh was determined to play a leading role in this action. As Sukhdev disclosed in a letter, strategy behind this action was to face the police and one who survived would make his statement. But the opportunity for sacrifice did not arise till the Assembly bombing in the April of next year. Bhagat Singh had always felt the necessity of doing something spectacular and stunning. A sacrifice was needed to warn the British Government and wake up his own countrymen out of slumber. The picture of August Vaillant throwing a bomb in the Assembly and making the statement shone brightly in his mind. In a letter written to Sukhdev just before the Assembly bombing action (8th April 1929), he declared that he was "prepared for the *voyage* in spite of all the sweet memory and in spite of all the charms of my life". [19]

While in jail, Bhagat Singh was prepared to die on a hunger strike demanding better facilities for political prisoners. He was unaware of the fact that jail authorities forcefully feed the hunger striking prisoners. He admitted this fact in a letter to Sukhdev during their hunger strike: "I tell you quite seriously that we believed we would die very shortly. Neither we were aware of the technique of forced feeding nor did we ever think of it. We were ready to die."[20] Forced feeding kept Bhagat Singh away from an early martyrdom. Despite it, Government records reveal that he had reached quite close to death during the hunger strike.[21]

Following the example of Russian anarchists and the French revolutionary Valliant, Bhagat Singh remained rigid on not offering his defence during his trial. He was fully convinced that he would get death penalty. He wrote to Sukhdev, "I am certain of capital punishment for me. I do not expect even a bit of moderation or amnesty."[22] In the same letter Bhagat Singh termed martyrdom as 'ideal death' and 'beautiful'.

In the opinion of his close associate Shiv Varma, Bhagat Singh considered death sentence as the greatest reward one could get in return for his love for motherland and he was proud that he was going to get it. Bhagat Singh's keen sense of foresight had helped him to conclude that a dead Bhagat Singh would be more dangerous to British Government than Bhagat Singh alive. He told his friends in jail that "after my hanging, the scent of my revolutionary thoughts will permeate the environment of our beautiful country. It will intoxicate the young men and they will become mad for freedom and revolution. Madness of the young men will drive British imperialists to the edge of their destruction. This is my firm belief. I am impatiently waiting for the day when I will get the highest reward for my services to the nation and my love for the people."[23]

He planned his march to martyrdom to invite maximum media publicity so as to arouse public sentiments and awakening. Soon after the award of death sentence (7th October 1930), Bhagat Singh wrote to Batukeshwar Dutt expressing his anxiety to embrace death for his ideals: "I will climb the gallows gladly and show to the world as to how bravely the revolutionaries can sacrifice themselves for the cause."[24]

Bhagat Singh had a well thought-out plan to utilize the time between the judgment (of the Lahore Conspiracy Case) and the execution. Even before the judgment, he had written to Sukhdev, "I wish that release calls for us should be made collectively and globally. Along with that, I also wish that when this movement reaches its climax, we should be hanged."[25]

Pressure was put on him from many quarters including Motilal Nehru to file an appeal in the Privy Council to gain the necessary time to secure a general amnesty for all political prisoners. Bejoy Kumar Sinha, Bhagat Singh's revolutionary colleague serving life sentence, was allowed to meet him to discuss the issue of appeal. Sinha vividly recalled Bhagat Singh's reaction, "*Bhai aise na ho ki phansi ruk jai* (Brother, let it not happen that the hanging is stayed)."[26] Bhagat Singh's concern, as Sinha explained, was that "he had no illusions about any amnesty being granted but he feared that as the prosecution evidence was weak and the trial had been conducted *ex-parte* the death sentence might be commuted on appeal and he would then be deprived of the opportunity of furthering the cause of the revolution by dying for it."[27]

Intensity of the country wide efforts to save Bhagat Singh – mass mercy petitions, protest meetings, Gandhiji's efforts, adjournment motion in the Central Assembly, prayers in places of worship, and processions created a general impression that commutation of death sentence was quite probable. This prospect unnerved the stoic Bhagat Singh for a while. It seemed that his life long quest was going to be unfulfilled in the end. In Bejoy Kumar Sinha's words, "He almost yearned to die. And sitting in his condemned cell ... [feared] that the people's agitation might not come in the way of the fulfilment of his one sole desire, so near to his heart".[28] Pran Nath Mehta, the lawyer of Bhagat Singh, tried to cajole him to allow a mercy petition to be submitted so as to strengthen the hands of leaders who were trying to save him. Bhagat Singh cleverly dodged Mehta by submitting a petition himself before the lawyer and his team could draft the mercy petition. Bhagat Singh's petition was designed to make the commutation impossible by declaring themselves as war prisoners, asking to be shot dead.

His last letter to Kultar Singh shows his preparedness for the moment of reckoning, the glorious death, for which he was waiting so long. He wrote:

"Koi dam ka mehman hun ai ahle mehfil,

Chiragh-e-sehar hun bujha chahta hun"

(I am a guest only for a few moments, my companions,

I am the lamp that burns before the dawn and longs to be extinguished)

"Meri hawa mein rahegi khayal ki khushboo,

Yeh musht-e-khaq hai, fani rahe na rahe" [29]

(The breeze will spread the essence of my thoughts,

This self is but a fistful of dust, whether it lives or perishes)

A day before his hanging, Bhagat Singh was asked by prisoners of the Second Lahore Conspiracy Case locked up in the same jail, something could be done if he desired to live. Bhagat Singh's reply presented a rational basis of his choice for death:

"It is but natural that I should desire to live. I do not want to conceal this, but it is conditional in the sense that I do not want to live with my freedom curbed. My name has become a symbol of revolution and the ideals and sacrifices of revolutionary party have placed me on a high pedestal. It is such a high pedestal that I may not be able to do justice to it as a living being. My weaknesses are not known to the public. If I am saved from the gallows, they would become known to everybody. Thus the symbol of revolution would fade and even dissolve, but if I die wreathed with smiles, Indian mothers would wish their children to emulate Bhagat Singh, and thus the number of formidable freedom fighters would increase so much that it would be impossible for the satanic forces of imperialism to stop and stem the march of revolution"[30].

When marching to the gallows, trio of Bhagat Singh, Sukhdev and Rajguru sang the couplet which was so dear to them:

"Dil se niklegi na mar kar bhi vatan ki ulfat,

Meri matti se bhi khushbu-e-wafa aayegi"

(Death may mingle my mortal remains with dust,

My love for my country shall never part;

The fragrance of that love will ever dart,

Like fountain from the depth of my heart.)[31]

Bhagat Singh had visualised the impact of his martyrdom on the national struggle for independence. He considered martyrdom as an essential weapon to wrest freedom by awakening the dormant power of the youth. A beautiful poem named *Liberty* by Walt Whitman copied by Bhagat Singh in his prison notebook explained his quest:

"These corpses of youngmen,

Those martyrs that hang from the gibbets-

Those hearts pierced by the grey lead,

Cold and motionless as they seem, live elsewhere

With unslaughtered vitality.

They live in other youngmen, O kings!

They live in other brothers again ready to defy you!

They were purified by death-

they were taught and exalted!

Not a grave for the murder'd for freedom,

But grows seed for freedom, in its turn to bear seed.

Which the winds carry afar and re-sow, and the

rains and the snows nourish.

Not a disembodied spirit can the weapons of

tyrants let loose

But it stalks invincibly over the earth, whispering,

counselling, cautioning."[32]

Bhagat Singh became a symbol of martyrdom and revolt against the British rule. Soon after his execution, *The People* (weekly newspaper from Lahore) wrote: "Bhagat Singh is not only one more martyr. For thousands today he is *the martyr*"[33]. Subhash Chandra Bose termed Bhagat Singh as "not a person, but a symbol. He symbolises the spirit of revolt that has taken possession of the country".[34] A look at the vast amount of contemporary literature, both in prose and poetry, produced after his execution and subsequently banned by the British Government is sufficient to show that Bhagat Singh's sacrifice kindled patriotic feelings throughout the length and breadth of the country.

Thus, right from his childhood till his last moments, Bhagat Singh remained a firm believer in the tradition of martyrdom, which could awaken the slumbering Indian masses and specially the youth. The epithet- *Shaheed-i-Azam* or 'the Prince among Martyrs' befits him because he invited his martyrdom, and resisted all efforts to save his life. There cannot be an iota of doubt that if there was any continuity in his thought process, it was intense patriotism; if there was a persistent dream, it was the freedom of the motherland; and if there was one passion which seized him throughout his short life, it was to embrace martyrdom.

Seventy nine years after his death, Bhagat Singh still remains the symbol of martyrdom. His name automatically comes to our mind whenever the word '*Shaheed*' or '*martyr*' is pronounced.

Millions of Indians, irrespective of region, religion, language, caste or political affiliation, adore him and draw inspiration from his sacrifice. His photographs adorn the walls of 'pan' shops, barbershops, *dhabas* (small eateries), homes and schools throughout the country. Masses are oblivious of the ideological debates, later attached with Bhagat Singh. Masses of this nation worship Bhagat Singh as a patriot and a martyr only and not as an ideologue. For them the romance of Bhagat Singh is integral to his martyrdom alone.

Notes & References

1. Virender Sindhu, ed., *Sardar Bhagat Singh, Patra Aur Dastavej*, 1975, p. 18.

2. Shiv Varma, ed., *Selected Writings of Bhagat Singh*, 1996, p. 125.

3. Manifesto of the Hindustan Socialist Republican Association, cited in, Ibid., p. 154.

4. Page 24 of Bhagat Singh's jail notebook.

5. Raja Ram Shastri, *Amar Shaheedon Ke Sansmaran*, 1981, p. 97.

6. Ibid., pp. 22-24.

7. Rajaram Shastri, op. cit, pp. 97-98.

8. Ibid., pp. 89-90.

9. Sohan Singh Josh, *My Tryst with Secularism*, 1991, p. 133.

10. Rajaram Shastri, op. cit., pp. 99-100.

11. Comrade Ramchandra, *Ideology and Battle Cries of Indian Revolutionaries*, p. 32.

12. Chaman Lal, ed., *Bhagat Singh Ke Sampoorna Dastavej*, 2006, pp. 49-51.

13. Ibid., p. 54.

14. English rendering by Shiv Varma, op. cit., pp. 51-52.

15. *Kirti*, March 1928, cited in Chaman Lal, op. cit. p. 92.

16. Virender Sindhu, *Mere Krantikari Sathi*, 1977, p. 49.

17. Page 31 of Bhagat Singh's jail notebook.

[18] Bhagat Singh's letter to Kultar Singh dated 3 March 1931. English translation from A.G. Noorani, *The Trial of Bhagat Singh*, 2005, p. 231.

[19] Shiv Varma (ed.) *Selected Writings of Bhagat Singh,* op. cit., p. 63.

[20] Ibid., p. 96.

[21] N.A.I. Home Political, F.36/III, 1930.

[22] Shiv Varma, op. cit., p. 98.

[23] Ibid., pp. 44-45.

[24] Ibid., p. 102.

[25] Ibid., p. 99.

[26] Bejoy Kumar Sinha, "He Marched to Death" '*Mainstream*', March 21, 1964.

[27] Ibid.

[28] Ibid.

[29] Bhagat Singh's letter to Kultar Singh, dated 3 March 1931. English translation from A.G.Noorani, *The Trial of Bhagat Singh*, op. cit., pp. 231-232.

[30] Manmathnath Gupt, *Bhagat Singh and His Times*, Delhi, 1977, p. 194.

[31] Translation adopted from Ramchandra, *Ideology and Battle Cries of Indian Revolutionaries*, 1989, p. 102.

[32] Pages 21-22 of Bhagat Singh's jail notebook.

[33] *The People*, 29th March 1931.

[34] Gurdev Singh Sidhu, (ed.), *The Hanging of Bhagat Singh: The Banned Literature*, 2007, p. 6.

10

Gandhi vs. Bhagat Singh: Myths and Facts

Although it is clear that Bhagat Singh cherished a burning desire to become a martyr for the independence of the country and cleared all hurdles in his way, the executions of 23rd March 1931 marked the collapse of the hopes of millions of Indians who had believed that Mahatma Gandhi would be able to save the lives of the revolutionary trio. More so, the event provided a potent weapon in the hands of opponents of Gandhiji who used it to malign him and charged him for disregarding the feelings of the entire nation. Leftists of that time and specially those outside the Congress fold were virulently anti- Gandhi and wanted to cash upon Bhagat Singh's newly born tremendous popularity and project him as a rival to Gandhi and his creed of non-violence.

Soon after Bhagat Singh's execution, Gandhiji had to face the 'Red' demonstrators in the Karachi session of the Congress, shouting slogans of "Gandhi go back", "Down with Gandhism", "Gandhi's truce has sent Bhagat Singh to the gallows", and "Long Live Bhagat Singh".[1] He was also presented with black flowers which he accepted gracefully. Yashpal, a bitter critic of Gandhi, one of his books was titled '*Gandhivad Ki Shav Pariksha*' (Post-Mortem Examination of Gandhism), wrote in his memoirs: "Gandhiji considered it moral to put government pressure on the people for prohibition but he considered it immoral to put people's pressure on foreign government to commute the sentences of Bhagat Singh etc."[2] Communist Party's line on the execution of Bhagat Singh was put forward in Gopal Thakur's *Bhagat Singh: The Man and*

His Ideas (1953): "Congress leadership had just then thwarted
the second mighty struggle in ten years by hustling the country into
an ill conceived compromise with the Government. With its betrayal
it was no surprise that Gandhiji entered into a pact with Lord
Irwin without securing a commutation of the death sentences."
Leftist scholar revolutionary, Manmathnath Gupta also bitterly
attacked Mahatma Gandhi over the issue of Bhagat Singh. He
devoted an entire chapter- "What Gandhi Did and Did Not Do
for Bhagat Singh" in his work; *"Bhagat Singh and His Times"*
(1977). Manmathnath Gupta went as far as to impute motives for
Gandhiji's 'apathy' towards the fate of Bhagat Singh:

> "It is not very difficult to assess why he (Mahatma Gandhi)
> was so apathetic,….He was by nature allergic to the very idea
> of revolution and consequently to revolutionaries. Secondly,
> the tremendous amount of publicity which Bhagat Singh was
> receiving could not have exactly gladdened Gandhi's heart.
> Apart from this he was cocksure that India was at last, at the
> end of its travail and he did not like all this at this juncture,
> which was not a disquieting nuisance to him, but seemed to be
> robbing him of his hard earned glory."[3]

Another biographer of Bhagat Singh, G.S. Deol, *Shaheed
Bhagat Singh: A Biography*, (1969), also held Mahatma Gandhi
responsible for Bhagat Singh's execution: "If the Mahatma had
wished, he could have insisted and got their commutation agreed
to. But a 'leader' who could go to the extent of stating to the
Viceroy, that "if the boys should be hanged, they had better be
hanged before Congress (Karachi) Session, than after it" could
hardly be expected to secure the commutation of the death
sentences of Bhagat Singh and his comrades."[4]

Like Manmathnath Gupta, A.G. Noorani has also dedicated
an entire chapter – "Gandhi's Truth" in his book, *'The Trial of
Bhagat Singh: Politics of Justice'* (1996). While disagreeing with
the harsh approach of Manmathnath Gupta, Noorani reaches the
conclusion:

"Gandhi alone could have intervened effectively to save Bhagat Singh's life. He did not, till the very last. Later claims such as that "I brought all the persuasion at my command to bear on him" (the Viceroy) are belied by the record which came to light four decades later. In this tragic episode, Gandhi was not candid either to the nation or even to his closest colleagues about his talks with the Viceroy, Lord Irwin, on saving Bhagat Singh's life."[5]

Both Noorani and Manmathnath Gupta have extensively quoted from an article by D.P. Das in '*Mainstream*' in its Independence Day Number in 1970. Das also concluded: "neither Gandhi nor Irwin had told the whole truth. There is a gulf of difference between the public statements of the two principal actors (Gandhi and Irwin) and the whole truth".[6] Das opined that Gandhi did not put enough pressure on Lord Irwin to save Bhagat Singh's life while publicly he said- "I pleaded with Viceroy as best I could". Charging Gandhi of deception, Das wrote in a sarcastic tone:

"It will be rash to run into a cynical conclusion about Gandhi.... Gandhi wanted to save the Pact from being wrecked. He genuinely believed that the Delhi Pact was much more important than the lives of one revolutionary here or another there. Bhagat Singh and his comrades were the tragic cases that arose at the time which almost stood between a settlement with Irwin by Gandhi."

"Gandhi had no difficulty in making his choice or option. In the light of his understanding, the course he took was the only one available in the circumstances. It is true it led him to the path of small deception for a cause which he considered to be noble and patriotic. Moreover, there was no serious reason for him to be particularly concerned with the Lahore Case which was the symbol of the cult of violence quite inimical to the principle he cherished.... Gandhiji's public statements on Bhagat Singh case should not be taken seriously. Take the case of the murder of Bali, the monkey king of Ramayana, by Rama. Even the murder was justified on ground of policy of statecraft".

"So Gandhi's deception should not make us cynical about him. Nor should the discovery of his deception for a cause considered noble by him be taken as an indication of any absence of nobility in him. He was indeed a great Indian. Let Bhagat Singh episode be just a spot in his career and a condonable spot. Have not we condoned the spot in the moon, Yudhishthira and Rama?"[7]

Gandhiji's critics fail to understand that, he had more to gain from commutation or suspension of death sentences of Bhagat Singh and his comrades than the contrary. Gandhiji was well aware that his failure to stop their execution will make the people in general and younger element of the Congress in particular, angry. Moreover the executions would inevitably glorify the revolutionaries and popularise the ideals underlying the revolutionary violence and thus it will be a tactical setback in his fight with the forces favouring use of violence in the battle for *swaraj*. While in the course of his talks with Lord Irwin, he had warned the Viceroy that hanging will make Bhagat Singh a national martyr.[8] Whereas if Gandhiji had succeeded in saving the lives of Bhagat Singh, Sukhdev and Rajguru, it would have been seen as the victory of non-violence over violence and moral victory of Gandhi over the revolutionaries.

Gandhiji's stand in the Bhagat Singh's case must be seen in the light of his approach towards the use of violent means for patriotic purpose, in general. He had deep rooted faith in the futility of violence and efficacy of non- violence. Gandhiji had always reiterated that means (non-violence) are more important than the end (*Swarajya*). To him non-violence was not only a policy but the creed. He had adopted a consistent stand towards revolutionary activities since 1908. He had no doubts about the patriotic impulse behind political violence but such patriotism, according to him, was 'misguided'. While commenting upon the murder of Mrs and Mr Kennedy by Khudiram, a Bengali revolutionary in 1908,

Gandhiji wrote in his newspaper *'Indian Opinion'* (May 1908), "Indian people will not win their freedom through these methods."[9] In the same year Madan Lal Dhingra was convicted for assassination of Curzon Wyllie. Mahatma Gandhi responded to the death sentence of Madan Lal Dhingra in *Hind Swaraj*, "Those who believe that India has gained by Dhingra's act and other similar acts in India make a serious mistake. Dhingra was a patriot, but his love was blind. He gave his body in a wrong way; its ultimate result can only be mischievous".[10] When Collector Jackson was murdered near Nasik in 1909, Gandhiji wrote, "The assassin is quite convinced in his mind that he is acting in the interest of the country, but it is difficult to see what good assassinations can do, whenever assassinations have taken place, they have done more harm than good."[11] In the case of Gopi Mohan Saha, a Bengali revolutionary executed in 1924 for murder of a European, Mr. Day in Calcutta in mistake for Sir Charles Tegart, the Commissioner of Police, Gandhiji had termed Saha's action as misguided love for the country and disapproved emphatically of all political murders.[12] He termed Saunders' murder as a *dastardly act* but blamed the government for provoking the act: "The fault is of the system of Government. What requires mending is not men but the system ..." At the same time he underlined the utter futility of such acts: "Freedom of a nation can not be won by solitary acts of heroism even though they may be of the true type, never by heroism so called."[13]

Gandhiji was opposed to all forms of violence including the violence justified by the law – prison sentence and the capital sentence. He emphasised this fact at a public meeting in Delhi on March 7, 1931: "I cannot in all conscience agree to anyone being sent to gallows, much less a brave man like Bhagat Singh."[14]

Mahatma Gandhi elaborated his stand on Bhagat Singh and revolutionary violence at Karachi session of Congress, three days after the execution of the Bhagat Singh, Sukhdev and Rajguru,

"You must know that it is against my creed to punish even a murderer, thief or a dacoit. There can be no excuse for suspicion that I did not want to save Bhagat Singh. But I want you to realise Bhagat Singh's error. If I had an opportunity of speaking to Bhagat Singh and his comrades, I should have told them that the way they pursued was wrong and futile. I declare that we can not win *swaraj* for our famishing millions, for our deaf and dumb, for our lame and crippled, by the way of the sword. With the Most High as witness I want to proclaim this truth that way of violence cannot bring *Swaraj*. It can only lead to disaster. I wish to tell these young men with all the authority with which a father can speak to his children that the way of violence can only lead to perdition".[15]

Gandhiji showed extraordinary admiration for Bhagat Singh and his revolutionary colleagues. He wrote in *Navjivan* on 29th April, 1931:

"Many attempts were made to save their lives and even some hopes were entertained, but all was in vain. Bhagat Singh did not wish to live. He refused to apologize; declined to file an appeal. If at all he would agree to live, he would do so for the sake of others; if at all he would agree to it, it would be in order that his death might not provoke any one to indiscriminate murder. Bhagat Singh was not a devotee of non-violence, but he did not subscribe to the religion of violence; he was prepared to commit murder out of a sense of helplessness…. These heroes had conquered the fear of death. Let us bow to them a thousand times for their heroism."[16]

A wrong impression has been created that Gandhiji became interested in Bhagat Singh's fate only a few weeks before his execution. As far back as 4th May 1930, a day before he was arrested, Gandhiji had written to the Viceroy, strongly criticizing him for the creation of the special Tribunal to try the revolutionaries in the Lahore Conspiracy Case: "You have found a short cut through the law's delay in the matter of the trial of Bhagat Singh and others by doing away with the ordinary procedure. Is it any wonder if I call all these official activities a veiled form of Martial Law?"[17]. On 31st January, 1931, five days after he was released from prison, he spoke in Allahabad on the subject of Bhagat Singh's execution in context of the forthcoming talks with the Viceroy: "Those under a death sentence should not be hanged. My personal religion tells me not only that they should not be hanged but also that they should not even be kept in prison. However, that is my personal opinion and we cannot make their release a condition."[18]

Coming to the tense events leading to 23rd March 1931, after the dismissal of the Petition for Special Leave to Appeal in the Privy Council on 11th February 1931, it became quite apparent that only an intervention by the Viceroy in the form of commutation alone could save the lives of the revolutionary trio. A nation wide signature campaign for a memorandum to be submitted to the Viceroy praying for commutation of death sentence to one of transportation for life was started (See chapter *Making of the Legend: Jail Life*). Revolutionaries and their sympathisers were also convinced that only Gandhiji's efforts could now save the lives of Bhagat Singh, Sukhdev and Raj Guru. Chandra Shekhar Azad himself met Jawahar Lal Nehru in this regard and requested him to make Bhagat Singh's release a precondition in Gandhi-Irwin talks. Azad also gave some sort of commitment regarding revolutionary activities if Bhagat Singh was spared.[19] In second or third week of February 1931, Azad sent Yashpal to talk to Jawahar Lal Nehru. Jitendra Nath Sanyal met Gandhiji personally through the intermediary of Jawahar Lal Nehru.[20] As he has written, Gandhiji promised to move in the matter but enjoined on him to keep the mater to himself.[21] Durga Devi Vohra (Durga Bhabhi) also met Gandhiji in this regard.[22] A delegation of Naujawan Bharat Sabha including Comrade Ram Chandra, Comrade Ganpat Rai and Kranti Kumar also met Gandhiji, first in Allahabad and later in Delhi.[23] Like Sanyal, Comrade Ramchandra was also advised by Gandhiji to keep this matter secret. Death of Chandra Shekhar Azad on 27th February 1931, in an encounter with the police in

Allahabad, dealt a heavy blow to any understanding between Gandhiji and revolutionaries over the question of suspension of revolutionary activities to facilitate the commutation of the condemned revolutionaries. This was hardly surprising because with Azad's death, virtually the entire leadership of revolutionaries was either dead or in the prison. Hopes of the commutation were strengthened by the fact that Gandhi-Irwin talks were round the corner. There was intense pressure on Gandhiji from Congress men and the general public alike to negotiate for Bhagat Singh's life during his parleys with the Viceroy. Lord Irwin was also feeling the weight of the public opinion but in his case pressure was counter balanced by the pressure from British bureaucracy, especially from the Punjab, against any delay or commutation of the execution of death sentences of Bhagat Singh and his comrades.

As Anil Nauriya has pointed out in his articles in *Mainstream*[24], Mahadev Desai's diary[25] (volume 14) in Gujarati reveals hitherto unknown efforts of Gandhiji to save the lives of the revolutionary trio even before the Gandhi - Irwin talks commenced. Mahadev Desai noted on 14th February in his diary (page 43), "Gandhiji asked me to go to Sastri (V. Srinivas Sastri) and talk to him about Bhagat Singh to see if they (M.R. Jayakar, Tej Bahadur Sapru, and Sastri) could help prevent hanging of Bhagat Singh." Mahadev Desai then went to see V. Srinivas Sastri and wrote in his diary (page 43-44), "Sastri said he would first take up the ethical ground because he would like to emphasise the need to do away with the sentence of death altogether." Tej Bahadur Sapru also agreed to move the Viceroy on the question of commutation of death sentence.[26]

Gandhi – Irwin talks began on 17th February 1931 and continued till 5th March when Gandhi-Irwin Pact or Delhi Pact was arrived at. According to the terms of the Pact, Congress suspended Civil Disobedience Movement and Government accepted some of the demands of the Congress. During this period (17th February to 5th March), Gandhiji and Irwin met eight times and spent together 24 hours in negotiations.[27] Gandhiji entered the talks without making Bhagat Singh's issue a precondition. As Gandhiji explained in *Young India* of 2nd April, 1931:

> "The Working Committee had agreed with me in not making commutation a condition precedent to truce. I could therefore only mention it apart from the settlement. I had hoped for magnanimity. My hope was not to materialise. But that can be no ground for breaking the settlement."[28]

Gandhiji raised the issue of Bhagat Singh with Viceroy on 18th February. Gandhiji reported on his interview with the Viceroy:

> "I talked about Bhagat Singh. I told him, "This has no connection with our discussion, and it may even be inappropriate on my part to mention it. But if you want to make the present atmosphere more favourable, you should *suspend* Bhagat Singh's execution". The Viceroy liked this very much. He said "I am very grateful to you that you have put this thing before me in this manner. *Commutation of sentence is a difficult thing, but suspension is certainly worth considering*". (Emphasis added)

> "I said about Bhagat Singh: "He is undoubtedly a brave man but I would certainly say that he is not in his right mind. However, this is the evil of capital punishment, that it gives no opportunity to such a man to reform himself. I am putting this matter before you as a humanitarian issue and desire *suspension* of sentence in order that there may not be unnecessary turmoil in the country. I myself would release him, but I cannot expect any government to do so. I would not take it ill even if you do not give reply on this issue."[29]

Lord Irwin, in his report to the Secretary of State on the same day, penned his position on the issue of commutation:

> "He (Mahatma Gandhi) did not plead for commutation, although he would, being opposed to all taking of life, take that course himself. He also thought it would have an influence for peace.

But he did ask for postponement in present circumstances. I contented myself with saying that, whatever might be the decision as to exact dates, I could not think there was any case for commutation which might not be made with equal force in the case of any other violent crime. The Viceroy's powers of commutation were designed for use in well known grounds of clemency, and I could not feel that they ought to be involved on grounds that were admittedly political."[30]

Reports of both Gandhiji and Irwin make it amply clear that Gandhiji asked for postponement or suspension of the execution and not the commutation. Gandhiji has been criticised on this account. Was Gandhiji interested only in postponement? Why did he make this move?

Legally, (as Viceroy himself also admitted) after the Privy Council's decision, Viceroy's commutation stood no chance. That Congress leadership had already explored the legal aspect was admitted by Gandhiji in a letter to C. Vijayaraghvachari dated 29th April 1931: "the legality of the convictions was discussed threadbare by jurists like Sir Tej Bahadur with the Viceroy and you know what great influence he had with him. But it was all of no avail…"[31] Hence, in place of the commutation, Gandhiji asked for the *suspension* of the sentences. Gandhiji's plan was to prolong the suspension and wait for a proper stage when a favourable environment was created in which he could ask for the remission of the sentences or even the release of the condemned revolutionaries. Gandhiji's strategy for suspension of the sentences worked well initially. The Viceroy, who was wary of even considering the case of commutating, immediately agreed to consider the suspension. Gandhiji's confidence about his success was based on the emerging situation. At that stage it looked improbable that British Government would go for execution as the public support for Bhagat Singh was rapidly increasing and the Delhi Pact was still to be ratified by the Congress. Gandhiji hoped that, in the meantime Congress would fulfil the settlement on its part and thus would be in better position to demand the issues outside the settlement. He echoed these sentiments at a public meeting in Delhi on March 7, 1931:

"It is still open to us to secure the release of all you have named....and that can be done if you will implement the settlement. Let 'Young India' stand by the settlement and fulfil all its conditions, and if, God willing, Bhagat Singh and others are alive when we have arrived at the proper stage, they would not only be saved from the gallows but released."

"But I will address to 'Young India' a word of warning. These things are sooner asked for than obtained. You want to secure the freedom of these condemned of violence. There is nothing wrong in it.....But I tell you, even you could not save them unless you fulfil the conditions of the settlement. You can not do so by violent means. If you pin your faith to violence, take it from me that you will not only not secure Bhagat Singh's release but will have to sacrifice thousands of Bhagat Singhs...."

"I beseech you then, if you want the release of the prisoners, to change your methods, to accept the settlement, and then come and ask me about the Garhwalis and Bhagat Singh. Come to me six months hence, after you have implemented the settlement and gained in strength, and ask me the question you are asking today and I promise to satisfy you."[32]

A secret part of Gandhiji's prolongation strategy was that he hoped to use the time in getting guarantee from the revolutionaries to shun violence if Bhagat Singh's life is spared. Gandhiji hoped to use this guarantee as a 'carrot' or a bargaining point with the British Government for the release of revolutionaries including Bhagat Singh.

Gandhiji, for the second time, raised the issue of Bhagat Singh with Lord Irwin on 19th March when they met to discuss the notification of the Pact at the Congress session at Karachi. Irwin recorded his conversation with Mahatma Gandhi in his minute:

"As he was leaving he asked if he might mention the case of Bhagat Singh, saying that he had seen in the press the intimation of his execution for March 24th. This was an unfortunate day, as it coincided with the arrival of the new president of the Congress at Karachi and there would be much popular excitement".

"I told him I had considered the case with most anxious care, but could find no grounds on which I could justify to my conscience *commuting* the sentence. As to the date, I had considered the possibility of postponement till after the Congress, but had deliberately rejected it on various grounds:

i. That postponement of execution, merely on political grounds when order had been passed seemed to me improper;

ii. That postponement was inhuman in that it would suggest to the friends and relatives that I was considering commutation; and

iii. That Congress would have been able legitimately to complain that they had been tricked by Government.

"He appeared to appreciate the force of these arguments and said no more".[33]

Next day, on 20th March, Gandhiji had a long conversation with Herbert Emerson, the Home Secretary. Emerson explained to Gandhiji in detail the Government's decision to go ahead with the executions:

"The question as to whether it (the execution) should take place before or after the Karachi Congress had been very seriously considered by the Government who realised the difficulties of either course, but thought it would have been unfair to the condemned persons to postpone execution and also not fair to Gandhiji to allow the impression to gain ground that commutation was under consideration when this was not the case. *He agreed that of the two alternatives it is better not to wait, but he suggested, though not seriously that the third course of commutation of the sentence would have been better still* (emphasis added). He did not seem to me to be particularly concerned about the matter. I told him that we should be lucky if we got through without disorder and I asked him to do all that he could to prevent meetings being held in Delhi during the next few days and to restrain violent speeches. He promised to do what he could ".[34]

Above mentioned accounts of Gandhiji's talks with Viceroy and Home Secretary on 19th and 20th March make it look quite obvious that Central Government and the Viceroy had taken the final decision regarding Bhagat Singh's execution before the Karachi session of the Congress. But, at the back of this inflexible and adamant attitude of the Viceroy and the Home Member lay the pressure built by the Punjab Government.

As it emerges from the correspondence between the Central Government and the Punjab Government, Viceroy had almost made up his mind to postpone the executions until Karachi Congress was over. He wanted to sound the Punjab Government which was in charge of executions, on this proposition. In an undated demi-official letter, Secretary of Home Department, Government of India wrote to Chief Secretary of Punjab Government, about the difficulties which might arise if Bhagat Singh was hanged before the Karachi Congress. Government of India suggested that "possible course is to wait until few days after the Karachi session was over."[35] Punjab Government mulled over this matter for some time. On 15th March the Government of India pressed the Punjab Government for a decision on this point. Punjab Government responded on 16th March. By clever reasoning, Punjab Government made a fool-proof case for the advantages that lay in executing Bhagat Singh etc. before the Karachi Congress. It put forward the view that if executions take place before the Congress Session, the resolutions at Karachi "would probably mere take the form of condolence to relations over the fate of the executed", but if the executions do not take place, "there is a danger that commutation of the sentences may be made a condition of future participation in discussion about constitution."[36] Punjab Government's advice left no option for the Central Government. On 17th March, Government of India informed Punjab that "Governor General in Council has declined to interfere on behalf of the persons under sentence of death in Lahore Conspiracy Case, namely Bhagat Singh, Shiv Ram Rajguru and Sukhdev. The Government of India accepts the view of Local Government that advantage lies in not waiting until after Karachi Congress, but they consider execution should be carried out not later than Monday 23rd and earlier if practicable."[37] On 18th March Punjab Government informed the Government of India about their decision to carry out executions at 7 p.m. on 23rd March and "the news will be made known in Lahore on early morning of March 24th."[38]

One of the last efforts of Gandhiji to save the lives of the three revolutionaries was the Asaf Ali's mission to get an undertaking from Bhagat Singh and his colleagues in jail, asking the revolutionary party to shun violence. Such a declaration, it was felt, would strengthen the hands of Gandhiji, in his final efforts to save the lives of Bhagat Singh and others. Mahadev Desai's diary also contains a paragraph for March 21, 1931, related to Asaf Ali's mission: "Asaf Ali had brought a letter praying clemency as from Bhagat Singh. Gandhiji rejected the draft and prepared a fresh draft which was more in keeping with Bhagat Singh's self–respect. Asaf Ali took this letter to Lahore."[39] Details of this unsuccessful mission are reconstructed from the contemporary press and interview of Asaf Ali himself.

Bhavisya, published in its issue of 9th April, a telegram sent by the correspondent of '*Free Press*' from Lahore for publication in various newspapers. The telegram, *Bhavisya* claimed, was censored and blocked by Government and hence could not be published. A portion of this telegram read:

"Mahatma Gandhi had got prepared a statement and sent it through Asaf Ali to Lahore to get it signed by Late Bhagat Singh and others; the objective behind this exercise was to facilitate the paper work regarding their death sentence.

Mahatmaji had also sent a message for these young men but Asaf Ali was not even permitted to meet them.

"After waiting at Lahore for three days he (Asaf Ali) received a letter from the Home Member of the Punjab Government stating that if Asaf Ali submitted to the Government a copy of the statement he had brought with him, his request for meeting with Bhagat Singh and others could be considered. Asaf Ali categorically declined the proposal and thus his meeting with Bhagat Singh could not materialize."[40]

The above account is corroborated by Asaf Ali himself in a statement which appeared in *Bhavishya* of 27th March, 1931 :

"I had come to Lahore from Delhi to meet Bhagat Singh with the permission of the Punjab Government with the intention of getting a letter from him for the Revolutionary Party instructing the Party to postpone their violent activities until there was hope of gaining independence through the non-violent movement of Mahatma Gandhi. I tried every possible means to meet him but without any success. I had made it clear to the authorities that my sole objective in meeting Bhagat Singh was to get help for the non-violent movement. I had also assured them that I hoped to get much success from this meeting. But the authorities' response to my requests smelt of their arrogance of power. My meeting with Bhagat Singh, I am confident, would have greatly helped in making the revolutionaries follow the path of Mahatma Gandhi. In a case that involved millions of Indians, patriots like Bhagat Singh would not have flinched a bit to admonish those who believed that a revolution was necessary to set right the political anomalies."[41]

Eighteen years after the incident, Asaf Ali, then Governor of Orissa, recalled his unsuccessful mission to save Bhagat Singh:

"When the Gandhi-Irwin pact was being negotiated much pressure was brought to bear on Gandhiji to secure reprieve for Bhagat Singh and his colleagues after they had been sentenced to death in the later Lahore conspiracy case.

Mahatma Gandhi did not find it consistent with his creed of non-violence to make a point of honour in respect of one found guilty of assassination. He did whatever he possibility could to plead with Lord Irwin, otherwise. A day before we left for the Karachi Congress, I approached Mahatma and showed him a draft which I had made, to be signed by Bhagat Singh and others circumspectly signifying a repudiation of the cult of violence should they agree to do so, hoping that after that it might be easier for Gandhiji to plead for their reprieve, I felt that Bhagat Singh had considerable regard for me and I argued with him he might agree to renounce violence. Mahatma turned to me and said, "go and try it if you feel like it". I went to Lahore and phoned up; the Home secretary was extremely polite and expressed his deep regret that Government would not allow me to interview Bhagat Singh. That was the last effort I made on Bhagat Singh's behalf."[42]

But strange as it may seem, Lord Irwin, who carried the final authority regarding the executions, was hesitant till the last day. Gandhiji was certainly aware of Viceroy's dilemma and so he redoubled his efforts to save Bhagat Singh and his comrades. Robert Bernays (a senior journalist working for *News Chronicle* (London) on a five month long visit to India, maintained a diary of his talks with a number of prominent Indian leaders and high ranking British officials. His diary, published in 1932, proved to be a sensitive and accurate chronicle of the events) noted in his diary on 21st March 1931, "Gandhi is delaying his departure (for Karachi Congress) here another day for further conversation with the Viceroy"[43] on the issue of Bhagat Singh's execution. On 21st March, Gandhiji met Irwin and again communicated his request for reconsideration of the impending executions.[44] Gandhiji met Irwin yet again on 22nd March to discuss the issue.[45] Viceroy *promised to consider* Gandhiji's submission. Sensing some hope, Gandhiji wrote a personal letter on the morning of 23rd (Monday) to the Viceroy. Mahadev Desai's diary mentions that on this day Gandhiji got up at 1 a.m. to write the letter which Devdas Gandhi took to Viceroy at 8 a.m.[46] In his final endeavour Gandhiji tried his best to convince the Viceroy (addressing him as *dear friend*) for the commutation of the death sentence citing public opinion, internal peace, offer of revolutionaries to shed violence, his own position, the possibility of a judicial error and the appeal to the *Christian sentiments* of Lord Irwin. He also offered to meet the Viceroy personally if necessary:

> 1, Darya Ganj, Delhi
>
> March 23, 1937

"Dear friend,

It seems cruel to inflict this letter on you but the interest of peace demands a final appeal. Though you were frank enough to tell me that there was little hope of your commuting the sentence of death on Bhagat Singh and two others, *you said you would consider my submission of Saturday.*

Dr Sapru met me yesterday and said that you were troubled over the matter and taxing your brain as to the proper course to adopt. If there is any room left for reconsideration, I invite your attention to the following.

Popular opinion rightly or wrongly demands commutation when there is no principle at stake, it is often a duty to respect it.

In the present case the chances are that, if commutation is granted, internal peace is most likely to be promoted. In the event of execution, peace is undoubtedly in danger.

Seeing that *I am able to inform you that the revolutionary party has assured me that, in the event of these lives being spared, that party will stay its hands, suspension of sentence pending cessation of revolutionary murders becomes in my opinion a peremptory duty.*

Political murders have been condoned before now. It is worth while saving these lives, if thereby many other innocent lives are likely to be saved and may be even revolutionary crime almost stamped out.

Since you seem to value my influence such as it is in favour of peace, do not please unnecessarily make my position, difficult as it is, almost too difficult for future work.

Execution is an irretrievable act. *If you think there is the slightest chance of error of judgement, I would urge you to suspend for further review an act that is beyond recall.*

If my presence is necessary. I can come, though I may not speak I may hear and write what I want to say,

"*Charity never faileth*". (Emphasis added)

I am

Your sincere friend"[47]

Mahatma's efforts failed to bear fruit. Bhagat Singh, Sukhdev and Rajguru were hanged the same evening on 7 p.m. As the news reached Gandhiji, according to an eyewitness account, he was "visibly moved and deeply shocked":

"As the news came (of the execution), Gandhi with head bowed over one hand stood for sometime in the open compound visibly moved and deeply shocked. It appeared later that he had till the last hoped that as a result of his private pleadings with the Viceroy, the executions would be stopped. As I sat with the Mahatma, in the third class carriage in which I was going to Karachi, I asked if he would express his real feelings even though the worst had happened. On strips of paper Gandhiji began writing and passing on the slips to me"[48]

As the above mentioned events show, the execution of Bhagat Singh, Sukhdev and Rajguru was the triumph of British bureaucracy especially of the Punjab, rather than the failure of Gandhiji. Bhagat Singh and his comrades' refusal to seek mercy and on the contrary demand execution in military style made the task very tough for Mahatma Gandhi. Viceroy remained indecisive till the very end and ultimately fell to the mounting pressure of British officers from the Punjab. Jatinder Nath Sanyal, who was watching the events related to his revolutionary colleagues very closely, opined that "most probably the viceroy had felt the influence of the public opinion on the matter, especially the request of Mahatma Gandhi. But the real citadel of power in India, the European ICS cadre, was deadly against the commutation, and the Viceroy ultimately yielded to their pressure".[49] Aruna Asif Ali, who along with her husband Asaf Ali had witnessed Assembly bombing and had accompanied Asaf Ali while visiting Bhagat Singh in jail, was another keen observer of developments related to the efforts to commute the death sentence. Recalling the events, she wrote later: "Irwin at one time almost submitted to Gandhiji's intercession. But the Punjab Governor of the day, rumours says, threatened to resign."[50] That the threat of resignation of British high officials of Punjab was a common knowledge is also suggested by memoirs of contemporaries like Kranti Kumar, Robert Barnays and C.S.Venu.[51] Censored and blocked telegram of *'Free Press'* (already mentioned) had categorically stated: "Free Press has come to know from reliable sources that, although Lord Irwin was himself not in favour of hanging Bhagat Singh etc, but almost all the English officers of the Punjab Government had threatened Lord Irwin that if he commuted the death sentences they will resign en mass."[52] *The People* of 22 March 1931 and *Abhyudaya* of 25 March 1931 also carried similar reports.[53]

As can be inferred easily, murder of Saunders and subsequent revolutionary actions had posed a direct challenge to the European civil servants serving in India. Huge popularity of Bhagat Singh only rubbed salt in their wounds. British judiciary had already done what it could do maximum- award of death sentence. Now it was the turn of the executive to put death sentence in practice.

British civil servants were against all sorts of compromise with the anti-government movement. Intelligence reports of that period mention that Gandhi-Irwin agreement "disheartened and depressed them and all other supporters of Government; for they believed they saw in the truce evidence of lack of determination on the part of Government in the last resort to maintain its authority".[54] In the case of commutation of the death sentence of Bhagat Singh, Rajguru and Sukhdev, they sabotaged all efforts, including Asaf Ali's mission, that could lead to commutation. Suggestion of the Punjab Government to hang the trio before the Karachi session was a masterstroke as it left Irwin without a sound argument. But when they found that Irwin was still vacillating they threatened to resign en mass. Fortnightly intelligence report of the Government for the fortnight ending 15 April 1931 also acknowledged, "there is no doubt that the carrying out of these executions has been in the nature of a much needed tonic to officials and supporters of Government".[55]

Gandhiji's efforts in the case of Bhagat Singh have been appreciated by his close associates like Sitaramayya, Mira Behn (Madeline Slade), Asaf Ali, and Aruna Asaf Ali. Sitaramayya was of the view that though the Gandhi Irwin settlement specifically denied pardon to these convicted of violent crimes, but Gandhiji had discussed the cases of Bhagat Singh and his companions with Lord Irwin and Viceroy had promised serious consideration.[56] Mira Behn who was staying with Gandhiji in Delhi during his negotiations with Lord Irwin, forthrightly wrote in her autobiography, *The Spirit of Pilgrimage*: "Bapu did his utmost to obtain a reprieve, and though the Viceroy could give him no definite assurance, still Bapu hoped and believed the remission would be granted, especially as the execution at such a moment would greatly intensify the anti-British feelings of the public."[57]

Lately, distinguished historian V.N. Datta has also reached the conclusion that "from the extracts of Gandhi – Irwin correspondence and also contemporary evidence, it is clear that Gandhi was deeply interested in saving Bhagat Singh's life, and was constant in his appeals to Irwin not to hang him." According to Datta, in order to understand Gandhi's role, "we have to relate his negotiations with the Viceroy to the political climate of the times, the pressure of public opinion, the role of the Viceroy, and the working of British bureaucracy, and Imperial system in India and England".[58]

Amit Kumar Gupta in a research paper entitled – '*The Executions of March 1931, Gandhi and Irwin*', presented a fine analysis of Gandhiji's strategy to save Bhagat Singh:

"Why did Gandhi at all ask for postponement of the executions instead of a forthright appeal for reprieve? To be fair to Gandhi one could argue with some force that a mere appeal for commutation to the Viceroy in February 1931, following a Privy Council ruling, was foredoomed to failure. After all Bhagat Singh's patriotism was not on trial. The Tribunal decided on what was a political crime and a premeditated murder. Nobody denied Bhagat Singh's legal guilt and Bhagat Singh and his comrades were the last persons to do that. On the question of reprieve and death penalty Bhagat Singh's own opinion was unequivocal... Under this circumstance judicial mercy from a British Viceroy stood little chance and Gandhi's understanding of law clearly grasped this. The only alternative to save the condemned to death was to exert political pressure. Political pressure in the form of public opinion was already there; otherwise it would not have been a point of discussion between Gandhi and Irwin. Gandhi could have, as he himself said, made commutation a condition of the Gandhi-Irwin Pact, which, of course, he was unwilling to do. His unwillingness is understandable in the context of the promise of a historic pact which occurred only rarely in a nation's life-time. A nation's fate could not be staked against the fate of some individuals. Besides, Gandhi and his Working Committee could not with justice champion the cause of violence by departing from their declared devotion to non-violence. In fact much of contemporary criticism of Gandhi on this point seems unreasonable. Thus when pressure through pre-condition appeared illogical Gandhi probably desired to add political manoeuvre to public opinion. He might have thought that if he could, by any remote chance, secure the suspension of executions, the Government would face great difficulty in carrying out the executions at all. The hope of ultimate success in a bargain is sometimes greater if demands are kept low at an initial stage. Gandhi was probably calculating that his apparently innocent request might be treated favourably by a Viceroy - anxiously preparing for a truce."[59]

In retrospect, the question whether Bhagat Singh could be saved or not should also be dealt from Bhagat Singh's perspective. Would he have liked to be deprived of his long cherished ideal of martyrdom? Would he have liked to survive at the mercy of Mahatma Gandhi, against whose political creed the revolutionary movement of 1920's was born? Would it not have been a symbolic defeat of the ideals of the revolutionary movement in the form of defeat of violence against non-violence? Gandhiji was aware of Bhagat Singh's steadfast resolve to die a martyr's death. Had Mahatma Gandhi succeeded in preventing Bhagat Singh from attaining martyrhood, would Bhagat Singh have commanded the same place which he commands at present in the galaxy of patriots? Perhaps in view of all these stirring questions; Bhagat Singh, Sukhdev and Rajguru, on 20th March 1931, closed the door on all efforts to save them by writing their 'mercy petition' to the Punjab Government: "....according to the verdict of your court we had waged war and we are therefore war prisoners. And we claim to be treated as such, i.e., we claim to be shot dead instead of being hanged."[60]

Notes & References

1. D.G. Tendulkar, *Mahatma: Life of Mohandas Karam Chand Gandhi, Vol.III, 1930-34*, 1961, p. 74.

2. Yashpal, *Simhavalokan*, 2005, pp. 404-405.

3. ManmathnathGupta, *Bhagat Singh and His Times*, 1977, p. 211.

4. Gurdev Singh Deol, *Shaheed Bhagat Singh: A Biography*, 1985, p. 93.

5. A.G. Noorani, *The Trial of Bhagat Singh: The Politics of Justice*, 1996, p. 252. Noorani's bias against Gandhi in context of the efforts to save Bhagat Singh has been thoroughly exposed by Anil Nauriya in a series of articles in *Maimsteam* in its issues dated April 6, 1996; April 13, 1996; June 22, 1996; June 29, 1996; and March 22, 1997.

6. D.P. Das, *Mainstream,* Independence Day Number, 1970.

7. Ibid.

8. The Earl of Halifax, *Fullness of Days*, 1957, p. 149. In a letter dated 8 May 1931, to Sir Darcy Lindsay of France, Gandhiji wrote: "I have no doubt whatsoever that the execution has surrounded these lives with a halo which they would not otherwise have had." (*Collected Works of Mahatma Gandhi*(here onwards *CWMG*), Vol. XLVI, p. 120).

9. *CWMG*, Vol.VIII, p. 133.

10. *The Selected Works of Mahatma Gandhi, Vol.III*, 1968, p. 133.

11. *CWMG*, Vol. X, p. 112.

12. S. Irfan Habib, *to Make the Deaf Hear: Ideology and Programmes of Bhagat Singh and His Comrades*, 2007, p. 88.

13. *CWMG*, Vol. XXXVIII, pp. 274-276.

14. *CWMG*, Vol. XLV, p. 273.

15. *CWMG*, Vol. XLV, p. 349.

16. *CWMG*, Vol. XLV, pp. 359-360.

17. *CWMG*, Vol. XLIII, p. 391.

18. *CWMG*, Vol. XLV, p. 133.

19. Yashpal, *Simhavalokan,* 2005, pp. 393-395.

20. Ibid. pp. 395-396.

21. J.N.Sanyal, *S. Bhagat Singh,* 1983, pp. 73-74.

22. Vachnesh Tripathi, *Krantimurti Duga Bhabhi*, 1996, pp. 33-34.

23 Memoirs of Kranti Kumar cited in K.C. Yadav and Babar Singh (eds.), *Making of a Revolutionary,* 2006, p. 171. Comrade Ramchandra has also written about meeting Gandhiji in context of Bhagat Singh (*Naujawan Bharat Sabha and HSRA*, pp. 139-140).

24 *Mainstream* issues dated April 6, 1996; April 13, 1996; June 22, 1996; June 29, 1996; and March 22, 1997.

25 *Mahadev Desai's Diary, Vol.14,* 1974.

26 All references of Mahadev Desai's diary have been cited from Anil Nauriya, "Execution of Bhagat Singh: Some Clarifications On Noorani's Narrative", *Mainstream,* April 6, 1996, p. 30.

27 D.G. Tendulkar, *Mahatma:Life of Mohandas Karamchand Gandhi, Vol.III,1930-1934,* 1961, p. 56.

28 *CWMG*, Vol. XLV, p. 352.

29 *CWMG*, Vol. XLV, p. 198.

30 *CWMG*, Vol. XLV, pp. 196-197.

31 *CWMG*, Vol. XLVI, pp. 51-52.

32 *CWMG*, Vol. XLV, pp. 272-273.

33 *CWMG, Vol. XLV,* pp. 315-316.

34 N.A.I. Home Political File, 33/I & KW, 1931.

35 N.A.I. Home Political File, 4/21/31, 1931.

36 Ibid.

37 Ibid.

38 Ibid.

39 Mahadev Desai's diary (page 171) quoted by Anil Nauriya in *Mainstream,* April 6, 1996, p. 30.

40 *Bhavisya,* Allahabad, 9 April 1931. Also published in *Amar Shaheed Sardar Bhagat Singh*, Snehlata Sehgal (Tr.), op.cit., pp. 289-290.

41 *Bhavisya,* Allahabad, 27 March 1931. Also published in Snehlata Sehgal (Tr.), op.cit. pp. 293-294.

42 *Commonweal,* Pune, 23 March 1949.

43 Robert Bernays, *Naked Faquir,* 1932, p. 213.

44 *CWMG, Vol. XLV,* p. 320; *Gandhi 1915-1948: A Detailed Chronology,* compiled by C.B. Dalal, 1971, p. 87.

[45] *Gandhi 1915-1948: A Detailed Chronology*, op. cit.

[46] Mahadev Desai's diary (page 171) quoted by Anil Nauriya in *Mainstream*, 6 April, 1996, p. 30.

[47] *CWMG, Vol.XLV*, pp. 333-334.

[48] J.N. Sahni's account, cited in Prem Bhasin, "Bhagat Singh and Gandhi's Truth", *Mainstream*, July 27, 1996.

[49] J.N. Sanyal, op. cit., p. 74.

[50] *Fragments from the Past, Selected Writings and Speeches of Aruna Asaf Ali*, 1989, p. 102.

[51] *Homage to Martyrs*, Shaheed Ardha Shatabdi Samaroh Samiti, Delhi, 1981, Hindi Section, pp. 85-86; Robert Barnays, op. cit. pp. 211-212; C.S. Venu, *Sirdar Bhagat Singh*, 1931, Microfilm, N.A.I. , p. 48.

[52] *Bhavisya,* 9 April 1931(translated from Hindi).

[53] *Abhyudaya,* 25 March 1931.

[54] *Terrorism in India, 1917-1936,* 1937, p. 42.

[55] N.A.I. Home Political File, 18/IV/1931.

[56] Pattabhi Sitaramayya, *History of the Indian National Congress*, 1935, Vol. i, p. 442.

[57] Mira Behn, *The Spirit's Pigrimage*, 1960, p. 124.

[58] V.N Datta's keynote address at the International Conference on *"Bhagat Singh and His Times"* organised by the Indian Council of Historical Research in collaboration with the Institute of Punjab Studies, Chandigarh in September 2007. Excerpts from the address were published in *The Tribune* of December 23, 2007 under the title, *"Bhagat Singh Trial and Execution: Gandhi Tried His Best for Reprieve"*. Datta has since revised and enlarged the address into a book- *Gandhi and Bhagat Singh*, 2008.

[59] Amit Kumar Gupta, *The Executions of March 1931, Gandhi and Irwin*, Bengal: Past & Present, Vol. XC, January- June 1971, pp. 111-112.

[60] Shiv Varma, *The Selected Writings of Shaheed Bhagat Singh*, 1996, pp. 132-133.

11

Was Bhagat Singh a Marxist?

(1)

The year 2006 marked the 75th anniversary of the martyrdom of Bhagat Singh, Sukhdev and Rajguru and Chandra Shekhar Azad. The years 2007-2008 marked the birth centenary of Bhagat Singh as well as of Sukhdev. The whole country felt enthused to commemorate and remember the sacrifices of these great freedom fighters and martyrs. Government of India in a Gazette of India Extraordinary notification dated 2nd May, 2006 included 75th anniversary of Bhagat Singh's martyrdom as well his birth centenary among the five national anniversaries to be celebrated, other three being: 150th anniversary of the first war of independence of 1857, 60th anniversary of India's Independence, and centenary of adoption of *Vande Matram* as the national song. The Government also announced its decision to establish a 'Bhagat Singh Chair' in a university to facilitate systematic studies of the revolutionary movements in general and Bhagat Singh in particular.

The Anniversary years (2006-2008) have also witnessed a spate of books, booklets, research papers and articles on Bhagat Singh. A perusal of this vast literature showed that much of the literature produced on Bhagat Singh during recent times has come from the pen of Indian Marxists. The Marxist writings on Bhagat Singh show a marked deviation from his image ingrained in public mind, that of Shahid-i-Azam (the great martyr) in the cause of the freedom of the motherland. In place of focusing on the great martyr's contribution to the national movement, the Marxist publicists tried to dilute Bhagat Singh's original identity as a patriot and a martyr and in its place present him as a Marxist ideologue. In fact they had started their preparations in 1990s, much before the Government of India or the public arose to the occasion. "Bhagat Singh's significance lies in his thought and philosophy", says a Communist booklet written in 1998, "Indian masses do not adore him merely because of his sacrifice and martyrdom."[1] In the same year (1998), Vinod Mishra, the General Secretary of CPI (ML) in his introduction to "Why I am an Atheist" wrote that Bhagat Singh is the real hero (*jananayaka*) among the freedom fighters because like Lenin, Bhagat Singh urged the young men to work to generate class consciousness among the workers and peasants and build a Communist party of professional revolutionaries.[2] To propagate this line of interpretation, Indian Communists launched a countrywide propaganda campaign involving their political parties, youth organizations, intellectuals and artists during his birth centenary. Every faction of the fragmented Communist movement in India is trying to project the ideology and image of Bhagat Singh in its own mould. For example, the CPI (M), in order to sell its political programme to the masses in general and youth in particular, in one of its official publication, called upon to consciously take to the people "four remarkable strands in the life, work and thought of Bhagat Singh and his comrades..... (a) uncompromising struggle against imperialism (b) unflinching resistance to communalism and caste oppression (c) unbending opposition to bourgeois land-lord rule, and (d) unshakable faith in Marxism and Socialism as the only alternative before the society."[3]

So, while the nation in general sees in Bhagat Singh a source of inspiration for every Indian, a symbol of courage and supreme sacrifice, the Indian Communists are toiling hard to present Bhagat Singh as a party icon. Their objective, is to use Bhagat Singh as a peg to hang their agenda on. Instead of analyzing the causes of fall of Communism due to the vast chasm between dream and reality, and the fading contemporary relevance of Marxism, they are striving to sell a dying ideology through the iconic status of Bhagat Singh, which he earned by inviting his own martyrdom. By laying claims on one of the most revered icons of Indian nationalism, they hope to survive the ideological disaster that Communism is facing globally.

Throughout the world, Marxism as an ideology is fighting a losing battle for survival. Indian Communists are doing no better. It is only because Bhagat Singh happens to be the most popular icon of the youth that the Leftists are so eager to hijack his popularity to sell their failed and discredited ideology. The Indian Left, in the hour of its worst ever crisis looks towards an icon like Bhagat Singh as a redeemer and especially so because international Communist icons like Lenin, Stalin and Mao are being relegated into the dustbin of history in their own countries. In this context, for the Indian Communism, Bhagat Singh has come to symbolize all which it claims to stand for. In the words of a CPI(M) publication:

> "Bhagat Singh has a special relevance to contemporary India, with the increasing aggressiveness of American imperialism bearing down on the country and the world; with millions of workers, peasants, agricultural labourers and even sections of the middle classes becoming prime targets of the rapacious strategy of imperialist globalization; with the economy and political sovereignty of the country itself being threatened by the worst form of neo-colonialism; and with all kinds of communal, castiest and terrorist forces out to dynamite the country's unity and integrity."[4]

In its desperation to attack its adversaries, the Marxist scholarship is resorting to attribute writings to Bhagat Singh, of which there is no substantial evidence to have been authored by Bhagat Singh. For example Nazirul Hasan Ansari's article – "Bhagat Singh for Today", published in *Mainstream* thrice (in issues dated March 27, 1993 and August 11-17, 2006 and October 2007) quotes substantially from an unsigned writing, *Sampradayik Dange Aur Unka Ilaj,* published in *Kirti* in June 1928. We have tried to examine the question of the authorship of all such polemical articles attributed to Bhagat Singh by the Communist publications, in the chapter *Literary Heritage of Bhagat Singh: A Re-examination.*

A recent line taken up by the Indian Communists is to monopolize its claims on Bhagat Singh's legacy – no one but only the Left has the right to commemorate Bhagat Singh. Eminent Marxist historian Irfan Habib has made a statement suggesting this approach.[5] An editorial in *Liberation,* the mouth piece of CPI (ML) in its issue of October 2006 also writes:

> "Bhagat Singh can be an inspiring icon only for the revolutionary people of India and they shall celebrate his birth centenary to uphold his lustrous revolutionary legacy….Beyond Gandhi and Nehru and defying the Advanis and Man Mohans, and the Bushes and Blairs, the future of India is still waiting to be discovered. In this mission of transforming the present and discovering the future, Bhagat Singh remains and will remain most relevant both as a guide and as an unexhausted source of energy and inspiration."[6]

In the words of Shamsul Islam, a Left activist: "if the British physically murdered Bhagat Singh, Rajguru and Sukhdev on 23rd March 1931; then it had become the duty of the system which we had borrowed in the name of independence, to kill the ideology of these martyrs."[7] The very title of this article "*Kyon Bhulaya Gaya Bhagat Singh Aur Unke Sathion Ko*" is a blatant lie and distortion. Marxist historian K.N. Panikkar also feels that Bhagat Singh has been deliberately neglected: "The birth centenary of Bhagat Singh is not being observed as an event of national importance or accorded official patronage reserved for national heroes. The reason for this neglect is worth exploring. Is it because the questions he raised about imperialism and economic exploitation are uncomfortable for the present ruling elite?"[8] Panikkar then gives credit to the Left for salvaging Bhagat Singh: "Yet, Bhagat Singh has not been entirely forgotten either, thanks to individuals and organizations who recognize the value of radical ideas and interventions in society."[9]

To protect its exclusive claims on Bhagat Singh, the Left has started reacting in an offensive manner to any non-Marxist interpretation of Bhagat Singh. In Chaman Lal's words:

"There is a great deal of effort today by various forces to appropriate the legacy of Bhagat Singh. The mainstream nationalist historiography, and its concomitant political current, the Congress, holds him up as a selfless patriot, but totally ignores his strong anti- Congress stance. In particular, the Congress eludes Bhagat Singh's Marxist ideology. Far greater injustice is done to Bhagat Singh by the Hindu Right- the RSS and its affiliates – who are also out to appropriate the revolutionary's legacy. *In an effort that can only be termed obscene, the Hindu Right would have us believe that Bhagat Singh was a votary of a greater Hindu homeland and a devotee of Bharat Mata.* Even a mere glance through the Notebook and other writings of Bhagat Singh is enough to expose these as lies."[10](Emphasis added)

An example of Left's ideological intolerance on the issue of Bhagat Singh can be seen in the following incident. When Hindi weekly *Panchajanya* brought out its Bhagat Singh number on 25th March 2007, Left raised a foul cry. Kishore Jamdar wrote an 'open letter to editor of *Panchajanya*' which was published in several forums including *Hamsa* (edited by Rajendra Yadav) and *Filhaal* (edited by Preeti Sinha). Jamdar squarely accused the RSS and its ancillary organisations: "You don't have any concern for Bhagat Singh's ideology. Your only purpose is to cash his popularity, even if this requires distortion of history which is a child's play for you."[11] Shamsul Islam, also expressed himself in equally derogatory tone on the issue of Bhagat Singh number of *Panchajanya* in his booklet *Golwalkar Ya Bhagat Singh*, published by Sahmat Muktnad.[12] Are these people really ignorant that Bhagat Singh's mother Vidyavati was very close to the Hindu movement till her last and Kultar Singh, Bhagat Singh's younger brother had been an office bearer of Jansangh and an M.L.A.?

Even Virender Sindhu, the niece and biographer of Bhagat Singh, has always been close to the RSS as she married a dedicated RSS worker Naresh Bhartiya, a known literary figure in Britain. Before her book was published, Virender Sandhu, had sought the blessings of RSS Chief Golwalkar. Golwalkar replied in a letter dated 13th September 1968, expressing his joy at the coming out of the life and work of Bhagat Singh. The Left got too panicky when the RSS chief K. Sudarshan was invited by Bhagat Singh's relatives and admirers to pay a visit to Bhagat Singh's paternal village Khatkar Kalan to pay his homage to the martyr.

In a similawr vein, Prakash Karat, General Secretary of CPI (M), while speaking at a national seminar[13] on Bhagat Singh in Bombay, commemorating the centenary celebrations, used the occasion for hitting at his political rivals:

"Entire outlook and the ideology which Bhagat Singh came to subscribe was the very anti-thesis of the Hindu communal ideology and politics espoused by the RSS and the Hindu Mahasabha..... To cover up the strong secular, anti - communal socialist ideology which Bhagat Singh came to represent, that the RSS reduces him to a pantheon of heroes which includes V.D. Savarkar and Aurobindo Ghosh who represented Hindu radicalism.... To reduce Bhagat Singh to a brave young martyr minus his clear vision of an India free from communal and casteist vices and a society based on Socialism is to do injustice to his memory."[14]

Karat summed up his speech by emphasizing that "Bhagat Singh should be a shining exemplary to counter the reactionary and retrogressive forces."[15]

Rahul Foundation, a Lucknow based extremist Left group (established in 1993-94), which does not believe in parliamentary democracy, has played an active role in decimating Bhagat Singh's Marxist image. The Foundation's declared objective is to bring about a 'new proletarian revolution' after destroying the present societal setup based on rampant capitalism which it claims was the unfulfilled dream of Bhagat Singh and his comrades.[16] The Foundation strives to establish proletariat's control over production, government and society through a 'revolution'. To give shape to its designs, it has established a web of ancillary organisations.[17]

To give fillip to its programme, the Rahul Foundation launched an ambitious three year campaign called *Smriti Samkalp Yatra* (23 March 2005-28 September 2008), commemorating 75 years of martyrdom of Bhagat Singh, Sukhdev, Rajguru, Chandra Shekhar Azad and Ganesh Shankar Vidyarthi; the birth centenary years of Bhagat Singh and Chandra Shekhar Azad; and the 150th anniversary of 1857 Revolt, all of which fell in the above mentioned three year period. During this period, its volunteers disseminated Foundation's literature on Bhagat Singh as also on international Communist heroes like Marx, Lenin, Stalin, and Mao. They also endeavored to enroll new volunteers as well as create new organizational centres, using the legacy of the martyrs. As part of these celebrations, the Foundation published a 692 page collection of documents of Bhagat Singh and his comrades at a very low price, besides separately publishing Bhagat Singh's jail note book and other booklets. Satyam, the editor of the collection, has written in the introduction that Bhagat Singh's significance lies in the challenges posed by new forms of imperialism, capitalism and failure of the party democracy in India:

> "When the whole country is being crushed under the plundering indigenous and foreign capital and its hegemonic power; when the polarization between the labour and capital is sharpening; when the worldwide decisive struggle (prophesied by Bhagat Singh) against imperialism is becoming more and more inevitable; when the real face of naked power represented not only by the Congress but also all the parties in the Parliamentary system and the phony leftists have been fully exposed; when Bhagat Singh's apprehensions have been proven right, the time has come for the labouring masses and the revolutionary youth to involve themselves whole-heartedly in the complicated task

of preparing for a new revolution against imperialism and indigenous capitalism."[18]

"The growth and development of Bhagat Singh, Bhagwati Charan Vohra etc. seems to have been similar to that of Mao-Tse-Tung and Ho Chi Minh, who, while learning from the international leadership, studied the concrete realities in their respective countries and formulated their own revolutionary strategies, skills and tactics. There is an objective basis to assume that if Bhagat Singh had remained alive and had an opportunity to form a Communist Party of his own, or had he, after joining the Communist Party, given it a new direction according to his own understanding, perhaps the history of the Communist movement or even the history of this country would have been written differently." [19]

In a booklet entitled *Vicharon Ki Saan Par* (2006), Satyam rejects any claim that Communist Party (CPI (M) and CPI) may have on Bhagat Singh's legacy:

"The Communist Party of India, that had come into existence prior to the martyrdom of Bhagat Singh, could have realized the dreams of the Indian proletariat by organizing them on a mass scale. But this could not happen because of the party's ideological and organizational weaknesses and also because a large section of its leadership was opportunistic. After their defeat in Telengana in 1951, the Communist Party became a line of defence for the capitalist establishment by adopting the parliamentary system completely. Thus it lost the right to being heir to the ideals and dreams of Bhagat Singh."[20]

Similar contempt is conveyed by *Filhaal*, a radical Left Hindi monthly in its Bhagat Singh special number of April 2007:

"At this time the ideological distinction among the parliamentary parties has disappeared. Acting as brokers for the imperialistic capital and joining it in the loot have become the creed of parliamentary politics. The Left Front Government, which claims to be the protector of the interests of peasants and workers, is now shooting them dead ... Unemployment is increasing and the plight of the masses deteriorating day by day ..... Communal and caste frenzy is on the rise. All the ruling classes are bent upon crushing democracy ... Superstition and all kinds of reactionary ideas are becoming dominant in new ways. In such times, the ideological heritage of Hindustan Socialist Republican Association of Bhagat Singh and Chandra Shekhar Azad is still our guiding light. This heritage contains all the guiding principles for liberation from all kinds of exploitation and oppression, as well as for progress, and can show us the way to make our present and future better."[21]

Thus each of the Communist factions is trying to project itself as the true inheritor of Bhagat Singh's revolutionary party HSRA. Each faction is publishing and using its own set of selected documents, attributed to Bhagat Singh and his comrades.

(2)

There is no denying the fact that Bhagat Singh got attracted to the socialist ideology during the last few years of his short life. His attraction to Socialism is rooted in the after-math of the Kakori case (1925) when the Hindustan Republican Association (HRA) was on the verge of extinction and needed to be reorganized. In his autobiographical essay "Why I am an Atheist" (written in 1930 in jail), Bhagat Singh has dealt with this subject. Bhagat Singh and his colleagues, who were left with the task of reorganization, felt that objectives and methods of the revolutionary party also needed to be revised. Police crackdown and subsequent convictions had exposed the weakness of the secret revolutionary activities. The earlier methods of the revolutionary party and their consequences - decoities to meet financial needs, lack of contact with the masses leading to lack of public sympathy- all these made Bhagat Singh to rethink. Rooted in the opposition to Indian National Congress' non-violent struggle, the revolutionary party was desperately in need of an alternative ideological position. In this context, Socialism as an ideal of economic emancipation and equality since the French

Revolution of 1789, gave Bhagat Singh a dream to fight for. The Bolshevik propaganda had declared the revolution in Russia to be immensely successful. Anti-imperialist image of Soviet Russia and the untested dream of an idealistic society had a romantic effect from a distance. Bhagat Singh, a young man of nineteen, developed a romantic curiosity to know Marxism and Leninism which claimed to have created in Socialist Russia a dreamland of society, free of exploitation and inequality. In his own words, he started studying "something of Marx, the father of communism, and much of Lenin, Trotsky and others- the men who had successfully carried out a revolution in their country."[22] Since the arrival of Raja Ram Shastri in Lahore in 1926, Bhagat Singh and his colleagues were able to get such literature from Dwarka Das Library. A book seller called Rama Krishna & Sons of Lahore was able to arrange for them even the banned books from England.

Bhagat Singh's insistence on re-christening of the party by the addition of the word 'Socialist' to HRA to make it Hindustan Socialist Republican Association (HSRA) during the September 1928 Delhi meeting is symbolic in that regard.

A leaflet in the handwriting of Bhagat Singh declaring Saunder's murder, dated 18 December 1928, pasted on the walls of Lahore after the murder, mentioned the dream of exploitation-less society.[23] But it was not until his stay in jail, in the last couple of years of his life that Bhagat Singh took up the cause of Socialism through his writings. Significantly, none of Bhagat Singh's writings or statements dealing with Socialism or Marxism can be dated prior to his arrest in 1929. The first writing in which elements of Socialism can be clearly traced is his joint statement with Batukeshwar Dutt in the Sessions Court on 6th June 1929 which presents elaboration of their conception of a Socialist society.[24]

During the trial in Lahore Conspiracy Case, Bhagat Singh and his fellow undertrials sent a telegram on Lenin's death anniversary on 21 January 1930: "We wish success to the great experiment

Russia is carrying out. We join our voice to that of the international working class movement. The proletariat will win, Capitalism will be defeated. Death to Imperialism."[25]

Two other oft-quoted writings attributed to Bhagat Singh dealing with the Marxist- Leninist conception of society and politics are *Introduction to Dreamland* and *Message to the Political Workers*. Both of these pieces are believed to have been written inside the jail during the last few months of his life on 15th January 1931 and 2nd February 1931 respectively. In these writings, Bhagat Singh comes across as a political thinker believing in mass action to reconstruct the society on a socialistic basis rather than merely being an advocate of violent means. Bolshevik revolution in Soviet Russia is seen as the role model for bringing up a revolution and subsequent reconstruction of society. In his Introduction to *Dreamland*, a poetical composition by Lala Ram Saran Dass, Bhagat Singh writes: "We the revolutionaries are striving to capture in our hands and to organize a revolutionary government which should employ all its resources for mass education, as is being done in Russia today. After capturing power, peaceful methods shall be employed for constructive work, force shall be employed to crush the obstacles."[26] But it must be kept in mind that publication of *Introduction of Dreamland* after more than three decades of its writing calls for an explanation. (See above chapter *Literary Heritage of Bhagat Singh: A Re-examination*).

In *Message to the Political Workers*, a controversial writing attributed to Bhagat Singh, the objective of the revolutionary party is described as complete independence, meaning, not merely transfer of power from British to Indian hands but to transfer power to those hands that are committed to a socialistic society. For this it is necessary to organize workers and peasants. In the same document Bhagat Singh distanced himself from the utility of violent methods: "Let me announce with all the strength at my command, that I am not a terrorist and I never was, except perhaps in the beginning of my revolutionary career. And I am convinced that we cannot gain anything through these methods. One can easily judge it from the history of the Hindustan Socialist Republican Association."[27] But this essay, different versions of which were circulated at different times, has issues regarding its genuineness. (See above chapter: *Literary Heritage of Bhagat Singh: A Re-examination*)

In his last letter to the British authorities (20 March 1931),[28] Bhagat Singh emphasized that the war against imperialism was also a war against exploitation and inequality. This war shall continue until the exploitation of toiling Indian masses is continued, irrespective of the fact whether the exploiters are British or Indian. The war "shall be waged ever with new vigour, greater audicity and unflinching determination till the socialist republic is established and the present social order is completely replaced by a new social order, based on social prosperity, and thus every sort of exploitation is put to an end and the humanity is ushered into the era of genuine and permanent peace."[29]

The documentary evidence quoted above leaves no doubt about the last phase of Bhagat Singh's rapid ideological journey towards Socialism and Marxism. But, at the same time, it cannot be said that Bhagat Singh had adopted Marxism to such an extent that he had shrugged off all his earlier influences which made him what he was. Testimonies of his revolutionary comrades and contemporaries are a valuable source of information in this regard. Asaf Ali, who was his counsel in the Assembly bomb case and who read out the famous statement in the Sessions Court later recalled that Bhagat Singh was not smitten by Communism.[30] Yashpal also expressed doubts whether Bhagat Singh would have agreed with the Communist Party, had he lived.[31] Most qualified statement on the subject comes from Ajoy Ghosh, revolutionary colleague of Bhagat Singh who later became the general Secretary of Communist Party (1951-1962), when he declared in 1945, "We did not look upon communists as revolutionists - revolution for us meant primarily armed action."[32] As far as Bhagat Singh's ideology was concerned,

Ghosh admitted candidly "It would be an exaggeration to say that he (Bhagat Singh) became a Marxist."[33]

References from Bhagat Singh's prison note-book are often cited as proof of his conversion to Marxism. The jail notebook contains copious notes from the books which he read in jail, and citations from many authors including Marx and Lenin. About the jail notebook, A.G. Noorani seems to be nearer the truth when he says, "The notebook testifies to his vast reading and his readiness to learn. He was a blind follower of no leader and uncritical supporter of no ideology … It is not possible to say in what directions his study and reflection would have taken him over the years, had he but lived. The notebook is very catholic in its selection of quotations."[34]

Bhagat Singh's atheism is also sometimes cited as an evidence of his conversion to Marxism. But his celebrated essay *"Why I am an Atheist"* makes is very clear that Bhagat Singh's atheism had nothing to do with Marxism. In this essay, Bhagat Singh has described his evolution into a confirmed atheist, from his days in National College (1921), to the end of 1926. Bhagat Singh's studies of Marxism started later. His atheism was a product of his sensitive mind, profound humanism and rational approach. It cannot be attributed to any philosophical or ideological conviction. He himself admitted: "Let me admit at the very outset that I have not been able to study much on this point. I had a great drive to study the oriental philosophy but I could not get any chance or opportunity to do the same."[35] He saw the reality around him in terms of human miseries: "This world of woes and miseries, a veritable, eternal combination of numberless tragedies. Not a single soul being perfectly satisfied."[36] Rampant inequality, exploitation, suffering and poverty moved him to question the idea of omniscient, omnipotent God and His purpose to create a world full of suffering. Later, through his studies, the concern for a just, equitable and poverty-less society coupled with his yearning for independence into a vision of independent, socialist India.

It must not be forgotten that he was not even twenty-four when he became a martyr. He was continuously evolving and his short revolutionary career witnessed rapid ideological cross-currents. It will be a foolhardy exercise to speculate what his ultimate destination would have been, had he not died so young. Also, during his ideological evolution, he retained all elements which he considered useful in meeting his ultimate objective- freedom of the motherland. He was ready to follow any path and ideology which brought freedom of the country nearer. That Bhagat Singh's ideological moorings rested on varied foundations viz. traditional as well as modern, Indian as well as foreign, is clear from the following extract from his joint statement with Batukeshwar Dutt in the Sessions Court, Delhi wherein they said, "The new movement which has arisen in the country, and of that dawn we have given a warning, is inspired by the ideals which guided Guru Gobind Singh and Shivaji, Kamal Pasha and Raza Khan, Washington and Garibaldi, Lafayette and Lenin."[37] Patriotism formed the bed rock of his ideology in which all the other influences got integrated or absorbed.

(3)

Bhagat Singh's attraction to Socialism and the appearance of this ideology in the political domain of India during the freedom movement ought to be studied in the context of the contemporary situation in India and abroad.

The impact of 1917 Bolshevik Revolution

News of Russian Revolution of 1917 generated a new wave of hope and enthusiasm in the heart of Indian revolutionaries. Like the Russo- Japanese war of 1905, which was seen as an Asian victory over Europe, the change of power in Russia in 1917 was regarded as the defeat of Western colonial powers led by the Great Britain at the hands of an Eastern power. As Indian patriotism was essentially anti-British, Bolsheviks' capture of power in Russia created in India a natural curiosity mixed with admiration for them and particularly Lenin, the main architect of the 'Revolution'. Soon after this event, nationalist press in India started detailed reporting on the events in Russia as well as Lenin, which led to development of great interest in Socialism in 1920s and 1930s. The widespread enthusiasm in India for Russian Revolution and Socialism cut across the political and ideological spectrum. The official report on the Indian constitutional reforms, published in 1918, also conceded: "The Revolution in Russia and its beginning was regarded in India as a triumph over despotism notwithstanding the fact that it has involved that unhappy country in anarchy and dismemberment; it has given an impetus to Indian political aspirations."[38] British Government in India, since long suffering from Russo-phobia, also started counter propaganda against Bolshevism and Lenin, disallowed literature on the subject and thus helped in popularizing Bolshevism and Lenin by default.

It is important to note that in the early years following the Russian revolution, Indian writings on Russia were not well informed. A glance at the early Indian literature on Russia and Lenin leaves no doubt that its authors saw the events in Russia with a romantic eye, as a solution to all problems which arise due to exploitation and oppression of man by man and of a country by another country. In fact, the most potent cause of Indian affection towards Bolshevik Russia was the distinct possibility of Russian help and support to Indian nationalist forces engaged in their struggle against the British rule in India. In the opinion of L. V. Mitrokhin, who did pioneering research on the influence of Lenin in India, early literature on Russia and Lenin had "one common shortcoming: inadequate knowledge of Marxism and lack of correct information ... about the Soviet Union. These writings were not able ... to provide satisfactory analysis of the events taking place in the Russia".[39] Moreover the propaganda techniques of the Bolsheviks in Russia and the Russo-phobic attitude of the British Government in India left little scope for knowing what exactly was happening in Russia.

Along with the educated classes, contemporary Indian political leaders, with the conspicuous exception of Mahatma Gandhi, visualized Russian events as an auspicious signal for national movement in India. Lokmanya Tilak who was in London in 1918 is reported to have held that the victory of Russian Revolution would greatly help the Indian freedom movement.[40] Another leading extremist leader, Bipin Chandra Pal wrote in 1919, "Today after the downfall of German militarism, after the destruction of the autocracy of the Czar, there has grown up all over the world a new power, the power of the people determined to rescue their legitimate rights – the power to live freely and happily without being exploited and victimized by the wealthier and the so-called higher classes.[41] Third member of the trio of Lal, Bal & Pal, Lala Lajpat Rai was also favourably inclined towards Socialism and Bolshevism in 1920. During his Presidential address at the first session of All India Trade Union Congress, in Bombay in 1920, Lajpat Rai said, "My own experience of Europe and America leads me to think that Socialistic, even Bolshevik truth is any day better, more reliable and more human than Capitalist and Imperialist truth."[42] In the Indian National Congress itself, a Left wing was emerging in the late 1920's with popular youth leaders like Jawahar Lal Nehru and Subhas Chandra Bose.

Jawahar Lal Nehru visited Russia for the first time in 1927 and at once became a great admirer of that country. On his return to India, he wrote his impressions in a series of articles in the press which were published in a book *Soviet Russia: Some Random Sketches and Impressions.* Though not an uncritical supporter, he declared Russia "as the greatest opponent of imperialism."[43] In his Presidential Address to the Lahore Congress of 1929, Nehru declared himself as 'a Socialist' and advocated a full 'Socialist programme' for India.[44] Few years later, in 1934, a socialist caucus within the Congress founded the Congress Socialist Party.

Bolshevik regime, World Revolution, and India

Bolshevik regime in Russia used all possible means to project the 1917 event as the transformation of Marx's theory into reality. Although, according to Marx, the Communistic revolution should have taken place in the great industrialised nations such as England and United States, where the proletariat was well organised, and not in a backward and poorly industrialised state like Russia. Nevertheless, Marxists the world over hailed the Revolution as the harbinger of a new era in history which would ultimately lead to the end of human misery and exploitation. The recent researches after the breakup of Soviet Union in 1991, helped by the opening of hitherto inaccessible secret archives of the Soviet regime, have thoroughly exposed the myth of the Revolution, hailed as the foundation event of world's 'first Socialist state'.

However, the new regime in Russia, with the help of the state sponsored propaganda, was able to project itself as an anti-imperialistic state and a friend of oppressed nationalities. Barely a few days after the revolution, on 24th November 1917, Russia declared the annulment of all secret treaties, and also the partition of Turkey and Persia by the Allied Powers. On 25th December 1917, Council of People's Commissars sanctioned an appropriation of two million roubles for assistance to revolutionary movements in different countries.[45] On 12th January, 1918, a Bolshevik appeal was addressed to Allied Powers, called for self-determination of all subjugated nations. Mesmerised by this propaganda, many began to see Soviet Russia as a veritable heaven where for the first time the dictatorship of the proletariat had been established.

Leaders of the Russian Revolution were very keen to turn the Revolution into the World Revolution, meaning thereby the establishment of communist regimes all over the world. Since in the Marxian scheme, the spread of capitalism and intensification of the misery of the working class were the necessary prelude for revolution, capitalist countries of Europe and North America were considered as prime targets. Bolshevik leadership was pretty sure that capitalist economies would not survive the post-war turmoil. Initially, Bolsheviks had reasons to cheer as there were Socialist and Communist uprisings across the Europe, notably in Germany,

Hungary and Finland. In the years 1918-1919, it seemed plausible that capitalism would soon be swept from the European continent. To guide and control the forthcoming World Revolution, Communist International or Third International (1919-1943) (henceforth Comintern), was created in March 1919. All the thirty-nine invitees to the First Congress of Comintern (2nd March – 6th March 1919) were from industrialized countries of Europe. Grigory Zinoviev, President of the first Congress of the Comintern, enthusiastically announced, "Europe is hurrying towards the proletarian revolution at a break-neck pace."[46]

Headquartered in Moscow, Comintern rose to become a massive structure of power and a gigantic organization claiming to represent the collective will of the Communist parties of different countries. It must be noted that the Bolshevik Party had changed its name to the Communist Party only in 1918. Socialist parties in different countries also rechristened themselves as Communist Parties and sought affiliation with the Comintern. There were 21 preconditions for a Communist Party to get recognition from the Comintern, among which the important ones were: dictatorship of the proletariat; legal as well as illegal means of struggle; Communist Parties to be built on the principle of 'democratic centralism', and the decisions of Comintern were binding on the parties.[47] From the very beginning Communist Party (of Russia) attained a pre-eminent position vis-à-vis Communist Parties of other countries, virtually dictating the Comintern policies.

But to the great dismay of Lenin and Trotsky, the impending revolution in Europe did not take place. One by one the Socialist uprisings were crushed. Following the collapse of the dream of revolution in the west, Comintern was compelled to focus its attention to the East. The new policy was to support nationalist movements in the Asia against the European colonial domination. This move was expected to serve twin purposes: undermine the European powers' strength and improve the national security of Soviet Russia. This change of policy is reflected in a secret memorandum by Trotsky to the Central Committee of the Russian Communist Party dated 5th August 1919. In this memorandum Trotsky wrote that "the road to India" might "prove at the given moment to be more readily passable and shorter ... than the road to Soviet Hungary." Since "the international situation is evidently shaping in such a way that the road to Paris and London lies via the towns of Afghanistan, the Punjab and Bengal."[48] Trotsky also recommended the setting up of a revolutionary academy somewhere in the Urals or Turkistan, which would be the political and military headquarter of the Asian revolution. Signalling the approval to the new policy, Lenin in a speech dated November 22, 1919 observed: "This revolutionary movement of the peoples of the East can now develop effectively ... only in direct association with the revolutionary struggle of our Soviet Republic against international imperialism."[49] Seven months later, in his draft thesis to the second Congress of Comintern, Lenin unambiguously declared, "There is no salvation for dependent and weak nations except in a union of Soviet Republics."[50]

Anglo - Russian rivalry had a long history. It had been the corner stone of the nineteenth century European politics. Russia, since the times of the Czars, had looked upon India as a weak link in the British Empire. After the Bolsheviks came to power in Russia in 1917, England remained the chief threat to Russia and the Revolution. The official report of the Government of India also pointed out that "it is in India that the Bolsheviks believe that they see the Achilles' heel of the British Commonwealth."[51] Apart from being a part of the enemy's empire, India also presented an exciting prospect for export of the Communist revolution. Also, success of the revolution in India was expected to inspire other colonies in Asia and Africa to adopt Communism. But, the export of the revolution to India was possible only in the garb of supporting her liberation struggle against the British. To unleash a Bolshevik propaganda campaign focussed on India, an Indian section of the Council for International Propaganda (Sovinterprop) was established at Tashkent in April 1920.[52] Shaukat Usmani who was in Russia at that time has written, "In Tashkent there were truckloads of literature in Turkish, Persian and English. The Eastern section of the COMINTERN had a room filled with such literature."[53] Moreover, besides literature, propagandists were also sent to India.

Indian revolutionaries approach Russia for help and Lenin woos Muslims

Much publicised anti-imperialist and pro-liberation declarations of the Bolshevik government attracted several groups of Indian revolutionaries in exile, first of which was led by Raja Mahendra Pratap, head of a Government in exile, stationed in Afghanistan. But nothing concrete could emerge out of their talks with Lenin due to acute ideological differences between the two sides. Failure of this initial effort notwithstanding, Russia authorities and Indian revolutionaries in exile got another opportunity to work together when Pan-Islamic movement rose against the British. Muslims were incensed at the treatment of their religious head Caliph at the hands of British in the post-war settlement. During the Caliphate Conference in Delhi, a *firman* (religious order) of Amir Amanullah of Afghanistan was read out in April, 1920, inviting the Muslims, for a holy war against the British.[54] Many Muslims joined the holy war (*Jehad*) and left India to proceed to Turkey via Afghanistan to fight against the British. They became known as Muhazirins. Some Muhazirins were able to reach Afghanistan and borders of Russian Turkmanistan. Both, the Bolsheviks and Indian revolutionaries in exile had their own plans to train the discontented Muslims and use them in attacking the British Indian territory with the help of Russian army.

Muslims occupied an important place in the Lenin's scheme against the western powers, especially Britain. Almost immediately after the revolution, the Council of People's Commissars had issued an appeal on December 3rd, 1917: 'To all the Working Muslims of Russia and the East':

"Comrades! Brothers! Great events are taking place in Russia ... In the face of these events, we turn to you, toiling and disinherited Moslems of Russia and the East ... Constantinople must remain in the hands of the Moslems ... When even the Indian Moslims, oppressed and tormented by a foreign yoke, are rising against their slave drivers – now it is impossible to keep silent. Lose no time in throwing off the yoke of the ancient oppressors of your land."[55]

To sway the Muslim mind, Russian propaganda emphasised upon egalitarianism as the supposed ideological commonality between Socialism and the *Koran*. Pamphlets like "*Bolshevism and Islam*", "*The Soviet Republic and Islam*", and the "*Republic and Islam*" were produced.[56] The impact of such propaganda can be illustrated in the words of Maulana Barkatullah, who, during an interview (May 6th, 1919) to Izevestia, echoed the voice of many Muslim Khilafatists who sought Soviet assistance at that time, "I am not a Communist, nor a Socialist ... but my political programme so far is to drive the English out of Asia ... In this sense, I came close to Communists, and, in this respect, we are your natural allies."[57] Shaukat Usmani, in a letter to M.N. Roy in June 1922 also echoed in similar vein,: "Islam preaches equality, and so does Communism. That is why I am a Communist".[58] Bolsheviks wished to bring the Muslim masses round to the idea of an alliance with Soviet Russia to gain her support in their struggle against colonial oppression.

(4)

Revolutionary Party's encounter with Communism

As mentioned earlier, Indian revolutionaries abroad were attracted to Lenin not for ideology but because of his anti-British rhetoric and hope of getting Russian help in the armed struggle against British Government in India. Revolutionaries of North India came in touch with ideas of Socialism and Communism through Sachindra Nath Sanyal, one of the most prominent leaders of the revolutionary movement in India and also a first rate intellectual.[59]

It was Sanyal who initiated Bhagat Singh into the Revolutionary Party in 1923. His well known book '*Bandi Jeevan*' and lesser known book '*Vichar Vinimaya: Ek Bharatiya Krantikari Ke Adhunik Vichar*' (published from Lucknow in 1938) provide a detailed account of his encounter with Communism. He was sentenced to life imprisonment in Banaras Conspiracy Case in 1915 but was released in 1920 as a result of Royal amnesty. Sanyal has written that he first heard about the revolution in Russia while serving the life term in Andamans. Like his fellow prisoners there, he was instantly attracted towards the new ideology of Communism but remained ignorant about its nuances until he came out of jail.[60] In the beginning of 1921, Sanyal started working in the labour movement at Jamshedpur where he worked for about nine months.[61] During this time he heard the name of Karl Marx for the first time and started reading whatever literature he could find on Russia and Lenin. On the basis of his limited knowledge, Sanyal started writing serialised articles on Russia and Lenin in a Bangali weekly *Shankha,* under the title *Lenin and Samasamyik Russia* (Lenin and Contemporary Russia).[62] These articles attracted the attention of M.N. Roy in Europe, who had emerged as the leading authority on India in the Comintern. Roy mentioned these articles in his journal *Vanguard of Indian Independence*.[63] Roy also sent an emissary, Kutbuddin, to meet Sanyal and invite him to Moscow to attend the ensuing Congress of the Comintern. Kutbuddin met Sanyal in September 1923 in Delhi on the occasion of Special Session of Congress. Sanyal has admitted that he became aware of the nuances of Communism for the first time as a result of his discussion with Kutbuddin.[64] Later, British authorities became aware of Sanyal's contacts with M.N. Roy.[65]

Sanyal enriched his knowledge about Communism by further studies and discussions. Sanyal's account reveals that several aspects of Communism greatly impressed him. He equated the negation of personal property in Communist society with *Sanyas* (renunciation), the highest stage of human development enshrined in Hindu religious texts.[66] Other aspects of Communism which attracted Sanyal were – exploitation-less society, no discrimination on the basis of wealth and state's monopoly of the means of production.

As the chief architect of Hindustan Republic Association (HRA), Sanyal's views on Socialism found place in the two documents of HRA: *Constitution of HRA* also known as *Yellow Paper* (1924) and a pamphlet *The Revolutionary* (January 1925). The *Constitution* put the object of HRA "to establish a Federated Republic of the United States of India by an organized and armed revolution ..... The basic principle of the republic shall be universal suffrage and the abolition of all systems which make any kind of exploitation of man by man possible."[67] The constitution also included the programme of starting labour and peasant organizations and to instil in minds of the proletariat that they are not for the revolution but the revolution is for them.

The Revolutionary explained the means to achieve the above objective further: "means of transportation and communication, mine and other kinds of every great industries.... shall be nationalized.... Electors will have the right to recall their representatives...Legislature will have the power to control the executives..... Ultimate objective of the party is to bring harmony to the world by respecting and guaranteeing the diverse interests of the different nations and states, and in this respect *it follows the footsteps of the great Indian Rishis of the glorious past and of Bolshevik Russia in the modern age*".[68] (Emphasis added)

But Sanyal was not a blind follower of Bolshevik ideology; he refused to agree with Marxian economic interpretation of history and theory of class struggle, historical materialism, and 'scientific' basis of Marxist atheism and also Marxists' abhorrence of Indian culture. Most remarkably, he analyzed the shortcomings of Marx's theory in the light of Indian culture and knowledge corpus.[69] Sanyal writes:

"For one who has not grasped the essence of Indian culture, it is not possible to perceive the demerits of Communism properly.

Therefore, one who does not have any love for the Indian culture, one who doesn't have faith in the distinctive usefulness of the Indian culture for the progress of human civilization cannot understand this programme; and one who has assumed that the principles of Communism are complete, indisputable and perfect is absolutely trapped in an illusion. Such a person cannot understand the action programme of our organisation."[70]

Sachindra Nath Sanyal made it amply clear that HRA, after careful deliberation, had avoided certain aspects of the Communist doctrine. He adopted only those elements of this doctrine which did not come into conflict with ancient Indian ideals. According to him the party avoided the name 'Socialist' because that would have ticked off many rich patriots who were helping the party. Sanyal stressed the fact that the only change brought about in September 1928, (when Hindustan Republic Association's name changed to Hindustan Socialist Republic Party) was the addition of the word 'Socialist' with the name of HRA, its programme remained unaltered.[71]

HSRA, Communism and Communist Party of India

As explained earlier (see above chapter: *Bhagat Singh in the Revolutionary Movement*), HSRA's re-emphasis on Socialism was part of the newly adopted strategy at their Delhi meeting (8th-9th September 1928). In the opinion of Bhagat Singh and others who favoured the change of name, addition of the word *Socialism* to the name of the party would convey the message that revolutionary group's activities were not merely confined to armed actions for liberating motherland but it had a larger objective - to establish a society devoid of inequality and exploitation.

On the basis of elements of Socialism in HRA's Constitution and rechristening of HRA to HSRA, some scholars have attempted to prove that the leaders of revolutionary party were working in close alliance with the Communist Party. It is important to note that up till the Meerut Conspiracy Case (1929-1932) Communist Party of India, though established in 1925, was nothing more than a handful of individuals in few cities being remote controlled by Moscow. Contemporary evidence also proves that ideology and course of action adopted by HSRA were independent of any Communist influence and moreover there were several areas of sharp disagreement between the two.

The fact remains that HSRA did not mark any major change in its working even after adding 'Socialist' to its name. The policy of terrorizing the tyrannical British officials and awakening the people by personal valour continued to be its major programme as can be seen by major actions of HSRA- killing of Saunders (17th December 1928), bomb explosion in the Central Assembly (8th April 1929) and attempt to blow up Viceroy's train (23rd December 1929). Also the fact remains that despite HSRA's public acceptance of the cause of socialism, it was not following any particular ideological stream. The multiplicity of inspirations and ideologies in the programme of HSRA is best expressed in the words of Bejoy Kumar Sinha, writing in 1939:

"We had been studying socialism and accepted socialistic ideas. Our movement however had not yet assumed a clear socialistic character.... The ideas inspiring our movement were a curious admixture of different political ideologies. The virile and the idealistic nationalism of Mazzini with its emphasis on revolutionary youths, the insurrection of the Blanquist type, the 'going-to-the-people movement' coupled with terroristic action of Russian Social Revolutionary Party, the October Revolution and its guiding ideology- Bolshevism- the influence of all these movements could be definitely traced in our ideas."[72]

Ajoy Ghosh recalled in 1945: "armed action by individuals and groups was to remain our immediate task. Nothing else, we held, could smash constitutionalist illusions, nothing else could free the country from the grip in which it was held."[73] The subtle change, though, was to take up 'actions' which were believed to be popular in nature or had the backing of the people in general.

The outlook of contemporary revolutionaries (of HSRA) about the then Communist Party is best explained in their own words. Ajoy Ghosh, a member of revolutionary party since 1923, who later joined the Communist Party and remained its General Secretary from 1951 to 1962, wrote in 1945: "Bhagat Singh and some others among us had already met a number of communist leaders. We felt sympathetic towards them and at one time even contemplated some sort of working alliance with them- Communists to organise the masses and conduct the mass movement, we of Hindustan Socialist Republican Association to act as its armed section. But when we learned that communist considered armed actions by individuals harmful to the movement, we dropped the idea ... We did not look upon communists as revolutionists - revolution for us meant primarily armed action."[74]

Jaidev Kapoor who was awarded life sentence in Lahore Conspiracy Case and who joined the Communist Party after his release in February 1946, also testified to HSRA members' talks with Communist leaders such as Muzaffar Ahmad and Shaukat Usmani. He said that there were some fundamental differences between HSRA and the Communists due to which the revolutionaries could not keep close contact with the Communist party.[75] He clarified the approach of the revolutionary group:

"On the basis of the assumptions and understanding of the times we had concluded that it is necessary to create the awareness, across our enslaved nation and particularly among the youth of this nation, that the fundamental cause of their sense of inferiority and poverty is our subject status. To achieve this, we shall have to take some bold and demonstrative initiatives."[76]

Yashpal has also thrown light on the relationship with the contemporary Communist leaders. In his words: "None of us was a Communist, nor could we ever be, in the sense in which the word communist is being used at present. Azad attained martyrdom on 27th February, 1931 and a few days after that I got an opportunity to exchange views with some Indian and European Communist leaders in Bombay. Despite agreeing with them in principle, I was not prepared to adopt their programme; and the Communists considered our programme as wrong."[77]

Sohan Singh Josh, a veteran Communist leader, emphasised the difference between the Marxist ideology of *Kirti* group with the ideology followed by Bhagat Singh's while referring to the period when '*Kirti*' group and Naujawan Bharat Sabha worked together during 1928-1931 (See the chapter *Bhagat Singh, The Naujawan Bharat Sabha and the Kirti Group: A Brief Encounter*).[78] Josh called Bhagat Singh (representing the ideology of HSRA) as impatient and immature, his thoughts as 'bookish revolutionary knowledge' and his viewpoint as *terroristic*.[79]

Communist opposition to the line of action adopted by Bhagat Singh was derived from the Marxist position on role of individual action versus role of the masses. In 1911, Trotsky had put forward the position on individual terrorism:

"In our eyes individual terror is inadmissible precisely because it belittles the role of the masses in their own consciousness, reconciles them to their powerlessness, and turns their eyes and hopes towards a great avenger and liberator who some day will come and accomplish their mission ... The more "effective" the terrorist acts, the greater their impact, the more the attention of the masses is focussed on them- the more they reduce the interest of the masses in self-organisation and self education."[80]

This position was further defined by Joseph Stalin:

"Let me explain that communists never have had, and never will have, any thing to do with the theory and practice of individual outrages, that communist never have had, and never will have anything to do with the theory and practice of conspiracies against individual persons. The theory and practice of the Comintern is based upon the idea of organising a revolutionary mass movement against capitalism. That is the true task of the communists."[81]

Communist party's official response to HSRA's policies and programme of action is best summed up in the collective statement of some of the Meerut Conspiracy Case accused- G. Adhikari, V. Ghate, K.M. Joglekar, P.C. Joshi, M.A. Mazid, Muzaffar Ahmad, S.S. Josh and Shaukat Usmani - all of them early leaders of the Communist movement in India:

"We oppose terrorism not because of any sentiment on the subject of violence but because we are convinced of its uselessness as a practical revolutionary party ... Individual terrorism is essentially a petty bourgeois policy ... It arises from an exaggeration of the role of the individual, who conduct the attack ... as the mass movement develops and its potentialities as a revolutionary force become clearer, the terrorists tend to some extent to come over the mass movement and such parties developed on the Socialist Revolutionary Party in Russia (or Agrarian Terrorist Party) and, at an earlier stage, the Socialist Republican Party in India. But while the policy of terrorism remains on the programme, it tends to absorb all the energies of the most active and self- sacrificing members and quite unnecessarily to deliver over to the police not only themselves but all their fellows. Consequently we oppose it even as subsidiary line of policy."

"We are, of course, not insensible to the revolutionary virtues displayed by the terrorists, nor of the advance which such parties as the Socialist Republican Army has achieved over orthodox nationalism. They represent an advance in as much as they oppose non-violence, they give up consciously all mystical obscurantist philosophies in favour of a realistic progressive outlook, they advocate, at any rate in theory, the mass revolutionary movement, and they show the necessity of illegal organisations and the way in which it may be afforded."

"But we consider that the courage and self-sacrifice of the terrorist are wasted and the advance they have made, important though it is, is not enough. They have advanced from the position of the bourgeois nationalism, but have reached only the limits of petty bourgeois nationalism. In order really to serve the cause of independence and national revolution they have to go one step further, to the mass revolutionary movement."[82]

One of the signatories of the joint statement was P.C. Joshi who later functioned as the General Secretary of the Communist Party of India from 1935 to 1948. P.C. Joshi later disclosed that "the stand we took in the joint statement made before the Sessions Judge of Meerut was squarely based on the Sixth Congress (1928) line" of the Communist International.[83]

Referring to the activities of Bhagat Singh and his comrades, a contemporary Communist journal *Workers' Weekly*, the weekly organ of the Communist Party in its issue of 13th November 1930, explained the policy of individual terrorism as a psychology of revenge and not revolution.[84] Veteran Communist leader B.T. Ranadive later attempted to justify the contemporary communist position: "It was not known at the time that Bhagat Singh and his comrades were turning towards socialism. Their slogans about proletariat and socialism were considered as expression of general sympathy of socialism, and not an acceptance of Marxism."[85] Ranadive's revelation about the contemporary Communist approach towards Bhagat Singh must be seen along with famous statement made by Ajoy Ghosh in 1945 – "It would be an exaggeration to say that he (Bhagat Singh) became a Marxist."[86]

As late as December 1951, the CPI was denouncing the means and methods adopted by the revolutionaries as counterproductive and irreconcilable with Marxism. In a 'Statement of Policy' adopted by CPI's Special Party Conference in Calcutta in December 1951, the party elaborated its approach on 'individual terrorism' under the heading – '*Perspective Tactical Line of the Indian Revolution*':

"Individual terrorism is directed against individuals of a class or system and is carried out by individuals or groups and squads. The individuals who act may be heroic and selfless and applauded or even invited by the people to act and the individuals against whom they act the most hated. Still such actions are not permissible in Marxism. And why? For the simple reason therein the masses are not in action. Therein, the belief is fostered that the heroes will do the job for the people. Therein, it fosters the belief that many more such actions will mean in sum total the annihilation of the classes or system. Ultimately it leads to passivity or inertia of the masses, stops their own action and development towards revolution and in the end results in defeat."[87]

Notes & References

1. Ravibhushan, *Ikkisvin Sadi Mein Bhagat Singh* (Bhagat Singh in twenty-first century), (written in 1998), Rahul Foundation, Lucknow, 2006, p. 19.

2. *Shahhid-i-Azam Bhagat Singh: Vichar Aur Sangharsh*, 2003, p. 11.

3. Ashok Dhawale, *Shaheed Bhagat Singh: An Immortal Revolutionary*, A CPI (M) publication, January 2007, p. 45.

4. Ibid., p. 44.

5. "Bhagat Singh Ka Smaranotsava Manane Ka Haqdar Kaun", *Nukkar Janam Samvad*, New Delhi, April-September, 2006.

6. *Liberation*, October 2006.

7. Shamsul Islam, "Kyon Bhulaya Gaya Bhagat Singh Aur Unke Sathion Ko," *Nav Bharat Times*, New Delhi, 20 March 1994.

8. *Frontline*, 2 November 2007, p. 4.

9. Ibid.

10. Chaman lal, *The Jail Notebook and Other Writings*, 2007, p. 21.

11. *Filhaal* (Patna), May-June 2007, p.17.

12. *Golwalkar Ya Bhagat Singh*, Sahmat Muktnad, 2007, p. 18.

13. Proceedings of this seminar organized by the Department of Civics and Politics of University of Mumbai were published in the form of a book containing 28 papers - Jose George, Manoj Kumar, and Avinash Khandare, (Eds.) *Rethinking Radicalism in Indian Society: Bhagat Singh and Beyond*, Rawat Publications, Jaipur, 2009.

14. *People's Democracy*, 15 April 2007.

15. Ibid.

[16] Naujawan Bharat Sabha, Disha Chhatra Sangathan, Bigul Mazdoor Dasta, *Krantikari Navjagaran Ke Teen Varsh (23 March-28 September 2008)*, n.d.

[17] 'Publication Division of Rahul Foundation', '*Shaheed Bhagat Singh Yadgaari*' Publication, '*Dastak*', and '*Parikalpana*' for publishing books etc.; '*Janchetna*' to act as a nodal agency for distribution of propaganda through fixed and mobile selling counters as well as book exhibitions; three periodicals- *Dayitva Bodh* (monthly magazine for the intellectual class), *Avvahan Campus Times* (fortnightly newspaper for students), *Bigul* (monthly dealing with labour issues); *Naujawan Bharat Sabha* (youth organisation), *Bigul Mazdoor Dasta* (labour organisation), *Disha Chhatra Sangathan* (student organisation), *Dehati Mazdoor Union* (Rural labour organisation), *Nari Sabha* (women organisation), *Dayitva Bodh Manch* (Organisation for intellectual class) and *Jagarook Nagrik Manch* (citizens' forum).

[18] Satyam, ed., *Bhagat Singh Aur Unke Sathiyon Ke Sampoorna Uplabdha Dastavej*, 2006, p. 18.

[19] Ibid, p. 20.

[20] *Vicharon Ki Saan Par*, 2006, p. 15.

[21] *Filhal* (Patna), April 2007, p. 2.

[22] "Why I am an Atheist", Shiv Varma, *Selected Writings of Shaheed Bhagat Singh*, 1996, p. 123.

[23] Shiv Varma, op.cit., p. 62.

[24] Ibid., pp. 69-70.

[25] Ibid., p. 77.

[26] Ibid, pp. 108-109.

[27] Ibid, p. 120.

[28] Published in *Bhavisya*'s special issue on Bhagat Singh on 9th April 1931.

[29] Shiv Varma, op.cit., p. 133.

[30] Asaf Ali, "An Outstanding Maker of History," published in *Commonwealth* (Pune) on 23 March 1949. This article was republished in M.M. Juneja, ed., *Selected Collections on Bhagat Singh*, 2007, pp. 125-132.

[31] Yashpal, *Simhavalokan*, 2005, p. 392.

32 Ajoy Ghosh, *Bhagat Singh and his Comrades,* 1979, p. 22.

33 Ibid, p. 28.

34 A.G. Noorani, *The Trial of Bhagat Singh: Politics of Justice*, 2005, p. xv.

35 Shiv Varma, op. cit., p. 127.

36 Ibid.

37 Ibid.

38 Zafar Imam, "The Rise of Soviet Russia and Socialism in India, 1917-1929," in B.R. Nanda, op.cit. p. 43.

39 L.V. Mitrokhin, *Everest among Men,* 1969, pp. 19-20.

40 Cited by G. Adhikari, Forward to L.V. Mitrokhin, *Everest among Men*, op. cit. p. 6.

41 Bipan Chandra, *India's Struggle for Independence*, 1989, p. 297.

42 S.G. Sardesai, *India and the Russian Revolution*, 1967, p. 39.

43 Vijay Sen Budhraj, op. cit. p. 37.

44 Ibid.

45 Sobhanlal Datta Gupta, *Comintern and the Destiny of Communism in India, 1919-1943,* 2006, p. 60.

46 Vijay Sen Budhraj, "The Communist International and Indian Politics," in B.R. Nanda, *Socialism in India*, 1972, p. 19.

47 Sobhanlal Datta Gupta, op. cit., p. 43.

48 Ibid., p. 249.

49 M.A. Persits, *Revolutionaries of India in Soviet Russia*, 1983, p. 38.

50 Jayantanuja, Bandyopadhyaya, *Indian Nationalism versus International Communism*, 1966, p. 105.

51 The Government Of India, *India in 1922-23*, p. 24, cited in Zafar Imam, op.cit., pp. 55-56.

52 M.A. Persits, op. cit., p. 6.

53 Shaukat Usmani, "Russian Revolution and India -III", *Mainstream*, July 15, 1967, p. 28.

54 M.A. Persits, op. cit., p. 70.

55 Jayantanuja Bandyopadhyaya, op. cit, p. 135.

56 M.A. Persits, op. cit., p. 54.

57 Ibid., pp. 47-48.

58 Ibid., p. 119.

59 Like Sanyal, another top leader of H.R.A., Jogesh Chandra Chatterjee was also in contact with some Communists. British intelligence reports mention that Jogesh Chandra Chatterjee had travelled to Pondicherry to meet R.C.L. Sharma, an agent of M.N.Roy. (D.Patrie, *Communism in India, 1924-27*, p. 120.).

60 Sachindra Nath Sanyal, *Vichar Vinimaya: Ek Bharatiya Krantikari Ke Adhunik Vichar,* 1938, p. 1.

61 Sachindra Nath Sanyal, *Bandi Jeevan,* 2006, p. 11.

62 These installments began in third issue in the Volume I of *Shankha* in 1921 and continued up to the 47th issue dated March 1922. (Satyendra Narayan Majumdar, *In Search of a Revolutionary Ideology and a Revolutionary Programme,* 1979, pp. 124-126).

63 Sachinindra Nath Sanyal, *Vichar Vinimay,* op. cit., p. 2. Sanyal was also on the list of the persons whom Charles Ashleigh, the British Communist emissary was to contact in India (D.Patrie, *Communism in India,* 1924-27, Edition Indian, Calcutta, 1972., p. 20.).

64 Sachinindra Nath Sanyal, *Bandi Jeevan, op. cit.,* p. 301.

65 A Government report noted: "On the 13th March 1925, the Director, Intelligence Bureau, received information that Sachindra Sanyal and M.N. Roy were in touch and acting in concert; that Sanyal had recently sent a messenger from India to Roy, who in turn had sent 200 pounds to Sanyal through an Indian sailor." (N.A.I. Home Political, 253, 1925, p. 14.)The same report also noted, "Jogesh Chatterji visited R.C.L. Sharma, in order to enlist support and funds through M.M. Roy, on behalf of H.R.A."(Ibid., p. 16.).

66 Sachinindra Nath Sanyal, *Bandi Jeevan,* op. cit., pp. 301-302.

67 H.W. Hale, *Political Trouble in India, 1917-1937,* 1974, p. 201.

68 Ibid., pp. 197-198.

69 Sachinindra Nath Sanyal, *Vichar Vinimaya,* op. cit., 1938, pp. 129-154.

70 *Bandi Jeevan,* pp. 313-314.

71 Ibid., pp. 315-316.

72 Bejoy Kumar Sinha, *In Andamans, The Indian Bastille,* 1988, pp. xiii-xiv.

73 Ajoy Ghosh, *Bhagat Singh and His Comrades,* 1979, p. 20.

74 Ibid., p. 22.

75 Transcript of interview with Jaidev Kapoor at NMML, p. 223.

76 Ibid., p. 224.

77 Yashpal, *Viplav* (Azad number*),* 1997, pp. 73-74.

78 Sohan Singh Josh, *My Tryst with Secularism,* 1991, p. 133.

79 Ibid., pp. 133-134.

80 Cited in Bhagwan Josh, *Communist Movement in Punjab,* 1979, p. 89.

81 Sir Horace Williamson, *India and Communism,* 1976, p. 229.

82 *Communist Challenge Imperialism from the Dock,* 1967, pp. 270-71.

83 P.C. Joshi, *Rajni Palme Dutt and Indian Communists*, cited in Gargi Chakravartty, *P.C. Joshi: A Biography*, 2007, p. 12.

84 B.T. Ranadive's Forward to Shiv Varma, *Selected Writings of Shaheed Bhagat Singh,* 1996, p. 9.

85 Ibid.

86 Ajoy Ghosh, op. cit., p. 28.

87 Cited in P.M.S. Grewal, *Bhagat Singh: Liberation's Blazing Star,* 2007, p. 57.

12

Ideological Hijacking of Bhagat Singh

It is shocking to know, as mentioned in the previous chapter, that by presenting Bhagat Singh as its hero, the Communist movement has reversed the position it took during the period between the late 1920's and 1953. During this period, on the instructions from the Communist International, Bhagat Singh and other Indian revolutionaries were referred to as *terrorists*. The Communist leaders of the time had declared openly that they were convinced of the *uselessness* of the revolutionary party. In November 1930, *Workers' Weekly*, the mouthpiece of the Communist Party dismissed the policy of revolutionary party as the '*psychology of revenge and not revolution*'. Up to 1951, the official position of the Communist Party of India (CPI) was to denounce the action programme of Indian revolutionaries as acts of individual terrorism which was *not permissible in Marxism.* (See above chapter: *Was Bhagat Singh a Marxist?*)

The great turnaround in the Communist Party's approach began in 1953, when under the leadership of Ajoy Ghosh, the Communists laid their claims on Bhagat Singh's legacy by linking his ideology with Marxism and Leninism. The explanation for this volte-face lay in the changed orders from Russia and new measures adopted to deal with the internal crisis faced by the Communist Party at that time.

Post independence, the CPI was facing serious internal problems which stemmed from the ideological dilemmas. The hardliners like B.T. Ranadive were not prepared to accept that

India had become independent on August 15, 1947. Ever fed on anti-Gandhism and anti-Congressism, they believed that no bourgeois party like the Congress could win the war of liberation against imperialism. "*Yeh Azadi Jhoonthi Hai*" (this independence is a farce) used to be a popular slogan of CPI those days and 15th August was observed as a 'Black Day'.[1] They still hoped to capture power through armed struggle in Telengana region in South India. Those who questioned this line were branded revisionists. Foremost victim of this policy of ideological intolerance was P.C. Joshi, under whose leadership (1935-48) the CPI was built from a stretch, who was disgracefully thrown out of the Party in February 1948, at Calcutta Congress of the CPI. The CPI, being wholly subservient to Communist Party of Soviet Union (CPSU) dictates, had taken a line that Indian Government was an agent of Anglo-American imperialism and the aim of the party should be to establish rule of Proletariat through violent struggle and chose Telengana as the first region to be 'liberated'. With the rise of Communist Republic of China in October 1949 under the leadership of Mao - tse Tung, CPI faced a new dilemma - the dilemma of divided loyalty between U.S.S.R. and Communist China. Who to follow? Stalin or Mao? Party leaders were engaged in a bitter internal feud over these burning questions. Divided leadership and unreasonable policies adopted by the CPI were also taking a toll of its organization. By 1950, membership of the CPI drastically fell to 9000, from 90000 in 1948.[2] Artists, writers and intellectuals once associated with the party were drifting away.[3]

After the end of Second World War in 1945, Soviet Union emerged as a super power but found itself embroiled in Cold War against USA, the other victorious super power. Both the superpowers were trying to woo the recently independent India towards their own camps. In this scenario, USSR's policy towards India suddenly changed radically in 1950 in the wake of geopolitical compulsions of the cold war with the American block. So, instead of encouraging a proletariat uprising in India, USSR now became eager to cultivate good relations with India to keep her out of the

Anglo-American block. At the same time India's warm relationship with the nascent Communist power China was not in USSR's greater interest, India being the first country to accord diplomatic recognition to the Communist Chinese regime in October 1949. To discourage pro-Chinese comrades, B.T. Ranadive, who favoured the China line, was replaced with C. Rajeshwar Rao as the General Secretary of the CPI. At the end of 1950, Stalin summoned some of the top ranking Indian Communist leaders to a secret meeting at Moscow. Rajeshwar Rao, Ajoy Ghosh, S.A. Dange and M. Basavpunniah clandestinely went to Moscow to attend the meeting.[4] In this meeting Stalin told the Indian delegation to recognize the independence of India, abjure the armed struggle in Telengana and instead work for "the united front of workers, peasants, intelligentsia and the national bourgeoisie".[5] As directed by the high oracle, CPI took a U-turn. Rajeshwar Rao, an advocate of the Chinese path, was replaced with more pro-Soviet Ajoy Ghosh as the General Secretary. In 1951, CPI celebrated 15th August as Independence Day for the first time.[6] In October 1951 Telengana struggle was formally withdrawn. In the same year CPI celebrated for the first time the birth anniversary of Mahatma Gandhi. On the behest of Soviet Union, Rajni Palme Dutt (RPD), Britain based Communist ideologue, directed Indian Communists to participate in the first general elections.[7] CPI henceforth became a parliamentary party renouncing the path of armed insurrection.

In order to break the isolation and change the Party's public image, CPI's new leadership had to cope with the question- How to identify itself with the legacy of the freedom movement? In addition to the above mentioned drastic changes in the CPI approach, one of the steps taken by Ajoy Ghosh was to, "turn towards integrating the fundamentals of Marxism-Leninism with the specific features of the history, conditions and revolutionary process"[8] in India. Bhagat Singh's iconic status, socialistic and radical inclinations made him a fit case for appropriation by the Communist Party.

Bhagat Singh's appropriation was not the lone strand in the new strategy. The entire Communist version of Indian history and in particular the national struggle against the British rule first presented by M.N. Roy (*India in Transition*, 1922) and then by Rajani Palme Dutt (RPD) (*India Today*, 1940), was revised and reinterpreted. Veteran Communist leader Mohit Sen elaborated the new stand: "For far too long had our national revolution been denied the status of a revolution. It had become fashionable to deride it, especially by Marxist historians who followed the lead of M.N. Roy and RPD. Gandhi, in particular, was derided as a compromiser, conservative, superstitious leader who put brakes on the revolutionisation of the masses, thereby ultimately helping the British colonialists. He was assessed as being, at best, the representative of the Indian capitalists. Nehru was assessed as his faithful lieutenant who deceived the masses, especially the youth, by his radical speeches and writings."[9] In pursuance of the newly adopted approach the Revolt of 1857 was also reinterpreted. The pre-1950 Communist understanding of the nature of 1857, based on the interpretation provided by M.N. Roy and RPD, was that of *a reactionary and feudal outburst*.[10] By 1957, P.C. Joshi was openly declaring that 1857 was "the first chapter of the history of Indian national movement against British imperialism".[11]

But how to reinterpret Bhagat Singh? Ajoy Ghosh was himself on record in 1945 that "it would be an exaggeration to call Bhagat Singh a Marxist". How to retrace that position? So naturally, Ajoy Ghosh avoided directly associating himself with the task of associating Bhagat Singh with Marxism because eight years back he had presented a contrary estimate of Bhagat Singh in his book '*Bhagat Singh and His Comrades*'. He summoned G.M. Telang, a political columnist; discussed Bhagat Singh at length with him and guided him in the task of projecting Bhagat Singh's image in a Marxist mould.[12] The outcome of this exercise was '*Bhagat Singh: The Man and His Ideas*' in 1953, published by People's Publishing House, CPI's official publication house. Interestingly, G.M. Telang wrote this book under a pseudonym - Gopal Thakur.[13] Shiv Varma (who was now a member of the Communist Party) in his Forward to the book, described it as the *first political biography* of Bhagat Singh, emphasizing that "Bhagat Singh should primarily be studied as a political figure."[14] Since then the Left has taken the position that Bhagat Singh's ideology is more important than his martyrdom and revolutionary activities. Shiv Varma also disclosed the perspective with which the book was written: "Bhagat Singh was a link between the Revolutionaries of the past and Communist movement of today".[15]

Thus in 1953, *Bhagat Singh: The Man and His Ideas*, became the first biography of Bhagat Singh written from the Communist viewpoint. G.M. Telang alias Gopal Thakur reached the conclusion that Bhagat Singh shared the understanding of the Communist pioneers on the course of Indian freedom struggle. But Telang could not escape raising the question, "What is then that kept him from joining the ranks of the early Indian Marxists?"[16] He answered that the difference between Bhagat Singh and Communists was limited to the immediate task at hand: "Bhagat Singh regarded immediate armed action by individuals or groups as important work while for the Communists, the foremost task was to organise the workers and peasants." The author rued the fact that though Bhagat Singh was coming nearer to accepting the organization of workers and peasants for their economic demands as important task along with fight for freedom, through his study of Soviet literature, British gallows denied him the opportunity of carrying out that task and further studying the works of Marx, Engels, Lenin and Stalin.[17]

Shiv Varma's reminiscences '*Sansmritiyan*' about his revolutionary colleagues were published in 1969. It also contained some documents as annexure including the '*Introduction of Dreamland*' (being published for the first time). In his opinion, Bhagat Singh was a pioneer among revolutionaries moving towards Socialism. But it did not mean that Bhagat Singh had comprehended all aspects of Marxism. According to Varma, as Bhagat Singh's end came nearer, his faith in the bright future of the country and toiling masses became stronger.[18]

Apart from the efforts of Indian Marxists in linking Bhagat Singh's ideology with Marxism, a notable contribution came from the Soviet side. From 1969 onwards, L.V. Mitrokhin, a Soviet scholar, made a vigorous effort to establish the Marxist - Leninist credentials of Bhagat Singh through his books – '*Everest among Men*' (1969), '*Lenin in India*' (1981) and '*Lenin and Indian Freedom Fighters*'(1988). In the first book, Mitrokhin devoted a full chapter to establish that Bhagat Singh was reading a biography of Lenin in his last moments, though Mitrokhin, even after exhaustive research, could not pinpoint the book itself. Mitrokhin revealed that the source of this story was Bejoy Kumar Sinha whom he met for the first time in 1967. Sinha himself was at that time under the influence of C. Rajeswar Rao, the then General Secretary of C.P.I.[19] Interestingly, at that time Sinha himself was collecting material for a work on Bhagat Singh, which, unfortunately, could not take the shape of a book. In '*Lenin in India*' too, a separate chapter on Bhagat Singh- "The Last Days of Bhagat Singh" was included in which Mitrokhin attempted to show a deep influence of Marx and Lenin on Bhagat Singh on the basis of the jail note book of Bhagat Singh: "While in prison, Bhagat Singh managed in only a short time to assimilate the tenets of Marxist theory. His life ended tragically when he was getting prepared to apply his knowledge of Marx in practice."[20] Mitrokhin also narrated in detail how Bhagat Singh *craved* to meet Lenin: "Such was the impact of Lenin's personality that even in far off colonial India those that were doomed to death imbibed the lines that described his life and work as one drinks from a life - giving spring."[21]

A Marxist historical critique of the ideology of Bhagat Singh and his comrades appeared in 1972 in the form of the Left historian Bipan Chandra's long article '*The Ideological Development of the Revolutionary Terrorists in North India in 1920's*'.[22] Bipan Chandra expressed the view that "Bhagat Singh and his friends were not great scholars of Marxism but they were not novices either. They had travelled some way and were gradually feeling, studying and thinking their way towards a scientific understanding of the problems of the Indian Revolution."[23] At the same time, Bipan Chandra had to admit that there were a "series of contradictions between their socialist ideology and their work…They merely generated a nationalist consciousness."[24] According to Bipan Chandra, Bhagat Singh, during his last days had become a socialist from a terrorist: "The Socialist within him had finally overcome the terrorist". But he did not abandon "the sense of heroic sacrifice which he had imbibed from terrorism."[25]

Seven years later, in 1979, we find Bipan Chandra elevating Bhagat Singh to a pre-eminent place among India's early Marxist ideologues.[26] In his opinion, Bhagat Singh's writings reveal a revolutionary who is totally committed to Marxism and also has the ability to give it a practical shape retaining all its complexities.[27] In the end Bipan Chandra sums up Bhagat Singh: "Bhagat Singh was a critical revolutionary mind in the best traditions of Marx, Engels and Lenin."[28]

In the same year (1979), another Marxist study on the ideological development of revolutionaries- *'In Search of a Revolutionary Ideology and a Revolutionary Programme'* by S.N. Majumdar, reached different conclusions. Majumdar, himself a revolutionary turned Marxist, was not prepared to call Bhagat Singh a Marxist, leave alone a Marxist scholar: "Bhagat Singh personified the conflicting trends and pulls working on the minds of the "terro-socialists"…... He could not shake off the influence of petty bourgeois romantic revolutionism."[29]

Among the various assessments of Bhagat Singh and his ideology, a candid assessment came from Sohan Singh Josh, who had worked closely with Bhagat Singh for some time in 1928. In his autobiography, *My Tyrst with Secularism: An Autobiography*, published in 1991, Josh declared Bhagat Singh and his comrades as nationalist revolutionaries, prepared to adopt any form of struggle to end the British slavery. Josh pointed out that Marxism failed to influence Bhagat Singh and his colleagues because of the failure of Kirti Kisan Party to strike roots in Punjab. Recording Josh's evidence at some length may not be out of place to view the matter in context:

"Bhagat Singh and his comrades were nationalist revolutionaries to the core who wanted to drive out the British rulers, gain independence and establish socialism in India............. they were neither terrorists nor anarchists, as these terms are known in English languages. They were most self-sacrificing, most honest and selflessly dedicated to the cause of liberating India. They hated exploitation of the working class and the Indian people by the blood sucking British imperialists and their allies and were willing to make any sacrifice for the upliftment of the working class."

"They were prepared to adopt any form of struggle to end the British slavery. Violent or non violent, peaceful or non peaceful, all means were justified in their eyes provided these advanced the cause of freedom. But their preference was for individual or group action they believed in meeting British terror with patriotic counter terror...... The working class and their party has not yet struck roots in backward Punjab to influence them with Marxist ideology. They were, in effect, impatient patriots who detested any wait-and- see or go-slow policy. They could no longer stand the continuous degradation, demoralisation and dehumanisation of the Indian people under the British rule and were ready to contribute their mite in the earliest liquidation of British despotism."[30]

Bhagat Singh's alleged wish to 'meet' and 'get acquainted' with Lenin was repeated by CPI leader A.B. Bardhan in a 31 page booklet which he wrote in 1984 for the All Indian Youth Federation activists. Bardhan also made extensive use of Bhagat Singh's prison note book to prove that Bhagat Singh's faith and conviction underwent a remarkable modification in the direction of becoming a Marxist from a revolutionary terrorist. About Bhagat Singh's final destination, had he escaped the gallows, Bardhan wrote:

"It is more than evident that Bhagat Singh was steadfastly evolving from a 'revolutionary terrorist' to a 'Marxist'. Fate did not provide him with opportunity to demonstrate his maturing into a Marxist-Leninist. But the course along which he had set his ship of life would assuredly have brought him in the Communist Movement, as it did to most of his colleagues, had not his life cut short in its prime by the British hangman's noose."[31]

Here it is worth pondering that would Bhagat Singh as Communist Party member would have become the icon of the youth as *Shahid-i-Azam*? What happened to the fate of his illustrious comrades who later joined the Communist movement? Who remembers them?

In the ideological colouring of Bhgat Singh, Shiv Varma moved a step ahead with the publication of '*Selected Writings of Bhagat Singh*' in 1986. Shiv Varma traced the ideological development of the revolutionary movement in the introduction to his compilation. As Varma made it clear, the compilation was brought about with the objective of clearing the deliberate 'distortions' about revolutionaries in general and Bhagat Singh in particular, such as: "Revolutionaries started as and remained Hindu nationalists till the end......The object of the movement was just to drive out the British and establish a Hindu Raj in India....They upheld only the socialistic ideals of the Soviet Russia but not the dictatorship of the proletariat established in that country."[32] About Bhagat Singh he drew the inference that Bhagat Singh accepted Socialism as a goal in 1928, but hangovers from the past still remained. Intense studies in jail and discussions ultimately made him a confirmed Marxist just near his end. On the basis of a newly discovered version of a document dated 2nd February 1931, Shiv Varma concluded: "Bhagat Singh comes out openly for Marxism, for communism and for a communist party."[33] Doubts regarding the genuineness of this document have been discussed in the chapter: *Literary Heritage of Bhagat Singh: A Re-examination.*

The Foreword of the *Selected Writings* was written by veteran Communist leader B.T. Ranadive, who differed from Shiv Varma's assessment about the ideology of Bhagat Singh. In Ranadive's opinion, Bhagat Singh was making his way towards acceptance of Marxism as a guide for the practical tasks facing the country, *but his understanding of Marxsim was not complete.*[34] Citing examples from Shiv Varma's version of a document dated 2nd February 1931, Ranadive showed that Bhagat Singh was confused about the role of the party in open political work and underground work. Moreover, "for this party Bhagat Singh relies only on the youth, not understanding the class character of such a party and its class basis....This confusion notwithstanding, Bhagat Singh made the transition from individual action to mass revolutionary movement, from individual revolution to class revolution and class struggle. And he succeeded in linking it with the immediate needs of the national revolutionary struggle against the British. But a certain conflict always remained in his mind - the conflict between the immediate demands of an advanced revolutionary ideology and the keen personal desire for immediate militant action and self immolation."[35]

An interesting deviation from the stand taken by the Party ideologues on Bhagat Singh is witnessed in Hans Raj Rahbar's *Bhagat Singh and his Thought* (Delhi, 1990). The author claims that his work is the first biography of Bhagat Singh written from the angle of dialectical materialism. Rahbar believes that the nationalised (Indian) version of Marxism and Leninism, which he claims was established by Bhagat Singh, is in fact the ideology of Bhagat Singh. Bhagat Singh and not the Communist Party of India, was the real representative of Marxism in India.[36] Rahbar's contempt for the Communist Party of India vis a vis Bhagat Singh is worth quoting :

"The communist leaders had branded Bhagat Singh and his comrades as terrorists, and by describing themselves as true Marxists, they tried to claim the credit of being revolutionaries. Thus, the void that was created after the disintegration of HSRA remained unfilled. Bhagat Singh and his comrades not only called themselves Marxists, they also acted like Marxists. On the contrary, the Communists were Marxists in words and not in deeds…Bhagat Singh and his comrades very well understood the difference between what the Communist leaders professed and what they practiced. This is why their joint front in Naujawan Bharat Sabha with them did not last long… Although the Communist leaders did exploit the reputation of Bhagat Singh and his comrades for their own benefit, yet they never followed the path of revolution which the latter had opened by sacrificing their lives. The Communists had neither the courage nor the wisdom to do so. Even those of Bhagat Singh's comrades, who joined the Communists Party after being released from jails, as the proverb goes, turned into salt in the salt mine."[37]

From the late 1980s, a shift in the Left stand on Bhagat Singh can be clearly noticed. From here onwards, Left writings do not merely portray him as a symbol of socialism and anti- colonial resistance alone. They are also using his iconic image to fight their political battles against their political rivals, neo-imperialism,[38] globalization, and communalism (read *Hindutva).* Reasons behind this shift can be easily ascertained in the grave ideological crisis that Communism is facing globally. The embracing of capitalism by Eastern Europe, fall of Communism in the erstwhile USSR and its disintegration, and adoption of market economy by Mao's China are some of the events that have shaken the very foundations of the Communist ideology and exposed the failures of the Communist experiment in various parts of the world. Recent researches have exploded the larger than life image of communist legends such as Lenin, Stalin and Mao. The so-called 'scientific' essence of the Scientific Socialism as propounded by Marx has itself come under a cloud of doubts as it was based on 19th century philosophy of science. Capitalism is growing by leaps and bounds and new Communist revolutions as predicted by Marx are nowhere in the offing. Also, in the era of new economic opportunities, youth who used to be earlier attracted towards socialist ideology no longer find any appeal in the Left. A well known political commentator has aptly remarked: "Communism is no longer an ideology which appeals to India's young..... Communism is increasingly seen as a failed, undemocratic (tyrannical even) system that epitomizes bureaucratic dictatorship."[39]

Notes & References

[1]   Devendra Swarup, *Did Moscow Play Fraud on Marx? The Mystery of Marx-Engels' Articles on 1857*, 2007, pp. 64, 66.

[2]   Gargi Chakravartty, *P.C. Joshi: A Biography*, 2007, p. 89.

[3]   Ibid.

[4]   Inder Malhotra, "The Great Communist Split" in *The Indian Express*, New Delhi, 20 September, 2010, p. 11.

[5]   Ganesh Shukla, *A Dialogue with Dange*, in Mohit Sen (ed.), *Indian Communism: Life and work of S.A. Dange*, Patriot Publishers, New Delhi, 1992, pp. 137-138, cited in Devendra Swarup, op. cit., p. 71.

[6]   Devendra Swarup, op. cit., p. 76.

[7]   Ibid, pp. 71-72.

[8]   Mohit Sen,'s Preface to *Bhagat Singh and His Comrades,* 1979, p. 14.

[9]   Mohit Sen, *A Traveller and the Road*, 2003, p. 154.

[10] M.N. Roy and Abani Mukherji, *India in Transition,*1922, Reprint 1971, pp. 20, 158-160. & Rajani Palme Dutt, *India Today*, 1940, Reprint 1997, pp. 195, 306, 440.

[11] *New Age*, August, 1957, p. 55.

[12] Mohit Sen, *A Traveller and the Road,* op. cit., p. 138.

[13] Ibid.

[14] Shiv Varma, *Foreward* to *Bhagat Singh: The Man and His Ideas,* 1953.

[15] Ibid.

[16] Gopal Thakur, *Bhagat Singh: The Man and His Ideas*, 1953, p. 40.

[17] Ibid., p. 42.

[18] Shiv Varma, *Sansmritiyan*, 1974, p. 46.

[19] Srirajyam Sinha, *Bejoy Kumar Sinha: A Revolutionary's Quest for Sacrifice*, 1993, pp. 171-177.

[20] L.V. Mitrokhin, *Lenin in India,* 1981, p. 125.

[21] Ibid., p. 115.

[22] Bipan Chandra, "The Ideological Development of the Revolutionary Terrorists in North India in 1920's," in B.R Nanda, (ed.), *Socialism in India,* 1972, pp. 163-189.

[23] Ibid., pp. 174-186.

[24] Ibid., p. 187.

[25] Ibid., p. 188.

[26] Introduction to *Bhagat Singh: Why I am an Atheist and Introduction to the Dreamland,*, 1979.

[27] Ibid.

[28] Ibid.

[29] S.N.Majumdar, *In Search of a Revolutionary Ideology and a Revolutionary Programme,* 1979, p. 181.

[30] Sohan Singh Josh, *My Tyrst with Secularism: An Autobiography*, 1991, pp. 143-144. Also see Sohan Singh Josh, *My Meetings with Bhagat Singh and on Other Early Revolutionaries,* 1976, p. 19.

[31] A. B. Bardhan, *Bhagat Singh: Pages from the life of a Martyr,* 1984, p. 27.

[32] Preface to Shiv Varma, ed., *Selected Writings of Bhagat Singh,* 1996, pp. 14-15.

[33] Shiv Varma, ed., *Selected Writings of Bhagat Singh,* 1996, p. 42.

[34] Ibid., pp. 8-9.

[35] Ibid.

[36] Hans Raj Rahbar, *Bhagat Singh: Ek Jwalant Itihas,* 2004, p. 6.

[37] Hans Raj Rahbar, *Bhagat Singh and His Thought,* 1990, pp. 195-196.

[38] "Reading Bhagat Singh's jail notebook and court statements, replace the word "British" with "American" and today's reality is not far away....The Indian rulers of today fit into the category of those "pure Indian" won through "petty concessions" by US imperialism, but in

the words of Bhagat Singh- "the war shall continue". (Chaman Lal, *Remembering Bhagat Singh on the 75th Anniversary of His Martyrdom*, 23 March 2006, www.monthlyreview.org).

[39]   *Hindustan Times*, 19 August 2007, p. 10.

Appendices

Appendix -A

Collected Works of Bhagat Singh in chronological order

Amarjeet Chandan, ed., *Collected Works of Bhagat Singh and his Comrades* (Punjabi), Balraj Sahni Yadgar Library Publication, Amritsar, 1974.

Virender Sindhu, ed., *Sardar Bhagat Singh, Patra aur Dastavej*, Rajpal & Sons, New Delhi, 1975.

Virender Sindhu (compiler), Bhagat Singh, *Mere Krantikari Sathi*, Raj Pal& Sons, Delhi, 1977.

Bipan Chandra, ed., Bhagat Singh, *Why I Am Athiest*, Sardar Bhagat Singh Research Committee, Delhi, 1979.

Shiv Varma, ed., *Selected Writings of Bhagat Singh*, National Book Depot, New Delhi, 1986.

Jagmohan Singh and Chaman Lal, eds., *Bhagat Singh Aur Unke Sathion Ke Dastavej*, Rajpal & Sons, New Delhi, 1986.

Jagmohan Singh and Chaman Lal, eds., *Bhagat Singh aur Unke Sathion Ke Dastavej,* Rajpal & Sons, New Delhi, 1991(revised edition).

Jagamohan Singh and Chaman Lal, eds., *Bhagat Singh Aur Unke Sathion Ke Dastavej*, Rajkamal, New Delhi, 1997.

Satyam, ed., *Shaheed-e-Ajam Ki Jail Note Book*, Vinod mishra (tr.), Parikalpana Prakashan, Luknow, 1999.

Bhoopendra Hooja, ed., *A Martyr's Notebook*, Indian Book Chronicle, Jaipur, 2002.

Ved Swaroop Narang and Gyan Kaur Kapur eds., *Shaheed Bhagat Singh Ki Jail Diary*, Raj Publishing House, Jaipur, 2002.

Shaheed e Ajam Bhagat Singh: Vichar Aur Sangharsh, (AISA, INAUS) Samkaleen Prakashan, Patna, 2003.

Chaman Lal, ed., *Bhagat Singh Ke Sampoorna Dastavrej*, Aadhar, Panchkula, 2006.

Satyam, ed., *Bhagat Singh Aur Unke Sathion Ke Sampoorn Uplabdh Dastavej*, Rahul Foundation, Lucknow, 2006.

Raj Shekhar Vyas, ed., *Mein Bhagat Singh Bol Raha Hun*, 3 vols. Praveen Prakashan, New Delhi, 2006.

K.C. Yadav and Babar Singh, eds., *The Fragrance of Freedom, The Writings of Bhagat Singh*, Hope India, Gurgaon, 2006.

Chaman Lal, ed., *Bhagat Singh Ke Rajnaitik Dastavej,* National Book Trust, New Delhi, 2006.

Gupta, D.N., ed., *Selected Speeches and Writings of Bhagat Singh*, National Book Trust, New Delhi, 2007.

Chaman Lal, ed., *Bhagat Singh: The Jail Note Book And Other Writings*, LeftWord, New Delhi, 2007.

K.C. Yadav, and Babar Singh, (eds.), *Bhagat Singh: Ideas on Freedom, Liberty and Revolution; Jail Notes of a Revolutionary,* Hope India, 2007.

Chaman Lal, ed., *Dastavejon Ke Aaine Mein,* Publication Division, Ministry of Information and Broadcasting, Government of India, New Delhi, 2007.

Appendix B

Bhagat Singh's letters to his family, friends, colleagues and press

Addressee	Dated	Special Feature
Three letters addressed to grandfather	(i) 22July 1918 (ii)7 July1919[1] (iii)14 Nov. 1921	Letters to grandfather are in Urdu. They begin with '*Om*'.
Two letters to aunts	(i) 24 Oct.1921 (ii)15 Nov.1921	Letters to aunts are in Gurmukhi
Two letters to father	(i) while leaving home in 1923 (ii)Published in *The Tribune* on 4th October 1930[2]	Both letters are undated
Three letters to Kulbir Singh(younger brother)	(i)16 Sep.1930. (ii) 25th Sep.1930. (iii) 3rd March 1931	All letters are from jail
Letter to Kultar Singh (younger brother)	3rd March 1931	
Letter to Amarchand	undated (may be dated to mid 1927)	
Four letters to Jaidev Gupta	(i) 24 Feb.1930[3] (ii) 28 May 1930[4] (iii) 3 June 1930[5] (iv) 24 July 1930[6]	
Two letters to Sukhdev	(i)undated	(written just before going to Assembly bomb action on 8th April 1929)

	(ii) undated	(written in jail after the end of hunger strike)
Letter to Harikishan,	Undated (1930)[7]	
Letter to Promila (B.K. Dutt's sister)	17th July 1930	
Letter to B.K. Dutt,	Undated,	written after being awarded death sentences (7th October 1930)
Letter to editor of '*Maharathi*'	27th February 1928	
Letter to editor of '*Modern Review*' (co-authored with B.K. Dutt)	24th December 1929	
Letter to colleagues (undergoing trial in the Second Lahore Conspiracy Case) in the adjoining barrack in Lahore Central Jail	22nd March 1931	

Appendix- C

Letters to British authorities (Twelve)

(i) Letter to police authorities after release from jail in 1927, undated.[8]

(ii) Letter to Inspector General, Punjab Jails dated 17th June 1929

(iii) Notice of hunger Strikes, dated 17th June 1929

(iv) Letter to Home Member, dated 24th July 1929

(v) Letter to Punjab Jail Enquiry Committee, dated 6th September 1929

(vi) Telegram to Home Member, dated 20th January 1930

(vii) Memorandum to Home Department, dated 28th January 1930

(viii) Letter to Special Magistrate, dated 11th February 1930

(ix) Letter to Governor General on establishment of Special Tribunal, dated 2nd May 1930

(x) Letter to Commissioner, Special Tribunal, dated 5th May 1930

(xi) Letter to Commissioner, Special Tribunal on reorganisation of Special Tribunal, dated 25th May 1930

(xii) 'Mercy petition'(so called) to Governor, Punjab, dated 20th March 1931

Appendix- D

Statements in the court (jointly with B. K. Dutt)

(i) Statement in the Sessions Court (read by Asaf Ali) dated, 6 June 1929.(According to Bhagat Singh's counsel Asaf Ali, substance of the statement was according to Bhagat Singh's own draft, the actual language and the sequence of the sentences was of Asaf Ali)[9]

(ii) Statement in the High Court (January 1930)

Appendix- E

Messages from Jail, Jointly with other co-accused (Four)

(i) Message to Punjab Students Conference, dated 19th October 1929

(ii) Telegram to IIIrd International, dated 24th January 1930

(iii) Telegram to Kakori case prisoners, dated 5th April 1930

(iv) Telegram to Hindustani Association, Berlin, dated 5th April 1930

Appendix- F

Pamphlets ascribed to Bhagat Singh (Three)

(i) Pamphlet pasted in Lahore after Saunders' murder, dated, 18 December 1928

(ii) Pamphlet pasted in Lahore after Saunders' murder, dated, 23 December1928

(iii) Pamphlet thrown in the Central Legislative Assembly on 8 April, 1929

Appendix- G

Writings ascribed to Bhagat Singh published before 8th April, 1929 (except the articles published in the *Phansi* number of *Chand* published in November, 1928)

Title of Writing	Date of Publication	Name & Place of Publication	Name of Author
Vishwa-Prem	15 & 22 Nov. 1924	*Matwala*, Calcutta	Balwant
Yuvak	16 May 1925	*Matwala*, Calcutta	Balwant
Punjab Ki Bhasa Aur Lipi Ki Samasya	Written in 1925 or later, but published on 28th Feb. 1933	*Hindi Sandesh*	Bhagat Singh
Holi Ke Din Rakta Ke Chheetein	15 Mar.1926	*Pratap*, Kanpur	Ek Punjabi Yuvak
Kakori Ke Veeron Se Parichay	May 1927	*Kirti*, Amritsar	Vidrohi
Kakori Ke Shaheedon ki Phansi ke Halaat	Jan.1928	*Kirti*, Amritsar	Vidrohi
Kuka Vidroh-1	Feb.1928	*Maharathi*, Delhi	B.S. Sindhu
Letter to Editor of Maharathi	Feb.1928	*Maharathi*, Delhi	Bhagat Singh

Chitra Parichaya	March 1928	*Maharathi,* Delhi	
Madan Lal Dhingra	March 1928	*Kirti,* Amritsar	Vidrohi
Arajaktavaad I (Anarchism)	May 1928	*Kirti,* Amritsar	Unsigned
Dharam Aur Hamara Swadheenta Sangharsh	May 1928	*Kirti,* Amritsar	Unsigned
Arajaktavaad II	May 1928	*Kirti,* Amritsar	Unsigned
Sampradayik Dange Aur Unka Ilaaj	June 1928	*Kirti,* Amritsar	Unsigned
Satyagriha Aur Hartalain	June 1928	*Kirti,* Amritsar	Unsigned
Achhoot Samasya	June 1928	*Kirti,* Amritsar	Vidrohi
Arajaktavaad III	July 1928	*Kirti,* Amritsar	Unsigned
Vidyarthi Aur Rajniti	July 1928	*Kirti,* Amritsar	Unsigned
Naye Netaon Ke Alag Alag Vichar	July 1928	*Kirti,* Amritsar	Unsigned
Roos Ke Yugaantkari Naashwadi	August 1928	*Kirti,* Amritsar	Unsigned
Lala Lajpat Rai Aur Naujawan	August 1928	*Kirti,* Amritsar	Unsigned

Yugaantkaari Maa	Sep.1928	*Kirti,* Amritsar	Unsigned
Kuka (II) Vidroh*	Oct. 1928	*Kirti,* Amritsar	Vidrohi
Aayrish Swatantrata Yudh(Transl. of My Fight for Irish Freedom in Hindi)		*Pratap,* Kanpur	Balwant
The Philosophy of the Bomb	Jan.26, 1930	Secretly published by Chandra Shekhar Azad in Kanpur	Kartar Singh

* *Kuka Vidroh (I)* was published in Maharathi in February 1928. Numbering in bracket has been given for the sake of convenience.

Appendix- H

List of biographical sketches of martyrs published in the *Phansi* number of *Chand* of November 1928

S.No.	Title	Author's Name
1	*Kuka Vidroh Ke Balidaan*	Nirbhay
2	*Chapekar Bandhu*	Sainik
3	*Kanhai Lal Dutt*	Vanshi
4	*Satyendrakumar Basu*	Kisan
5	*Madanlal Dhingra*	Basant
6	*Amirchand*	Gautam
7	*Awadhbihari*	Vidrohi
8	*Bhai Balmukund*	Ramesh
9	*Basantokumar Visvas*	Vidrohi
10	*Bhai Bhag Singh*	Natwar
11	*Bhai Watan Singh*	Chakresh
12	*Mewa Singh*	Kovid
13	*Pt. Kanshi Ram*	Bandi
14	*Gandha Singh*	Lakshaman
15	*Kartar Singh Sarabha*	Balwant
16	*V.G. Pingley*	Virendra
17	*Jagat Singh*	Surendra
18	*Balwant Singh*	Mukund
19	*Doctor Mathura Singh*	Brajesh
20	*Banta Singh*	Girish
21	*Ranga Singh*	Ghanshyam
22	*Vir Singh*	Yadav
23	*Uttamsingh-*	Pathik

24	*Doctor Arud Singh*	Pathik
25	*Babu Harinaam Singh*	Agyat
26	*Sohanlal Pathak*	Subodh
27	*Deshbhakt Sufi Amba Prasad*	Agyat
28	*Bhai Ram Singh*	Bhanu
29	*Bhan Singh*	Dhanesh
30	*Yatindranath Mukerji*	Ek Yuvak
31	*Nalini Vakchya*	Suryanath
32	*Udham Singh*	Pancham
33	*Gendalal Dikshit*	Ramprasad 'Bismil'
34	*Khushiram*	Ek Darshak
35	*Gopimohan Saha*	Bhavbhuti
36	*Bomeli Yudh Ke Chaar Shahid*	Madhusen
37	*Dhanna Singh*	Chaturanan
38	*Banta Singh Dhamiyan*	Senapati
39	*Varyam Singh Ghugga*	Bhushan
40	*Kishan Singh Gargajja*	Mohan
41	*Santa Singh*	Vir Singh
42	*Dalip Singh*	Kapil
43	*Nand Singh*	Natnath
44	*Karma Singh*	Prabhat
45	*Ramprasad 'Bismil'*	Prabhat
46	*Rajendranath Lahiri*	Santosh
47	*Roshan Singh*	Rupchandra
48	*Ashfaqullah Khan*	Shri Krishna

Notes & References

[1] Newly discovered letter at NMML, published in *Jansatta* (Hindi), 28 March 2007; *The Tribune*, 8 April 2007. In these articles, Chaman Lal has mentioned Nehru Memorial Museum and Library (NMML), New Delhi as the source of four new letters. But despite repeated efforts, the present author failed to locate their original copies in NMML.

[2] All collections and books except G.S. Deol (1985) give date of writing of this letter as 4th October 1930.

[3] Newly discovered letter, *Jansatta* (Hindi), 28 March 2007; *The Tribune*, 8 April 2007.

[4] Ibid.

[5] Ibid.

[6] Ibid.

[7] Published in *The People*, 14 June,1931.

[8] This is one of the new additions, claimed to have been discovered in Nehru Memorial Museum and Library and first published in *Jansatta* (Hindi) of 28th March2007and *The Tribune* of 8th April 2007. Surprisingly, Chaman Lal, author of these articles, has himself not included this letter in his latest collection of Bhagat Singh's documents, *Shaheed Bhagat Singh: Dastavejon Ke Aaieene Mein* (2007).

[9] Asaf Ali's interview in *Commonwealth* (Poona), 23rd March 1949, republished in, M.M Juneja, ed., *Selected Collections on Bhagat Singh*, 2007, p. 129.

Bibliography

List of Files Seen at National Archives of India, New Delhi

Branch	File-Number & Year	Subject Matter
Home Political	F.67, 1924	*Akali Jatthas* proceeding to Jaito
Home Political	F.253, 1925	Activities of Revolutionaries in Bengal
Home Political	F.375, 1925	Manifesto of HRA
Home Political	F.38/III, 1925	Train decoity by revolutionaries at Kakori
Home Political	F.254, 1926	Bomb explosion in Lahore on 16 October 1926
Home Political	F.139/III., 1926	Custody of Jogesh Chandra Chatterjee in Kakori Case
Home Political	F.53, 1927	Judgment of Special Session Judge of Lucknow and Chief Court of Oudh in Kakori Case
Home Political	F.32, 1927	Internal political situation in India

Home Political	F.1, 1928	Internal political situation in India
Home Political	F.25/2, 1928	Examination and interception of seditious literature in past
Home Political	F.18/XVIII, 1928	Communist correspondence with Moscow
Home Political	F.17, 1929	Political situation in India
Home Political	F.192, 1929	Bomb outrage in Legislative Assembly
Home Political	F. 202, 1929	Forcible feeding during hunger strike
Home Political	F.242, 1929	Treatment of prisoners during trial
Home Political	F. 28/II, 1929	Translation of *My Fight for Irish Freedom*
Home Political	F.192/KWI, 1929	Investigation in Delhi Bomb Case
Home Political	F.21/XXII, 1929	Question in Leigislative Assembly (LA) regarding strikes in connection with Simon Commission's visit.
Home Political	F.21./57, 1929	Question in LA regarding treatment of under trials in Lahore Case
Home Political	F.21/XXIII, 1929	Question in LA regarding boycott of Sirnon Commission
Home Political	F.25/65, 1930	Passport granted to Hansraj Vohra

Home Political	F.23/18, 1930	Question in Parliament regarding ill treatment of political prisoners in India
Home Political	F.29/IV, 1930	Proscription of book – *India in Bondage*
Home Political	F.4/15, 1930	Discovery of bomb factory in Delhi. Arrest of Kailash Pati
Home Political	F.4/14, 1930	Revolutionary conspiracy in Jullundhar
Home Political	F.130 & K.W., 1930	Activities of Naujawan Bharat Sabha (NBS)
Home Political	F.4/8, 1930	Appointment of inspector of explosion in connection with the Assembly Bomb Case
Home Political	F.172, 1930	Obstruction tactics adopted by accused in Lahore Conspiracy Case
Home Political	F.137, 1930	Petition by Bhagat Singh and Dutt
Home Political	F.498, 1930	Activities of NBS at Karachi
Home Political	F.244 & K.W., 1930	Re-examination of rules relating to under trials
Home Political	F.11/30, 1930	Activities of NBS at Peshawar
Home Political	F.18/III, 1930	Internal political situation in India
Home Political	F.36/III, 1930	Hunger strike in jail
Home Political	F.23/2, 1930	Question in Parliament regarding Prevention of Seditious Meetings Act 1908

Home Political	F.4/7, 1930	Saunders' murder
Home Political	F.4/13, 1930	Attack on Viceroy's train and progress of Delhi bomb case
Home Political	F.4/10, 1930	Attack on Punjab Governor's life
Home Political	F.36/IV, 1930	Hunger strike of Bhagat Singh and Dutt
Home Political	F.133, 1930	Note by Director of Intelligence Bureau on the political situation with special reference to revolutionary crime and terrorism
Home Political	F.29/7, 1931	A leaflet of Hindustan Ghadar Party
Home Political	F.18/I/1931	Internal political situation in India
Home Political	F.18/IV, 1931	Report on political situation in the Punjab
Home Political	F.4/21, 1931	Banning of processions and meetings after the execution of Bhagat Singh and others
Home Political	F.9/XI& K.W., 1931	Publication in *Daily Worker*, New York of certain Charges against Saunders
Home Political	F.152/31, 1931	Recommendations for dealing with Civil Disobedience Movement
Home Political	F.27/5,1931	Prosecution of J N Sanyal, Ramchandra & Bhoopendra Nath Sanyal

Home Judicial	F.152/1/1931, K.W.	Mass petition and Bhagat Singh's mother's petition for commutation
Home Political	F.4/12,1931	Appeal for funds to perpetuate the memory of Bhagat Singh, Rajguru and Sukhdev
Home Political	F.11/15,1931	Statement of approver Kailashpati
Home Political	F.235,1931	Confiscation of pass supplied to Hindustan Times reporter by Judge in Delhi Conspiracy Case
Home Political	F.4/20,1931	Appeal to Privy Council against death sentence
Home Political	F.33/I & K.W., 1931	Gandhi's interview with Home Secretary on the issue of Bhagat Singh's impending execution
Home Political	F.33/II & K.W., 1931	Congress speeches on Bhagat Singh's execution
Home Political	F.208/1932	Speeches on Bhagat Singh in Karachi Congress
Home Political	F.150,1932	Translation of Tamil biography of Bhagat Singh
Home Political	F.48/4,1933	Fourth manifesto of Hindustan Socialist Republican Association
Home Political	F.44/64,1934	History-sheet of Ramkrishna

Transcripts of Interviews in Oral History Section of Nehru Memorial Museum and Library, New Delhi

Chhabil Das

Durga Devi Vohra

Feroz Chand

Jaidev Gupta

Jaidev Kapur

Kulbir Singh

Kultar Singh

Lajjavati

N.K.Nigam

Pran Nath Mehta

Ram Kishan

Satyabhakta

Books

Adhikari, G.M., *Communist Party of India and its Path to National Regeneration and Socialism*, Delhi, 1964.

Adhikari, Gangadhar, ed., *Documents of the History of the Communist Party of India*, vol. I, People's Publishing House, New Delhi, 1971.

Ahluvalia, Amar Nath, *Varlap* (Punjabi), Sanatan Dharam Steam Press, Lahore,1931, (N.A.I. Home Polilical,116,1932).

Amar Shaheed Sardar Bhagat Singh, Government of Punjab, Chandigarh, 1968.

Ananda, Prakasha, *A History of The Tribune*, The Tribune Trust, 1986, Delhi.

Aruna Asaf Ali, *Fragments from the Past, Selected Writings and Speeches of Aruna Asaf Ali,* Patriot Publishers, New Delhi, 1989.

Azad, Baba Prithvi Singh, *Baba Prithvi Singh: The Legendry Crusader, An Autobiography,* Bharatiya Vidya Bhavan, Bombay, 1987.

Bakshi, S.R., *Bhagat Singh*, Anmol Publication, New Delhi, 1990.

Bakshi. S. R., *Bhagat Singh and His Ideology*, Capital Publishers, New Delhi, 1981.

Bandyopadhyaya, Jayantanuja, *Indian Nationalism versus International Communism*, Firma K.L. Mukhopadhyay, Calcutta, 1966.

Bardhan, A.B., *Bhagat Singh: Pages from the Life of the Martyr*, All India Youth Federation, New Delhi, 1984.

Barrier, N.G., *Banned Controversial Literature and Political Control in British India, (1907-47),* Manohar, New Delhi, 1977.

Basu, Jyoti et al (eds.), *Documents of the Communist Movement in India*, vols. I-IV, National Book Agency, Calcutta, 1997.

Basu, Jyoti, *History of the Communist Movement in India*, Vol. I, CPI (M) Publicaton and LeftWord, New Delhi, 2005.

Bhargava, Motilal, *Role of Press in the Freedom Movement*, Reliance Publishing House, New Delhi, 1987.

Bipan Chandra, *India's Struggle for Independence*, Penguin, Delhi, 1989.

Bismil, Ramprasad, *Atmakatha*, Atmaram & Sons, Delhi, 1958.

Bose, Subhash Chandra, *The Indian Struggle, 1920-1942*, Asia Publishing House, Bombay, 1967.

Buried Alive, Autobiography, Speeches and Writings of an Indian Revolutionary Sardar Ajit Singh, Gitanjali Publishing House, New Delhi, 1984.

Chakraborty, Trailokya Nath, *Thirty Years in Prison: Sensational Confessions of a Revolutionary*, Alpha-Beta Publications, Calcutta, 1963.

Chakravartty, Gargi, *P.C. Joshi; A Biography*, National Book Trust, New Delhi, 2007.

Challenge: A Saga of India's Struggle for Freedom, Nisith Pankaj Ray &others, (eds.), People's Publishing House, New Delhi, 1984.

Chandra, Bipan, *Bhagat Singh Aur Unke Sathiyon Ki Vichardhara Aur Rajniti*, Rahul Foundation, Luknow, 2006.

Chandra, Bipan, *Bharatiya Rastravad, Kuchh Nibandh*, Rajendra Prasad Pandey, (tr.), Jawahar Publishers and Distributors, New Delhi, 1996.

Chatterjee, Jogesh, *In Search of Freedom*, Messers. K.L.Mukhopadhyaya, Calcutta, 1967.

Chaturvedi, Banarasi Das (ed.), *Yash Ki Dharohar*, Atmaram & Sons, Delhi, 1968.

Chaturvrdi, Banarasidas, ed., *Shaheed Granthmala* (series), Atma Ram & Sons, Delhi, 1960-63.

Chauhan, Lal Bahadur Singh, *Krantiveer Bhagat Singh*, Atmaram & Sons, Delhi, 2004.

Chauhan, Shivdan Singh, ed., *Baba Prithvi Singh Azad Lenin Ke Desh Mein*, Navyug Publishers, Delhi, 1978.

Chopra, P.N., ed., *Who's Who of Indian Martyrs*, Ministry of Education, three volumes, New Delhi, 1969, 1972, 1973.

Communists Challenge Imperialism from the Dock, (The General statement of 18 Communists accused in the Meerut Conspiracy), Introduction by Mujjaffar Ahmad, National Book Agency, Calcutta, 1967.

Dalal, C.B., *Gandhi: 1915-1948, A Detailed Chronology*, Gandhi Peace Foundation, New Delhi, 1971.

Dange, S.A., *Gandhi vs. Lenin*, Liberty Literature Co., Bombay, 1921.

Das, Kiran Chander, *Amar Shaheed Jatin Das*, Department of Public Relations, Chandigarh, 1950.

Datta Gupta, Sobhanlal, *Comintern and the Destiny of Communist Movement in India, 1919-1943*, Seri Baan, Calcutta, 2006.

Datta, V.N., *Gandhi and Bhagat Singh*, Rupa, New Delhi, 2008.

Deol, Gurudev Singh, *Shaheed Bhagat Singh: A Biography*, Publication Bureau,, Punjabi University, Patiala, 1969.

Dave, Kapil Prasad Mahasukhbhai, *Bhagat Singh Kaunn* (Gujarati), Ahemdabad, n.d. (NAI Lib).

Deol, Gurudev Singh, *Shaheed-e-Ajam Bhagat Singh*, Deep Publication, Nabha, Ludhiana, 1978.

Deol, Gurudev Singh, *Shaheed Bhagat Singh: A Biography*, Punjabi University, Patiala, 1969.

Devi, Chandravati, *Shahid Sardar Bhagat Singh* (Hindi),Lahore,1931,(Home Political 4/36,1932).

Dewan, Manorama, *Inqalabi Yatra,* National Book Trust, New Delhi, 2006.

Dhankar, Jaiveer S., *A Short History: Hindustan Socialist Republican Association*, Sanjay Prakashan, New Delhi, 2004.

Dharamvir, *Bhai Parmanand Aur Unka Yug,* University Publication, New Delhi, 2005.

Dublish, Kaushalya Devi, *Revolutionaries and their Activities in North India*, B.R. Publications, Delhi, 1982.

Ewart, J., *Terrorism in India, 1917-36,* Government of India Press, Shimla, 1927.

Freedom Struggle Centenary Souvenir, 1857-1957, Delhi.

Gandhi, M.K., *Collected Works of Mahatma Gandhi,* Publication Division, Ministry of Information and Broadcasting, New Delhi, 1998.

Gopal, S., (ed.) *Selected Works of Jawaharlal* Nehru, Vol. 4, Orient Longman, New Delhi, 1973.

Gandhi, M.K., *Selected Works of Mahatma Gandhi*, Navajivan Publishing House, Ahmedabad, 1968.

Gaur, Dharmendra, *The Azad Episode, The Great Betrayal by his Treacherous Colleagues*, IBH Prakashan, Bangalore, 1979.

George, Jose, Kumar, Manoj and Khandare, Avinash, (Eds.) *Rethinking Radicalism in Indian Society: Bhagat Singh and Beyond*, Rawat Publications, Jaipur, 2009.

Ghosh, Ajoy, *Bhagat Singh and His Comrades,* People's Publishing House, Bombay, 1945.

Ghosh, K.C., *The Roll of Honour: Anecdots of Indian Martyrs*, Vidyabharati, Calcutta, 1965.

Gopal, S., *The Viceroyality of Lord Irwin, 1929-31*, Oxford at the Charlton Press, 1957.

Grewal, J.S., (Ed.), *Bhagat Singh and His Legend*, World Punjabi Centre, Patiala, 2008.

Grewal, J.S., *Sikhs of Punjab*, Oxford University Press, New Delhi. 1990.

Grewal, P.M.S., *Bhagat Singh: Liberation's Blazing Star*, LeftWord, New Delhi, 2007.

Guha, A.C., *First Spark of Revolution*, Orient Longman, Delhi, 1971.

Gupta, Manmathnath, *Bhagat Singh and His Times*, Lipi Prakashan, Delhi, 1977.

Gupta, Anand, *Lenin in India*, New Literature, Delhi, 1980.

Gupta, Manmathnath, *Bharat Mein Sashastra Kranti Ki Chesta Ka Romanchkari Itihas*, 1939.

Gupta, Manmathnath, *History of Indian Revolutionary Movement*, Bombay, New Delhi, 1972.

Gupta, Manmathnath, *Krantidoot Bhagat Singh Aur Unka Yug*, 1972.

Gupta, Manmathnath, *They Lived Dangerously*, People's Publishing House, New Delhi, 1969.

Gupta, Maya and Gupta, Amit, *Defying Death: Struggle against Imperialism and Feudalism*, Tulika, New Delhi, 2001.

Gupta, K.L., *Sardar Bhagat Singh*, Adarsh Press, Agra, 1931, (NAI Lib.).

Gurudutt, *Bhav Aur Bhavana*, Shashwat Vani, New Delhi, 2000.

Habib, S.Irfan, *To Make the Deaf Hear: Ideology and Programmes of Bhagat Singh and His Comrades*, Three Essays Collective, New Delhi, 2007.

Hale, H.W., *Political Trouble in India, 1917-1937,* Chugh Publications, Allahabad, 1974.

Halifax, The Earl of, *Fullness of Days*, Collins, London, 1957.

Hardas, Balashastri, *Armed Struggle for Freedom, 1857 to Subhash*, Jagriti Prakashan, Noida, 1998.

Harishankar, Rama, *Gandhi's Encounter with the Indian Revolutionaries*, Siddhath Publications, New Delhi, 1996.

Homage to Martyrs, Shaheed Ardha Shatabdi Sangharsh Samiti, Delhi, 1981.

Jackson, T. A., *Ireland Her Own: An Outline History of the Irish Struggle,* C. Desmond Greaves, Berlin, 1973.

Jeevaanthan, P.,(Tr.) *Nan Nastheegan Ain. (Why I Am An Athiest), Sardar Bhagat Singh*(Tamil), Bhagvthariya Noor Pathippur Khazhalagam, Erode,1934, (NAI Lib.).

Johar, K.L., *Martyr Bhagat Singh: An Intimate View*, Sneh Prakashan, Delhi, 2007.

Josh, Bhagwan, *Communist Movement in Punjab*, Anupama Publication, Delhi, 1979.

Josh, Sohan Singh, *Akali Morchon Ka Itihas*, People's publishing House, New Delhi, 1974.

Josh, Sohan Singh, *My Meetings with Bhagat Singh and on Other Early Revolutionaries,* Communist Party of India, Delhi, 1976.

Josh, Sohan Singh, *My Tyrst with Secularism: An Autobiography*, Patriot Publishers, New Delhi, 1991.

Josh, Sohan Singh, *The Great Attack, Meerut Conspiracy Case,* People's Publishing House, New Delhi, 1979.

Joshi, P.C., and Damodaran, K., *A Documented History of the Communist Movement in India, 1917-1922,* 2 vols., edited by Sobhanlal Datta Gupta, Sunrise Publication, New Delhi, 2007.

Joshi, P.C., Chattopdhyaya, Gautam and Kaushik, Devendra, *Lenin in Contemporary Indian Press,* People's Publishing House, New Delhi, 1970.

Juneja, M.M., *Biography of Bhagat Singh*, Modern Publishers, Hissar, 2008.

Juneja, M.M., ed., *Bhagat Singh Par Chuninda Lekh,* Modern Publishers, Hissar, 2007.

Juneja, M.M., ed., *Selected Collections on Bhagat Singh,* Modern Publishers, Hissar, 2007.

Karnik, V.B., *M.N.Roy,* National Book Trust, New Delhi, 2005.

Kaye, Cecil, *Communism In India, with Unpublished Documents from National Archives of India,1919-1924,* Editions Indian, Calcutta, 1971.

Khatri, Ram Krishna, *Shaheedon Ki Chhaya Mein*, Vishwa Bharati, Nagpur, 1983.

Khullar, K.K., *Shaheed Bhagat Singh: Kuchh Adhkhule Prasth*, Hem Publishers, New Delhi, 1981.

Kooner, K.S. and Sindhra, G.S., *Some Hidden Facts: Martyrdom of Shaheed Bhagat Singh,* Unistar, Chandigarh, 2005.

Lahore Ki Phansi (Hindi), Sri Yantralaya, Banaras, 1931(NAI Lib.).

Lal, Chaman, *Gadar Party Nayak Kartar Singh Sarabha,* National Book Trust, New Delhi, 2007.

Laushey, David M., *Bengal Terrorism and Marxist Left: Aspects of Regional Nationalism in India 1905-1942,* Firma K. L. Mukhopadhyaya, Calcutta, 1975.

Mahaur, Bhagwandas, Malkapurkar, Sadashiv and Varma, Shiv, *Yash Ki Dharohar*, Rahul Foundation, Lucknow, 2006.

Mira Behn (Madeleine Slade), *The Spirit's Pilgrimage*, Longmans, London, 1960.

Pal, Prakashwati, *Lahore Se Lucknow Tak*, Viplav Office, Lucknow, 1994.

Majumdar, Satyendra Narayan, *In Search of a Revolutionary Ideology and a Revolutionary Programme*, People's Publishing House, New Delhi, 1979.

Malhotra, Shanta, *Sreya Marg Ke Pathik*, K.K. Publications, New Delhi, 2000.

Manikyam, M. R., *Sardar Bhagat Singh- Jiitha Charitra*(Telgu), Madras, 1931 .(NAI Lib.).

Mathur, L.P., *Bhagat Singh: The Prince of Martyrs*, Avishkar Publications, Jaipur, 2002.

Mehar Ilam al Din, *Pyara Bhagat Singh* (urdu), Sanatan Dharam Press,1931(Home Political,4,1932).

Mehrotra, N.C., and Sharma, Poonam, *Uttar Pradesh Mein Krantikari Andolan Ka Itihas*, Atmaram and Sons, Delhi, 1999.

Memoirs: 25 Communist Freedom Fighters, People's Democracy, New Delhi, April 2005.

Misra, Prabhu Narayan, *Lahore Ki Suli*, Sri Press, 1931 (NAI Lib.).

Mitrokhin, L.V., Everest *Among Men: Notes about Early Indian Literature on Lenin,* Girija kumar Sinha, ed., Soviet Land Booklets, Delhi, 1969.

Mitrokhin, L.V., *Lenin in India*, Allied Publishers, New Delhi, 1981.

Mitrokhin, Leonid, *Lenin and Indian Freedom Fighters,* Panchsheel Publishers, New Delhi, 1988.

Mohan, Kamlesh, *Militant Nationalism in Punjab*, Manohar, New Delhi, 1985.

Muthukumarswami, M.N., *Sardar Bhagat Singh Charitram*(Tamil), Kadaloor Agencies, Tiruppathiripuliyar,1931.(NAI Lib.).

Nanda, B.R., (ed.), *Socialism in India,* Vikas Publishing House. New Delhi, 1972.

Naqqash-e-Fitrat, *Shan-e- Ajadi Ke Teen Parwane*(urdu),, Lahore, n.d. .(NAI Lib.).

Nath, Shaileswar, *Terrorism in India*, Delhi, 1980.

Nayar, Kuldip, *The Martyr: Bhagat Singh, Experiments in Revolution*, Har-Anand Publication, New Delhi, 2000.

Nayar, Kuldip, *Without Fear; The Life and Trial of Bhagat Singh*, Harper Collins, New Delhi, 2007.

Nigam, Nand Kishore, *Balidan*, Naya Hindustan Press, Delhi, n.d.

Noorani, A.G., *The Trial of Bhagat Singh: The Politics of Justice*, Oxford University Press, New Delhi, 1996.

Overstreet,G.D., and Windmiller, Marshall, *Communism In India,* The Permanent Black, Bombay,1960.

Parmanand, Bhai, *The Story of My Life* (Tranlated from Hindi by N.Sundra Iyer and Lal Chand Dhawan), The Central Hindu Yuvak Sabha, Lahore, 1934.

Patnaik, Ashok Kumar, *The Soviets and the Indian Revolutionary Movement, 1917-1929*, Anamika Prakashan, New Delhi, 1992.

Patriotc Poetry Banned by the Raj, National Archives of India, New Delhi, 1982.

Patriotc Writings Banned by the Raj, National Archives of India, New Delhi, 1984.

Persits, M.A., *Revolutionaries of India in Soviet Russia*, Progress Publishers, Moscow, 1983.

Petrie, David, *Communism in India*, 1924-27, Edition Indian, Calcutta, 1972.

Prabhakar, Vishnu, *Amar Shaheed Bhagat Singh*, Arya Prakashan Mandal, Delhi, 1998.

Pradhan, Ram Chandra, *Raj to Swaraj,* Macmillan, New Delhi, 2008.

Qatla-e- Begunah, Urf Shaheedan-e- Watan (urdu), Ram Prasad, Lahore, n.d. .(NAI Lib.).

Raghawan, G.N.S., ed., *M. Asaf Ali's Memoirs, the Emergence of Modern India,* Ajanta, Delhi, 1994.

Rahbar, Hansraj, *Bhagat Singh and His Thought*, Manak Publications, New Delhi, 1990.

Rahbar, Hansraj, *Bhagat Singh: Ek Jwalant Itihas*, Bhagat Singh Vichar Manch, Delhi,1990.

Ram, S., (ed.), *Shaheed Bhagat Singh: Patriotism, Sacrifice and Martyrdom*, Commonweal, Delhi, 2005.

Ramchandra, *Ideology and Battle Cries of Indian Revolutionaries*, Published by Author, New Delhi, 1989.

Ramchandra, *Naujawan Bharat Sabha and HSRA*, published by Author, New Delhi, 2003.

Rana, Bhagwan Singh, *Bhagat Singh: An Immortal Revolutionary of India*, Diamond Pocket Books, New Delhi, 2008.

Rana, Bhagwan Singh, *Bharat Ke Mahan Amar Krantikari Bhagat Singh*, Bhartiya Grantha Niketan, Delhi, 1988.

Saigal, Omesh, *Shaheed Bhagat Singh, Unique Martyr in Freedom Movement*, Gyan publishing House, New Delhi, 2002.

Ranadive B.T., and Jyoti Basu, *Role of the Communists in The Struggle For Independence*, A CPI (M) Publication, New Delhi, n.d.

Ranjan, Ravi and Singh, M.K., *Bhagat Singh*, K.K. Publications, New Delhi, 2009.

Roy, M.N., *India in Transition*, Nachiketa Publication, Bombay, 1971.

Sanyal, J.N., *Sardar Bhagat Singh* (English), Fine Printing Cottage, Allahabad,1931 (NAI Lib.).

Sanyal, Jatindra Nath, *S. Bhagat Singh*, Vishwa Bharati Prakashan, Nagpur, 1983.

Sanyal, Jitendra Nath, *Amar Shaheed Sardar Bhagat Singh*, Krantikari Prakashan, Mirjapur, 1970.

Sanyal, Jitendra Nath, (Translated into Hindi by Snehlata Sehgal) *Amar Shaheed Sardar Bhagat Singh*, National Book Trust, Delhi, 1999.

Sanyal, Jitendra Nath, *Amar Shaheed Sardar Bhagat Singh*, (translated into Hindi by Sneh Lala Sehgal), Rahul Foundation, Lucknow, 2007.

Sanyal, S.N., *Vichar Vinimay: Ek Bhartiya Krantikari Ke Adhunik Vichar,*Luknow, 1938.

Sanyal, Sachindra Nath, *Bandi Jeewan,* Atmaram & Sons, 1963.

Sardesai, S.G., *India and the Russian Revolution*, Communist Party Publication, New Delhi, August 1967.

Sarkar, Sumit, *Modern India*, Mcmillan, Madras, 1983.

Satyabhakta, *Krantipath Ke Pathik*, Sanskriti Sansthan, Bereilly, 1973.

Ṣharma, I. Mallikarjuna, ed., *In Retrospect, Vol.I: North India, Sagas of Heroism and Sacrifice of Indian Revolutionaries*, Ravi Sasi Enterprises, Hyderabad, 1999.

Sen, Mohit, *A Traveller And The Road*, Rupa, New Delhi, 2003.

Shaheed-e-Ajam Bhagat Singh: Vichar Aur Sangharsh, (AISA, INAUS), Samkaleen Prakashan, Patna, 2003.

Sharma, I. Mallikarjun, *Role of Revolutionaries in the Indian Freedom Struggle*, Marxist Study Point, Hyderabad, 1987.

Sharma, Ramvilas, *Bharat Mein Angreji Raj Aur Marxwad*, Rajkamal, Delhi, 1982.

Shastri, Chandrashekhar, *Bhartiya Atankavaad Ka Itihas*, Endaman Sahitya angir, Kanpur, 1939.

Shastri, Chatursen, *Meri Atmakahani*, Chatursen Shastri Sahitya Samiti, Delhi, 1963.

Shastri, Raja Ram, *Amar Shaheedon Ke Sansmaran*, Sadhna Sahitya Mandir Prakashan, Kanpur, 1981.

Shri Shiv Varma Abhinandan Granth, Sardar Bhagat Singh Smarak Samiti, Agra, 1985.

Sidhu, Gurudev S., *Hanging of Bhagat Singh: Banned Literature*, Unistar Books, Chandigarh, 2007.

Sindhu, Virender, *Yugdrista Bhagat Singh Aur Unke Mritunjay Purkhe*, Rajpal, New Delhi, 2004.

Singh, Swarn, *Path of Revolution, A Biography of Shaheed Bhagat Singh*, Wellwish Publishers, Delhi, 1998.

Sinha, Bejoy Kumar, *In Andamans, The Indian Bastille*, People's Publishing House, New Delhi, 1986.

Sinha, Bejoy Kumar, *The New Man in the Soviet Union*, People's Publishing House, New Delhi, 1971.

Sinha, Srirajyam, *Bejoy Kumar Sinha: A Revolutionary's Quest for Sacrifice*, Bhartiya Vidya Bhavan, Bombay, 1993.

Sitaramiyya, Pattabhi, *The History of The Indian National Congress, 2 vols.*, Padma Publication, Bombay, 1936 and 1939.

Sivannaidu, Penta, *Proscribed Telgu Literature and National Movement in Andhra*, 1920-40, Reliance Publishing House, New Delhi, 2002.

Sukhdev Raj, *Jab Jyoti Jagi*, Kranti Prakashan, Mirjapur, 1971.

Sundarajan Saroja, *March to Freedom in Madras Presidency*, Lalitha Publications, Madras, 1989.

Suri,Naresh and Mitra, Ragini, *Amar Shaheed Bhagat Singh: Vyaktitva Aur Vichar*, Anubhuti Prakashan, Allahabad, 1987.

Devendra Swarup, *Did Moscow Play Fraud on Marx?: The Mystery of Marx-Engels' Articles on 1857*, Historians' Forum, Delhi, 2007.

Tendulkar, D.G., *Mahatma: Life of Mohandas Karamchand Gandhi, Vol.III, 1930-34*, Publication Division, Ministry of Information and Broadcasting, Government of India, Delhi, 1961.

Thakur, Gopal, *Bhagat Singh: The Man and His Ideas*, People's Publishing House, New Delhi, 1962.

Thapar, Mathuradas, *Mere Bhai Shaheed Sukhdev*, Delhi, Praveen, 1992.

The Bomb Incident, Lok Sabha Secretariat, New Delhi, 1958.

The Earl of Halifax, *Fullness of Days,* Collins, London, 1957.

Tripathi, Vachnesh, *Kranti Ke Vo Lal Din*, Vikram Publication, Delhi, 2000.

Tripathi, Vachanesh, *Krantimurti Durga Bhabhi*, Hindi Academy, Delhi, 1996.

Tripathi, Vachanesh, *Krantikarion Ke Aitihasik Dastavej*, Akhil Bharati, New Delhi, 1998.

Ujala, Sohan Lal Singalia, *Shahid Samrat Sardar Bhagat Singh Ka Krantikari Samajik Darshan*, Samyak Prakashan, New Delhi, 2005.

Usmani, Shaukat, *Historic Trips of a Revolutionary: Sojourn in the Soviet Union*, Sterling Publishers, New Delhi, 1977.

Vaishampayan, Vishwanath, *Amar Shaheed Chandrashekhar Azad*, Rajkamal Prakashan, New Delhi, 2007.

Varma, Shiv, ed., *Bhagat Singh on the Path of Liberation. Jail Notes* edited by Bhupender Hooja, Bharati Pustakalaya, New Delhi, 2007.

Varma, Shiv, *Sansmritiyan*, Samajwadi Sahitya Sadan, Lucknow, 1969.

Varma, Shiv, *The Selected Writings of Shahhed Bhagat Singh*, Samajvadi Sahitya Sadan, Kanpur, 1996.

Venkalarayaiya, M.,(ed.). *The Freedom Struggle in Andhra Pradesh, Vol III. (1921-1981)*, Andhra Pradesh, 1965.

Venu, C. S., *Sirdar Bhagat Singh*, Published by the Author, Madras, 1931 (NAI microfilm)

Vidrohi, Ramesh, *Bhagat Singh: Jeevan, Vyaktitiva Aur Vichar*, Bhavana Prakashan, Delhi, 1975.

Vidrohi, Ramesh, ed., *Mahan Krantikari Dhanvantri*, Bhavana Publication, New Delhi, 1961.

Vidyalankar, Satyadev, *Didi Sushila Mohan*, Marwari Publication, Delhi.

Vidyalankar, Satyaketu, et al, *Arya Samaj Ka Itihas*, vol. VI, Arya Swadhayaya Kendra, New Delhi, 1987.

Vidyarthi, Sudhir, ed., *Shaheed Bhagat Singh: Kranti Ka Sakshya*, Rajkamal Prakashan, New Delhi, 2009.

Vohra, Asharani, *Krantikari Kishor*, Saras Sahitya Prakashan, Delhi,1988.

Vohra, Asharani, *Krantikari Mahilaiyen*, Publication Division, Ministry of Information and Broadcasting, Gonernment of India, New Delhi, 2006.

Vohra, Asharani, *Swadheenta Senani Lekhak Patrakar*, Prathibha Pratisthan, Delhi, 2004.

Vyas, Raj Shekhar, *Mritunjaya Bhagat Singh*, Grantha Academy, New Delhi, 1994.

Vyathit Hridaya, *Amar Shaheed: Sardar Bhagat Singh*, Himachal Pustak Bhandar, Delhi, 1995.

Waraich, Malwinder Jit Singh, *Bhagat Singh: The Eternal Rebel*, Publication Division, Ministry of Information and Broadcasting, Government of India, New Delhi, 2007.

Waraich, Malwinderjit Singh, Sidhu, Gurudev Singh, (eds.), *The Hanging of Bhagat Singh, The Complete Judgement and Other Documents*, Unistar, Chandigarh, 2005.

Williamson, Horace, *India and Communism*, Edition Indian, Calcutta, 1976

Yadav, K.C. and Singh, Babar, *Bhagat Singh: Making of a Revolutionary, Contemporary Portrayals*, Hope India, Gurgaon, 2006.

Yadav, K.C. and Singh, Babar, *Fragrance of Freedom*, Hope India, Gurgaon, 2006.

Yagnik, Bhadrakumar, ed., *Shahid Bhagat Singh* (Gujrati), Vasant Printing Press, 1931, (NAI Lib.).

Yashpal, *Simhavalokan*, Lokabharati, Allahabad, 2005.

Special numbers of newspapers and magazines

Abhyudaya, May 1931, Padya Kant Malviya, ed., Abhyudaya Office, Pyayag.

Chand (Phansi number), November 1928, Chatursen Shastri, ed., Allahabad.

Dr. Bhagwan Das Mahour Abhinandan Grantha, Vishwambhar Amrohi, Mahour Abhinandan Samiti, Gwalior.

Filhaal, April 2007, Patna.

Panchajanya, Kranthi Katha Ank, 25 October 1981, Vachnesh Tripathi, Bhanu Pratap Shukla, eds., Rastradharm Prakashan Ltd., Lucknow.

Panchajanya, Kranthi Sansamaran Ank, Vachnesh Tripathi, Bhanu Pratap Shukla, eds., Rastradharm Prakashan Ltd., Lucknow.

Panchjanya, November 1966, Rastradharm Prakashan Ltd., Lucknow.

Panchajanya, Bhagat Singh Ank, 25 March, 2007.

The People, Lajpat Rai Number, 13 April ,1929, Lahore.

Udbhavana, Bhagat Singh Vishesank, July- December 2007, New Delhi.

Articles in Journals, Newspapers etc.

Ali, Asaf, "An Outstanding Maker of History," *Commonwealth* (Pune), 23 March 1949.

Ansari, Nazirul Hasan, "Bhagat Singh for Today," *Mainstream,* (published thrice) 27 March 1993, 11-17 August 2006, 6 October 2007.

Bakshi, S.R., "Gandhi and Bhagat Singh," *Indian History Congress Proceedings,* 1982.

Bhatia, Prem, "Newspaper-Hawker's Wail," *The Tribune,* 28 March 1980.

Bhatnagar, R.K., "Did the Mahatma Do His Best to Save Bhagat Singh," *http://www.asiantribune.com,*

Bhattacharya, Dipankar, "Bhagat Singh ki Prasagikta," *Rastriya Sahara,* New Delhi, September 28, 2006.

Celly, Ashk, "Bhagat Singh, Bose and the Mahatma," *Mainstream*, July 21, 2007.

Chaman Lal, 8th April, 1929; "A Day to Remember," *http:// bhagatsinghstudy.blogspot.com*, December 4, 2008.

Chaman Lal, "Bhagat Singh Ki Phansi Gandhi Ki Naitik Haar," *http://bhagatsinghstudy.blogspot.com*, September 25, 2007.

Chaman Lal, "Dastavejon Mein Shaheed-e-Azam," *Jansatta*, April 25, 2007.

Chaman Lal, "Chand Durlabh Dastavej," *Filhaal*, Patna, May-June, 2007.

Chaman Lal, "Gandhi and Bhagat Singh," *http:// bhagatsinghstudy.blogspot.com*, December 4, 2008.

Chaman Lal, "Jinnah and His defence of Bhagat Singh," *http:// bhagatsinghstudy.blogspot.com*, January 19, 2008.

Chaman Lal, "Letters of a Martyr," *The Tribune*, 8 April, 2007.

Chaman Lal, "Memorandum Regarding Places of Freedom Struggle in Pakistan," *http://bhagatsinghstudy.blogspot.com*, October 8, 2007.

Chaman Lal, "Political Correspondence of Bhagat Singh," *Mainstream*, 22 March, 2008.

Chaman Lal, "Rare Documents of Bhagat Singh," *http:// bhagatsinghstudy.blogspot.com*, December 4, 2008.

Chaman Lal, "Sach Ki Khoj," *Jansatta*, 20 April, 2008.

Chaman Lal, "Stamp of the Martyr," *The Tribune*, 22 March, 2008.

Chaman Lal, "Remembering Bhagat Singh on the 75th anniversary of his Martyrdom," Monthly Review *http:// www.monthlyreview.org*, 23 March, 2006.

Chaman Lal, "Revolutionary Legacy of Bhagat Singh," *Economic and Political Weekly*, 15 September, 2007.

Chaman Lal, "Two Indian Epics on National Hero Bhagat Singh," *http://bhagatsinghstudy.blogspot.com*, December 4, 2008.

Chandra, Bipan, "Bhagat Singh, Communalism, and Religion," *New Thinking Communist*, 15 April, 1991.

Chopra, Suneet, "Bhagat Singh's Prison Notebook," *Student Struggle*, March, 1985.

Das, D.P., "Gandhi and Bhagat Singh," *Mainstream*, Independence Day Number, 1970.

Datta, V.N., "Bhagat Singh's Trial and Execution: Gandhi tried his best for reprieve," *The Tribune*, New Delhi, 23 December, 2007

Datta, V. N., "Symbol of Courage & Patriotism," *The Tribune*, 18 March, 2007.

Deol. G., "The Ghadarites and Shaheed Bhagat Singh," *People's Path*, March, 1968.

Gandhi, Tushar, "Gandhi and Bhagat Singh," *The Hindustan Times*, 17 June, 2002,

Gupta, A.K., "The Executions of March, 1931, Gandhi and Irwin," *Bengal, Past And Present*, Vol Xl, PartI, January-June, 1971.

Gupta, Manmathnath, "A Passage to Eternity," *The Tribune*, 26-27 March, 1988.

Gupta, Maya , "A Review of Revolutionary Terrorism in India,1927-1931," *Journal of Indian History* (Trivendrum), Vol. LV, PartIII, December,1977.

Habib, Irfan, "Bhagat Singh Ka Smaranotsava Manane Ka Haqdar Kaun," *Nukkar Janam Samvad*, New Delhi, April-September, 2006.

Habib, S. Irfan, "Bhagat Singh and Today's Challenges," *Nukkar Janam Samvad*, New Delhi, April-September, 2006.

Habib, S. Irfan, "Shaheed Bhagat Singh and his Revolutionary Inheritance," *The Indian Historical Review*, December 2007, New Delhi.

Habib, S. Irfan, "Bhagat Singh as Seen by Ramaswami Periyar," *The Hindu*, 22 March 2008.

Hashmi, Salima, "Pakistan Aaj Bhagat Singh Ko Khoj Raha Hai," *Filhaal*, Patna, October 2007.

Islam, Shamsul, "Bhagat Singh, Rajguru, Sukhdev,and the Hindutva Gang," *Mainstream*, 13-19 April, 2007.

Islam, Shamsul, "Kyon Bhulaya Gaya Bhagat Singh Aur Unke Sathion Ko," *Nav Bharat Times*, New Delhi, 20 March 1994.

Jamdar, Kishore, "Bhagat Singh Ka Bhagwakaran: Panchyajanya Ko Khula Patra," *Hansa*, September, 2007.

Jamdar, Kishore, "Panchajanya Ke Sampadak Ko Khula Patra," *Filhaal*, Patna, May-June, 2007.

Karat, Vrinda, "Bhagat Ingh Aaj Bhi Prasangik," *Nukkar Janam Samvad*, New Delhi, April-September, 2006.

Kaushik, R.K., "Missed Target of Bhagat Singh," *The Tribune*, 18 September 2002.

Krishnan, P.R., "Carry Forward Bhagat Singh's Secular, Anti-Imperialistic And Marxist Outlook," *People's Democracy*, 15 April, 2007.

Krisnam, Kavita, "Bhagat Singh Ki Virasat Aur Rang De Basanti," *Rastriya Sahara*, New Delhi, 23 March, 2006.

Mishra, Shiv Dutt, "Bhagat Singh Ko Bachane Ki Koshish Ki Thi Gandhi Ne," *Pratham Pravakta*, 1-15 September, 2007.

Mishra, Vinod, "Yuva Bhartiya Vidrohiyon Ke Prakash Stambh," *Rastritya Sahara*, New Delhi, 28 September, 2006.

Mittal, S.K., and Habib, Irfan, "The Congress and the Reolutionaries in the 1920s," *Social Scientist*, June 1982.

Mohan, Kamlesh, "Techniques of Revolutionary Propaganda in the Punjab, 1920-25," *Punjab: Past & Present* (Patiala), Vol.XI, Part I, April 1978.

Mohan, Kamlesh, "Bhagat Singh's Trial Quickens the Pace of India's March Towards Freedom," *Proceedings of Punjab History Conference*, Patiala, 1973, pp.175-191.

Mohan, Kamlesh, "His Contribution to the Ideological Aspect of Freedom," *Proceedings of Punjab History Conference*, Patiala, 1975, pp.221-230.

Mudrarakshas, "Dalit Prashn Aur Bhagat Singh," *Hindustan*, 8 April, 2007

Noorani, A.G., "A Farcical Trial," *The Hindustan Times*, 31 January, 1997.

Panikkar, K.N., "Celebrating Bhagat Singh," *Frontline*, Chennai, 2 November 2007.

Prasad, Bimal, "Remembring Bhagat Singh," *Mainstream*, 28 March, 1981. Reprinted in Mainstream, 24 March, 2007.

Puri, Harish K., "Bhagat Singh and the Ghadar Movement," *Mainstream*, 22 March, 2008.

Raj Kishore, "Bhagat Singh Ki Sambhavnayen," *Rastriya Sahara*, 25 March, 2007.

Raj Kishore, "Bhagat Singh Ko Ham Kya De Sakte Hain," *Jansatta*, 23 March 2007.

Raj, A.K., "Ravi Se Kauveri Tak Bhagat Singh Ki Khoj Mein," *Patna*, October 2007.

Rao, Niraja, "Bhagat Singh and the Revolutionary Movement," *Revolutionary Democracy*, Vol.III, No.1, April, 1997.

Sachadev, Aseem, "Dhara Ke Khikaf Khete Hue," *Janasatta*, 8 July, 2007.

Salil, Suresh, "Bhagat Singh: Vaicharik Virasat ki Prasangikta," *Rastriya Sahara*, 27 May, 2007.

Sehnavis, Chinmohan, "Impact of Lenin on Bhagat Singh's Life," *Mainstream*, (published twice) 4 April 1981, 6 October, 2007.

Sen, Arpita, "The Proscription of an Irish Text and the Chittagong Rising of 1930," *The Indian Historical Review*, New Delhi, December 2007.

Sharma, Raghav Sharan, "Phansi Dilana Kya Hinsa Nahin," *Pratham Pravakta*, 1-15 September 2007.

Sharma, Shalini, "Developing a Communist Identity: the case of Naujawan Bharat Sabha," *Journal of Punjab Studies*, Fall 2007.

Singh, Chander Pal, "Shahadat Ke Diwane The Bhagat Singh," *Pratham Pravakta*, 16 July, 2008.

Singh, Chander Pal, "Jail Mein Gujre Dinon Ke Gaurav Gatha," *Pratham Pravakta*, 1 August, 2008.

Singh, Chander Pal, "Bhagat Singh Ko Bachane Ko Vyagra The Gandhi," *Pratham Pravakta*, 16 August, 2008.

Singh, Chander Pal, "To Bhagat Singh Communist The!," *Pratham Pravakta*, 1 October, 2008.

Singh, Chander Pal, "Shahadat Harapne Ki Koshish," *Pratham Pravakta*, 16 April, 2010.

Singh, Hajara, "An Epoch-Making Escape from Lahore," *The Tribune*, 17 December, 1995.

Singh, Jagmohan Singh, "Unke Sapno Ka Bharat," *Rastriya Sahara*, New Delhi, 23 March, 2006.

Singh, Jagmohan, "Kaun Poora Karega Shahid-e-Aajam Ke Inquilab Ka Khwab," *Amar Ujala*, 23 March, 2007.

Singh, Jagmohan, "Liberate Him from Misinterpretation" (interview), *Frontline*, 2 November, 2007.

Singh, Kunwar Pal, "Bhagat Singh Kiske Saath Hain," *Jansatta*, 25 March, 2007.

Singh, Madan Gopal, "Before the Hanging," *Tehalka*, 20 October, 2007.

Singh, Mahip, "Krantidrista Ka Samman," *Dainik Jajaran*, 14 March, 2008.

Singh, R. Vikram, "Gandhi Ji Bacha Sakte The Bhagat Singh Ko," *Jansatta*.

Singh, Sri Bhagwan Singh, "Akale Nahin Hain Bhagat Singh," *Jansatta*, 13 June, 2007.

Singh, Sri Bhagwan Singh, "Jikra Parivash Ka, Fir Bayan Apna," *Jansatta*, 14 June, 2007.

Sinha, Bejoy Kumar, "He Marched To Death," *Mainstream*, 24 March, 2007.

Sinha, Bejoy Kumar, "Shaheed Bhagat Singh: Crusader for Socialist Cause," *The Tribune* (Ambala), 23 March, 1967.

Sinha, Bejoy Kumar, "Influence on Bhagat Singh," *Link*, 19 April, 1970.

Surjeet, Harkishan Singh, "Bhagat Singh Remains Our Symbol of Revolution," *People's Democracy*, 19 March, 2006.

Taneja, Nalini, "A Radical Legacy," *Frontline*, 2 November, 2007.

Uniyal, Ved Vilas, "Bhagat Singh Ko Bhunane Ki Koshish," *Amar Ujala*, 6 April, 2007.

Upadhaya, Umakant, "Sardar Bhagat Singh Arya Samaj Calcutta Mein," *Jan Gyan* (New Delhi), August 2006, pp. 27-29.

Shaukat Usmani, "Russian Revolution and India," *Mainstream*, July 1, July 8, July 15, July 22, July 29, and August 5, 1967.

Vidyarthi, Sudhir, "Batukeshwar Dutt Ko Bhula Dena Gunah Hai," *Filhaal*, Patna, September 2007.

Vidyarthi, Sudhir, "Shaheed Bhagat Singh:Ve Chaar Kitabein Aur Koot Bhas Ki Diary," *Filhaal*, Patna, September, 2007.

Virendra, "Was Bhagat Singh A Terrorist," *The Tribune*, 19 March, 1989.

Yachuri, Sitaram, "Shaheed Bhagat Singh's Birth Centenary, Abiding Relevance," *People's Democracy*, 30 September, 2007.

Yachuri, Sitaram, "Thereby Hangs a Tale," *Hindustan Times*, 23 March, 2006.

Vyas, Rajshekhar, "Kya-Kya Chhipa Hai Bhagat Singh Ki Jail Dairy Mein," *Pratham Pravakta*, 15 April, 2008.

Selected Communist Pamphlets on Bhagat Singh

Bhusan, Ravi, *Ikkiswi Sadi Mein Bhagat Singh*, Rahul Foundation, Luknow, 2006.

Dhavale, Ashok,, *Shaheed Bhagat Singh: An Immortal Revolutionary*, A CPI(M) Publication, New Delhi, 2007.

Grewal, P.M.S., *Jang-i-Azadi Ka Dhadakta Tara: Bhagat Singh*, CPI(M), Delhi State Committee, 2007.

Kumar, Ajay, ed., *Bhagat Singh: Smriti Mein Prerna, Vicharon Mein Disha*

Naujawan Bharat Sabha, Disha Chhatra Sangathan, Bigul Mazdoor Dasta, *Krantikari Navjagaran Ke Teen Varsh (23 March-28 September 2008)*, n.d.

Rakesh, Raj Kumar and Sharma, Manoj, *Bhagat Singh; Anvarat Jalti Mashal*, Rahul Foundation, Luknow, 2006.

Sabyasachi, *Shaheed-i-Azaam Bhagat Singh*, Yugantar Publication, Mathura, n.d.

Satyam, *Vicharon Ki Saan Par*, Rahul Foundation, Luknow, 2007.

Sharma, Rajendra, ed., *Golwalkar Ya Bhagat Singh*, Sahmat Muktanad, New Delhi, 2007.

Singh, Jaswinder, *Us Mure Hue Panne Se Aage,* Lok Jatan Prakashan, Bhopal, 2007.

Vidyarthi, Sudhir, *Bhagat Singh Ki Sunein* , Lok Prakashan Griha, Delhi, 2006.

Index

Lafayette, 153

Lahiri, Rajendra Nath, 36, 107

Lahore, 30-35, 37, 92, 100-01, 114-16, 151, 158, 160, 254

Lahore Conspiracy Case, 22-23, 60, 63-64, 94, 96, 103, 132, 139, 143, 153, 158, 170-71, 176-77, 194, 213, 221, 224, 233, 254, 270

Special Tribunal to try, 39

Lahore Conspiracy Case Ordinance, 176

Lahore High Court, 156

Lahore Jail, 34, 38, 64-65, 157, 160

Lahore Naujawan Bharat Sabha, 139, 140

Lahore Railway Station, 114

Lahori Gate, Delhi, 106

La Humanite of Paris, 153-54

Lajjavati, 25, 63, 69, 71-73, 162

Lajpat Rai, 28, 31-32, 34, 37, 89, 109, 114-15, 138, 197, 260

Lajpat Rai Day, 161

Language role in nation-building, 209

Lawrence, John, 83

Left ideological intolerance on Bhagat Singh issue, 249

Left Scholarship on Bhagat Singh, 24

Left Writings, 26, 48, 248

Lenin, 67, 70, 153, 246-47, 251, 254, 257-59, 262-63, 265-66, 283-86, 281

Lenin Day, 161

Lenin death anniversary, 254

Lenin woos Muslims, 264-65

Liberation, 248

Literacy heritage of Bhagat Singh, 47-49

London, 263

Looted govt. treasury, 107

Lucknow, 30, 63, 107-08, 110, 118

Lucknow Jail, 33

Lyallpur, 27, 34, 86, 90, 104

Mahabir Singh, 48, 116, 160, 174

Mahadev Desai's Day, 226, 234

Maharathi (Delhi), 52-53, 55, 61

Mahaur, Bhagwan Das, 25, 186-87, 190, 196-98

Mahendra Pratap, 264